"If we hope to reach young people today, we must both know their world and know them *in* their world. In *Youth Ministry as Mission*, Hull and Mays show us how missiology can help us see a way forward in youth ministry, humbly discovering the mission of God right where we are—where we, too, have been sent to become living translations of the gospel for young people."

—Brad M. Griffin,
senior director, Fuller Youth Institute;
author of *3 Big Questions That Change Every Teenager*

"With deferential scholarly humility, Mays and Hull have written a book that insists on integration over invention. Both hefty and substantive, it's also winsome. The authors eagerly synthesize diverse contributions in pursuit of truly helpful answers. Compelling theological clarity gives shape to culturally savvy youth ministry practice; a missional mindset flows into biblically faithful activity. Thought leaders contemplating future church and twenty-year-olds aligning weekly youth ministry efforts with God's purposes will find considerable value in this text. May our vision soar as we embrace life with Jesus among young people on mission!"

—Dr. Dave Rahn,
coauthor of *Disrupting Teens with Joy*

"The field of youth ministry is in need of an approachable, yet deeply theological, examination of cross-cultural missions. This is that book. Whether you are a devoted lay member, a seasoned youth pastor, or a youth ministry educator, this innovative and engaging book will be a valuable and timeless tool."

—Dr. D. J. Coleman,
student ministries pastor, Northwood Church

"*Youth Ministry as Mission: A Conversation About Theology and Culture* is a must-read for new and experienced youth ministers alike. Hull and Mays establish clear connections between youth ministry and Christian missiological principles that will provide fresh insights for communicating the gospel to and with youth. Their questions and suggestions for practical application have already encouraged our team to creatively engage our local church community in this important work."

—Caleigh Smith,
youth ministry director, Bulverde UMC;
advisory board member, Youth Becoming Leaders:
High School Christian Leadership and Global Transformations Institute

"As the director of the Global Center for Youth Ministry, I am thankful for this valuable resource from Brian Hull and Patrick Mays. This new book is a helpful tool for understanding the connection between contextualization, missions, and youth ministry. Hull and Mays not only present a powerful argument for youth ministry as missions, but they also grant student ministry leaders a tool for mobilizing their students to do missions. This book will help students and student ministers to develop a vision for global student ministry. We need the type of global movement the authors describe. This book is an important contribution to that movement."

—Tim McKnight,
ass⋯   ⋯uth Ministry and
⋯ Youth Ministry,
⋯ Divinity School

T0283737

"Hull and Mays's *Youth Ministry as Mission* makes a crucial contribution in developing new ministry pathways for twenty-first-century realities where missions is no longer geographic, but temporal and generational. In a constant-change context, traditional youth ministry that passes on the Christian faith in the image and worldview of the existing adult generation is obsolete and has resulted in large numbers of millennials and GenZs leaving churches. *Youth Ministry as Mission* provides a framework to interpret the next generation as an emerging culture and develop the means to both reach and enable youth to contextualize the gospel for their own generation's culture.

"*Youth Ministry as Mission* is not just another program but provides youth workers with the necessary theory and skills to bridge and reach changing generational cultures. I suspect *Youth Ministry as Mission* will be an essential youth ministry textbook for generations to come.

"I should know because Brian Hull trained my own son to be an effective youth pastor, overseeing a thriving 150-plus-member youth ministry."

—Samuel K. Law,
senior dean of Academic Affairs and
associate professor of Intercultural Studies, Singapore Bible College;
pastor-at-large, the Evangelical Chinese Church of Seattle

"What can youth ministry learn from missiology? Brian Hull and Patrick Mays masterfully weave together theological, missiological, and youth ministry scholarship to provide a compelling way forward for youth ministry. Age-old Christian practices such as incarnational witness and discernment are reintroduced to us through the lens of missions. Hull and Mays remind us of the significance the church plays in culture, while also providing concrete ways to engage youth culture. Hull and Mays model the significance of narrative throughout their analysis, making this resource accessible and relevant for those engaged in youth ministry in multiple contexts. I, for one, look forward to using this as a textbook in my undergraduate course on youth and culture!"

—Sarah F. Farmer,
assistant professor of Practical Theology and Community Development,
Indiana Wesleyan University;
coauthor of *Raising Hope: Four Paths to Courageous Living for Black Youth*

YOUTH MINISTRY AS MISSION

A CONVERSATION ABOUT THEOLOGY AND CULTURE

Brian Hull & Patrick Mays

KREGEL
MINISTRY

Published by Kregel Academic, an imprint of Kregel Publications, 2450 Oak Industrial Dr. NE, Grand Rapids, MI 49505-6020.

ISBN 978-0-8254-4729-7, print
ISBN 978-0-8254-6933-6, Kindle
ISBN 978-0-8254-7780-5, epub

Printed in the United States of America

22 23 24 25 26 / 5 4 3 2 1

To Carol, who has offered continual support and love. To my parents, who have prayed over me and supported me. To Dave Curtiss, who believed in me. To the students, teens, parents, and amazing adult volunteers who have journeyed with me as we learn together about God's great love in and through the lives of young people.
—Brian Hull

To my students at LeTourneau University: you continually impress me with your dedicated study, your challenging questions, your commitment to service, and your faithfulness to live the gospel. You inspire me to be a better professor, a better campus pastor, and a better person. I am forever grateful for our journey together.
—Patrick Mays

TABLE OF CONTENTS

1

INTRODUCTION

IN A GALAXY NOT SO FAR AWAY . . .

Bill looked around the room, amazed at the diversity.

"How did we get here?" he wondered. "Am I too old for this?"

Bill saw a room of forty teenagers talking and hanging out before the midweek youth service. He saw young people from a variety of ethnic and cultural backgrounds. He found it almost impossible to relate to the issues they faced on a daily basis.

Manny, a second-generation Mexican immigrant, was in the corner talking to Nephtalie, who was from Haiti. Both of these high school students had family struggles, in addition to the cultural barriers they described in connecting with other youth at school.

Bill just finished a conversation with Ken, a Chinese American, who was struggling with the pressure to get accepted into a top university. Bill knew that was part of the reason Ken's parents moved here ten years ago. The pressure on Ken was daunting.

Besides all the ethnic diversity in the room, Bill couldn't help but notice how society had changed for these teenagers. This was a group with more information at their fingertips than any other in the history of the world. There was no singular "youth culture"; rather, many youth cultures were represented in the room. The world was definitely different from the small, midwestern church Bill grew up in.

And their expressions of faith were different. It seemed to be harder and harder to distinguish the language of the "committed" youth from the "nominal" youth. Conversations about God were easy enough to initiate, but there was a reticence to describe one's relationship in any kind of rich, theological language. Perhaps the reluctance was because they didn't know the language. Bill wondered if he was the one to blame. After all, he was their youth minister!

Bill remembered fifteen years ago when he started in youth ministry at his home church in Iowa. He did not know everything then, but he did feel more comfortable with the cultural issues. Now he knew that the models of ministry he used then were less effective at sharing the good news with teens who were from so many different cultures, value systems, and religious backgrounds. He needed help, and he knew his volunteers needed help.

The next day, while puttering in his office, Bill stumbled upon some books on mission, dusty from neglect. He was reading as a diversion but began to be inspired by the content.

"Maybe I need a change," he mused.

He found himself praying, asking God if he was calling him to be a missionary somewhere, grasping for anything to avoid planning another ineffective youth group event. God surprised him with an answer.

"Yes, I want you to be a missionary . . . right where you are."

This moment brought a flash of insight for Bill. He realized that the reason he resonated with the mission books so much was that they were describing many of the things that he was already doing intuitively in his ministry to youth. His "desperate" acts to be relevant to his youth and their culture, both the failures and the successes, clearly had gaps. He knew that! But in these mission books, he began to learn a new vocabulary, giving life to old ways and opening up new worlds.

Sophia was a new youth pastor across town. She was very energetic and had little trouble attracting a crowd of young people. She could lip-synch Ariana Grande and Taylor Swift with the girls and shoot hoops with the guys. Her passion for music and sports was exceeded only by her passion to reach youth for Jesus. Even though she was only six years removed from being a high school student herself, she was very aware that the youth in her church were culturally different from her. Yes, there was the obvious skin tone difference, since her parentage was mixed-race. But there were also more subtle and sometimes deep differences. She was wondering how in the world she was going to keep relating with youth if they kept changing. She was already trying to connect with some of this year's fifth graders in the children's ministry, and she realized they lived in a different world from when she was in elementary school.

At a local youth pastors' networking meeting a couple of weeks ago, several youth pastors were complaining about "teens these days." She understood the frustration to some extent, but she also wondered if there were some problems with the current models of youth ministry in reaching the youth cultures of today.

At the meeting, she bravely raised the question. Most people in the room brushed her off. "Clearly a rookie," many thought to themselves.

But one youth pastor, Bill, came up to her afterward. He mentioned that he too had been asking some of those questions and had come across an author she might like to read. He handed her a book by some guy named Lesslie Newbigin.

"Take two ibuprofen, read this, and call me in a couple of weeks," he said.

THE IMPACT OF LESSLIE NEWBIGIN

After thirty-five years in the mid-twentieth century as a Presbyterian bishop in India, Lesslie Newbigin retired from missionary work and returned to his native Britain. He was astonished to find a timid, nonengaging church where there had once been a robust and sending church actively engaging the world. If one listens closely, Newbigin can be heard saying, "What happened? What did you do to the church?"

Newbigin began addressing this situation in his "retirement," and has since been called one of the most significant theologians of the late twentieth century. The main focus of his writing used the missiological principles he honed in India and as general secretary of the International Missionary Council on his own Western culture. His attack on the Enlightenment's "false dualism" and Christianity's failure to critique the rise of reason and empiricism laid a foundation for missiological engagement with post-Christian Western culture. By questioning the assumptions of this prevailing "plausibility structure," Newbigin showed how Christians could confidently assert the truth claims of the gospel in a "pluralist society." In short, he called for a missionary engagement with Western culture that included the recovery of the public truth of the gospel, the missional nature of the church, and a missional analysis of Western culture (1989).

His work has guided a renewal movement in the church. What he discovered might be the key to helping youth pastors like Bill and Sophia.

THE FRONT LINES OF YOUTH MINISTRY

Have you ever had two friends who have common interests but have never met each other? When you hang out with one friend, he or she sounds a lot like your other friend. For whatever reason, they have never met, but you feel like the world would be a better place if they just got together and talked.

We would like to introduce youth ministry and missiology to each other, so they can start having that conversation. In this book, we are going to familiarize our youth worker friends with some of the literature and ideas in missiology that we believe will help make a better youth leader by providing tools to analyze the current context.

As youth ministers, we are on the front lines of the American religious milieu that often makes youth ministry frustrating. The National Study of Youth and Religion (NSYR), led by Christian Smith and first introduced in the book *Soul Searching: The Religious and Spiritual Lives of American Teenagers*, helped the church name what was happening to the faith of most young people: Moralistic Therapeutic Deism (MTD). The NSYR revealed that many adolescents in Christian churches have a "misbegotten" faith that is only "tenuously" Christian. It consists of the following (Smith and Denton 2005):

1. A God exists who created and ordered the world and watches over human life on earth.
2. God wants people to be good, nice, and fair to each other, as taught in the Bible and by most world religions.
3. The central goal of life is to be happy and to feel good about oneself.
4. God does not need to be particularly involved in one's life except when God is needed to resolve a problem.
5. Good people go to heaven when they die.

Kenda Creasy Dean, who was a member of the original NSYR research team, was charged with the task of giving a pastoral response to the findings of the study. She addresses MTD in her book *Almost Christian*, saying that MTD is not "durable" or robust enough to last into adulthood. She invites the church to take this issue seriously by recognizing that youth ministry needs a different approach. She suggests an effective response involves the whole congregation engaging youth in a missionary way. She heartily draws on the work of missiologists Lamin Sanneh and Andrew Walls to indicate that mission is translation work, whether that translation occurs in a new geographic location or within an emerging generation. She writes,

The reason parents, pastors, and youth ministers should take Walls's theory of mission-as-translation to heart is simple: it is not just about witnessing to the gospel in new locales. Translation is how we hand on faith to our children. The principles that describe the gospel's transmission across cultures could just as easily describe the way we ferry faith across generations. (Dean 2010, 98)

This book aims to develop further the mission principles of gospel transmission to younger generations in more practical and theological ways, by connecting to missiology. We believe that youth ministry is mission work. Youth ministry is going to new lands, crossing cultural divides, living with a new people, learning a new language, translating stories and concepts, and transforming lives through sharing the good news of Jesus Christ. Whether you are a youth pastor like Bill and Sophia, a student studying youth ministry, the person who said "yes" to leading a youth Bible study, or the youth coordinator because the church board "suggested" it was your turn, you have this sense of the cultural gap between you and the youth you love.

The task of missiology is to study the history and work of missions and learn from it. We believe that the Christian faith is missionary. It joins with God's mission to reach out to the world so that God can be known (in the fullest form of knowing). We believe that good youth leaders—youth leaders who care—learn about the culture of the people they care about. This is mission work.

THE CONVERSATION

If we are going to be claiming that youth workers are missionaries, we want to explain what a missionary is. Following this introductory chapter, chapter 2 makes the connection between youth ministers and missionaries. Many Christians have a sense of what missionaries do. They go to a people, learn their language, and share the gospel. In this process is a fairly clear sense of leaving behind one's own culture and entering a new one. If youth ministry in today's context is essentially a missionary activity, as we suggest, then what do youth ministers (missionaries) do? This chapter begins the conversation between youth ministry and missiology with the classic article by Donald Larsen, "The Viable Missionary: Learner, Trader, Story Teller," and makes the case that youth minister work is missionary work. Dean's *Almost Christian* will be used as a primary example of how doing youth ministry as a missionary is essential in today's context.

Chapter 3 continues the conversation by exploring the theological foundation of youth ministry and missiology. In the first half of the chapter, a theology of mission will be delineated, drawing heavily on Christopher Wright's *The Mission of God* and *The Mission of God's People*, Andrew Walls's *The Missionary Movement in Christian History: Studies in the Transmission of Faith* and *The Cross-Cultural Process in Christian History: Studies in the Transmission and Appropriation of Faith*, and Timothy Tennett's *Invitation to World Missions: A Trinitarian Missiology for the Twenty-First Century*. The second half of the chapter will make a domestic application of this theology of mission, primarily following the extensive work of Lesslie Newbigin, particularly *The Gospel in a Pluralist Society*.

Chapter 4 leans into the connection between the incarnation and youth ministry. This chapter will consider the impact of the incarnation—God coming to humanity in his Son, Jesus Christ. The theology of this act of grace will be unpacked, and the implications for youth ministry will be explained. The incarnation as viewed in Andrew Root's *Revisiting Relational Youth Ministry* will be explored alongside missiology texts such as Darrell Guder's *The Incarnation and the Church's Witness*, Christopher Wright's *Mission of God*, and David Bosch's *Transforming Mission*.

Chapter 5 discusses the translatability of the gospel. Drawing heavily on the work of Lamin Sanneh's *Translating the Message* and Andrew Walls's indigenizing and pilgrim principles, gospel translatability is applied to the world of youth ministry. Darrell Whiteman's model and application of dynamic equivalence reveals the convergence of youth ministry and mission practice.

While the first five chapters of the book build a strong theological foundation for why the conversation with missiology is so important for youth ministry, chapters 6 through 13 connect to more practical applications. Chapter 6 explores tools for youth leaders to learn about the cultures of the youth around them, including differentiation between addressing the developmental level of teens and the ministry to teens in culturally attuned ways. Conversations with Stephen B. Bevans's *Models for Contextual Theology*, Robert J. Schreiter's *Constructing Local Theologies*, and Dean Fleming's *Contextualization in the New Testament* will highlight the chapter's argument.

When engaging in the task of learning a culture, the issue of cultural relativism is raised. Chapter 7 tackles this issue by outlining its development as an anthropological doctrine. Then a pragmatic critique questions the myth of primitive harmony and indicates that many societies have maladaptive practices, ones that do not provide adequate answers for their environments. A biblical critique suggests that God validates culture through the incarnation, but societies need transformation to conform to God's will. Four practices, then, are suggested for Christians to become effective cultural witnesses to the reality of God's incarnational transformation. When Christians are informed by historical and methodological relativism without subscribing to ethical relativism, they make powerful witnesses to God's kingdom in the world. Secular sources such as Robert Edgerton's *Sick Societies* and Ruth Benedict's *Patterns of Culture*, and sources by Christian missiologists such as Lamin Sanneh's *Translating the Message*, inform the discussion. These are missiological reminders for those who teach and work in youth ministry.

Chapter 8, a look at youth ministry as an interpretive community, will discuss the importance of understanding culture(s) within the context of a community. It will give some practical ways to empower the local church community to think, discern, and engage for itself in sustainable ways. Within this discussion, a missional ecclesiology will emerge, as we engage with David J. Bosch's *Transforming Mission*, W. Jay Moon's *African Proverbs Reveal Christianity in Culture*, Paul Hiebert's work on "critical contextualization," and the work of the Gospel and Our Culture Network (in particular, Lois Y. Barrett's *Treasure in Clay Jars* and Darrell Guder's *Missional Church*).

Chapter 9 will engage the importance of being able to tell and live out God's story in a way that recognizes the culture and language of a particular group of youth. This will include some examples from the authors' experiences in practicing mission in a youth ministry context. Vincent Donovan's *Christianity Rediscovered* will help set the stage for this chapter, with substantiation from Craig Bartholomew and Michael Goheen's *The Drama of Scripture*.

Chapter 10 will look into developing indigenous leadership, discussing the necessary shift toward empowering young people in leadership as they construct their own theologies, organizing people toward action, and giving voice to the issues of their lives. This chapter will build on the work of Henry Venn and Rufus Anderson, along with David Bosch's *Transforming Mission*. In addition to this mission literature, we will look closely at young people in leadership in Scripture and Christian history. Finally, the authors' own efforts in developing High School Christian Leadership Institutes will also be discussed.

The next three chapters turn the readers' attention to helping youth witness to their world through evangelism, service, and social justice. Chapter 11 grapples with evangelism in a multireligious context, which many youth face on a daily basis in their communities. Within such a context, how does one hold on to and communicate core beliefs in appropriate and effective ways? This requires an understanding of a theology of other religions and a missionary approach to the evangelistic task. Timothy Tennett's *Invitation to World Missions*, Michael Goheen's *Introducing Christian Mission Today*, and Winfried Corduan's *Neighboring Faiths* highlight the discussion.

Chapter 12 explores how to encourage youth to engage with key social justice issues within their communities, such as racial reconciliation, poverty, and civic engagement. Miroslav Volf's *Exclusion and Embrace* will be a good conversation partner here, as well as Jung Young Lee's *Marginality: The Key to Multicultural Theology* and Gustavo Gutiérrez's *Theology of Liberation*.

Chapter 13 takes a look at the role of service in youth ministry, particularly the short-term mission trip. Recent work by Simone Mulieri Twibell on the effectiveness and pitfalls of short-term mission trips, along with the classic work on pilgrimages and rites of passages by Victor Turner, will serve to help youth ministry leaders make informed decisions about the role of short-term mission trips in the scope of their youth ministries.

Chapter 14 concludes the book with a summary and an inspirational call for youth ministries to embrace their missional contexts.

This book is meant to be read and discussed. Hopefully, you will find some other people to join you in reading this book. You will find some questions for reflection at the end of each chapter to help you and your community engage the material, wrestling with what this kind of approach might mean for youth ministry moving forward in your context.

The story of Bill and Sophia, two youth pastors trying to learn a new way of approaching youth ministry, will weave its way through the book. Neither Bill nor Sophia are real people, but they represent dozens of conversations we've had over the years with youth leaders all over the world—youth leaders like you and me. Bill and Sophia, like all youth leaders, are on a journey as they learn this new way of approaching youth ministry. They and their views on youth, the church, and youth ministry will be changed.

THE CONVERSATION BEGINS

Sophia finished the last page of Newbigin's *The Gospel in a Pluralist Society*. So many thoughts streamed through her mind that she found it difficult to focus. She was excited, bewildered, and exhausted all at the same time. It seemed clear to Sophia that Newbigin saw the central character of the church as mission.

She wondered out loud, "If the church is in mission, then is what I do in youth ministry really mission work?"

Sophia recalled the missionaries she had met at her church's mission conference. She remembered the cultural artifacts and a few of the dramatic stories. She also remembered the appeals for money. But she realized she never got a sense of what they do on a daily basis.

She snapped out of her brain fog, grabbed her phone, and sent Bill a text: "What is a missionary?"

QUESTIONS FOR REFLECTION

1. Think about a time you had a realization, like Bill or Sophia, in
    which you recognized that circumstances had changed. What kind of
    change did this realization require of you?

2. As you begin reading the book, what do expect to learn from missions
    and missiological literature that could help youth ministry?

3. Look through the descriptions of the chapters. Which chapter(s)
    look(s) most interesting to you? Why?

4. What do you hope for in reading this book?

2

WHAT IS A MISSIONARY?

BILL SMILED AS HE READ SOPHIA'S TEXT. He recalled the time awhile back when he distinctly sensed God telling him, "Yes, I want you to be a missionary . . . right where you are."

GIVE ME THE ANSWER!

That moment of God's call was both exciting and confusing. It drove him to begin to read any book on mission that he could get his hands on. His initial enthusiasm began to wane, though, when his search for clarity resulted in more bewilderment. So many times he had heard well-meaning friends, mentors, and pastors say, "You don't have to be a missionary to follow God's call." It was always said in an effort to show that God calls and uses people in a variety of ways. He even found himself repeating this message to his youth. But now this message from God was ringing in his head: "I want you to be a missionary." Maybe, he began to think, there is something foundational about this missionary thing, something that gets at the heart of my ministry with youth. That thought compelled him to call Stan.

Stan and his wife, Sally, had been missionaries in the Czech Republic since 1994, right after the fall of communism. Recently retired, they had moved to the community to be close to family and had become an integral part of Bill's church in a short two years. They volunteered to help with some youth activities, and Bill had grown to appreciate their servant attitude, flexibility, and wisdom that came from their many years ministering cross-culturally. Stan and Sally (known to the youth as S²) quickly became fixtures of the youth group. The youth loved the fun-loving grandparent surrogates who were always ready for hugs, talks, and coffee. Bill, too, had come to rely on Stan's insights into life and ministry.

When Stan answered the call, Bill found himself blurting out, "What's a missionary?"

"Well, hello to you, too!" Stan mused.

"I'm sorry. I've been encamped in my office for a few days trying to get my mind around the missionary thing. I told you how I sensed God telling me that I needed to be a missionary."

"Yes, I remember."

"Well, when I told you, you gave me that crooked smile of yours and said that I would figure it out. So, I've been blowing the dust off these mission books sitting on my shelf, but now I want to hear from a real person. What is a missionary? And I have chosen you to give me the answer!"

"I guess I should be flattered," chuckled Stan. "I'll tell you what," he continued, "if you don't mind, I'd like to send you an article that helped shape my understanding of mission work. It's a short read and easily accessible."

"All right," said Bill, "I'll add it to my reading list."

"Right now, though, I want to give you some context for reading the article. My guess is that this message from God about being a missionary is throwing you for a loop because of the missionary stereotypes that are running through your mind," said Stan.

"Right," answered Bill. "I really don't think my youth will be able to relate if I show up wearing a pith helmet and khaki shorts."

"You may be surprised that pith helmets and khaki shorts were not regular attire for missionaries in Eastern Europe." Stan loved a little snark.

"Okay, Stan, deconstruct my stereotype."

"Mission derives from a Latin word that means 'to send,'" Stan began to teach. "The Catholic order, the Jesuits, used the term in the 1500s to describe their activity to gather unbelievers and the 'apostate' Protestants into the Roman Catholic Church. Protestants, by the nineteenth century, coopted the term to describe their activity in evangelizing non-Christians, typically in foreign lands. From this narrow use, mission, then, becomes something that professional missionaries do 'over there.' So we get the stereotypes of the helmet, the shorts, and the jungle. More recently, missiologists have worked to recover a more holistic sense of the word."

"Okay, slow down, Stan!" interrupted Bill. "I'm trying to take notes."

"No problem," replied Stan. "I could talk about this stuff all day."

After a pause for a sip of coffee, Stan continued, "I'll tell you what. Why don't we set a time to get together, and I'll walk you through the concept of mission."

A few days later, Stan came to Bill's office with a pile of books. "Are you ready?" asked Stan.

"Let's do it!" said Bill.

DEFINING MISSION

As Stan mentioned to Bill in their earlier phone conversation, the Jesuits in the sixteenth century first used the term *mission* in reference to human agency in spreading the Christian faith. Before then, mission rather precisely referred to the internal activity of the Triune God in sending the Son and the Holy Spirit (Bosch 1991). Timothy Tennent explains, "In short, the word *mission* was originally about God and *His* redemptive initiative, not about us and what we are doing. However, in popular usage within the church, it seems that mission has now come to refer almost exclusively to various tasks the church is doing" (2010, 54). The shift in usage of the term highlights the push and pull of understanding mission as primarily an activity of God or an activity of humans.

As the Protestant mission movement became a compelling worldwide force, culminating in the "Great Century" of Protestant missionary activity in the nineteenth century (Tucker 2004), the concept of mission broadened to include a number of meanings. These included, but were not limited to, the sending of missionaries, the work of missionaries, and missionary-sending organizations (Bosch 1991). The emphasis, though, even in this expansion of the term, tended to be on the role of human actors in the process of spreading the gospel to other places.

The twentieth century saw the fruit of the missionary enterprise, with Christianity expanding in geographic regions outside of the West. This, along with several other factors, have reshaped the mission context for today's church, according to Tennent (2010). He notes "seven megatrends that are shaping twenty-first century missions," two of which particularly confront the idea that mission is something that is done "over there." First is the reality that the West as a geographic entity or Western culture as a sociological force can no longer be considered Christian in any way that connects to historic or theological orthodoxy. Michael Goheen (2014) suggests that Western economic ideals, placing ultimate value on market-driven and profit-driven motives, are the chief shapers of Western culture. Simply put, Christianity is not the center of the Western experience, "and we find ourselves standing in the middle of a newly emerging mission field" (Tennent 2010, 11).

Second is the movement of Christianity to the periphery of Western culture and the simultaneous emergence of a vibrant Christianity in the Majority World,[1] challenging the "West-reaches-the-rest" missiological paradigm. Whereas before, those of us in the West "instinctively" knew that the "mission field" was in places like Asia and Africa, now mission is being accomplished multidirectionally. Statistically, about 70 percent of Christians live in the Majority World. Many of these Majority World churches are sending out a vital missionary force. At the dawn of the twenty-first century, close to 85 percent of the cross-cultural missionaries in the world came from outside the West. Scott Moreau (Moreau, Corwin, and McGee 2015, 16) identifies this phenomenon as "from everywhere to everywhere" mission, in which "almost every region of the world is now both sending and receiving people" who bear the gospel message.

The result of non-Western growth of the Christian church began to raise questions and critiques about how mission was traditionally viewed, leading Tennent (2010) to suggest that we need to pause for reflection, in order for mission to be useful for the twenty-first century.

Several missiologists and biblical scholars from the spectrum of theological positions offer different conceptions, redefinitions, and various emphases on the concept of mission. Four evangelical writers—Christopher Wright (2006), Timothy Tennent (2010), Michael Goheen (2014), and Scott Moreau (2015)—present thorough and useful discussions on defining mission. Each knowledgeably analyzes the current global context and carefully navigates divine and human agency. Wright (2006, 22–23), who expressing his dissatisfaction with the traditional use of the term, says "our mission (if it is biblically informed and validated) means our committed participation as God's people, at God's invitation and command, in God's mission within the history of God's world for the redemption of God's creation." In his effort to reinvigorate the concept of mission, Tennent (2010, 54) says, "Mission refers to God's redemptive, historical initiative on behalf of His creation." Goheen (2014) offers this concise statement: "Mission is participation in the story of God's mission."

---

1.   "Majority World" refers to the non-Western world.

Scott Moreau's effort serves to summarize the current contours of the evangelical understanding of mission in a three-part exposition. First, he defines missions as "the specific task of making disciples of all nations" (2015, 69). It consists of all the various work and activities of organizations, churches, and individual missionaries around the world who are moving beyond their borders to proclaim the gospel cross-culturally. Second, Moreau says mission "refers to everything the church does that points to the kingdom of God" (70). The church, then, is seen as "sent" by and for God into the world. It includes the specific task of making disciples of all nations, along with the wider witness of the church for God through other forms of witness and justice.

Third, Moreau indicates *missio dei*, the mission/sending of God, communicates the idea that God initiates mission. Wright (2006) suggests that the biblical story unveils God's initiative. God reveals himself to Israel and then in Jesus Christ, thereby confronting the idolatry of each age. God elects, forms, and sends a people in Israel and then the church, whose communal life demonstrates and witnesses to God's redemptive activity on behalf of his creation. This puts the emphasis on God's agency in the expansion of his kingdom on earth. The church, then, participates with God in his redemption of the world. In this scheme, *missio dei* is the overarching term that places God at the forefront and the center of mission. Mission focuses more on what the church is sent to do by God in the world, and missions is a subset describing the activity of making disciples and planting churches.

Overall, each puts the emphasis on God's redemptive initiative to the world with an invitation from God to his people to join him in the work.

A MISSIONARY TO YOUTH

"Wow!" exclaimed Bill. "That's a lot to take in all at once." He paused to take a sip of coffee and to peruse the notes he took on Stan's discussion of mission. "Let's see if I get this. Historically, mission was used to refer to the relationship of the Trinity, until around five hundred years ago when the Jesuits began to use it in regard to their work. From then, mission came to describe mostly human efforts in spreading the gospel around the world. Following the Protestant mission boom of the 1800s, Christianity became a vital force in the traditional mission fields outside the West. Now, with the weakening of Christian influence in the West, we have a situation in which the traditional mission sending areas are a mission field, too."

"Yes, that's a pretty good summary," responded Stan.

"I guess the other key part is that this emerging context has caused a rethinking of the concept of mission. I appreciated the writers you mentioned who are, in a sense, recovering the idea that mission begins as an activity with God. And God invites us to participate with him in mission." Bill stopped and pondered for a moment, then continued, "Okay, so I still want to know . . . what is a missionary?"

"I thought you'd never ask," Stan responded, laughing. "Seriously, though, Sally and I had to wrestle with that question when we started to consider being missionaries in the Czech Republic. Yes, the Czechs had been under communist rule that suppressed religious life for almost fifty years, but it seemed a bit incongruous to be doing mission work in the shadow of cathedrals. We did our research and discovered that about 90 percent of Czechs did not believe in God. Clearly, there needed to be a fresh retelling of the gospel in a way that could be understood in the current context. We sensed a calling from God to be missionaries there. So, we went and actually did what missionaries do."

"What's that?" asked Bill.

"We went to the Czech people, lived among them, learned their language and their culture. We built and nurtured relationships. We got to know them so well as both individuals and as a society that we were able share the gospel with them in a new way, a way that this generation had not heard before. First Thessalonians 2:8 became our guiding verse: 'So we cared for you. Because we loved you so much, we were delighted to share with you not only the gospel of God but our lives as well.'"

Stan took a breath, then said, "Another key factor is that we really tried to pay attention to where God was already at work among the Czechs. We partnered with local churches who had held on through the years of communism. We held 'theology on tap' conversations at our local pub. It was amazing to see these Czechs speak with freedom about their religious questions and longings after they had been bottled up for so many years. In short, we tried to follow God's agenda rather than our own. We wanted to see where God was already moving and join him."

"That's amazing," said Bill. "I can see why you and Sally are so great with our youth. You do the same kind of thing with them. Well, except for the pub part."

"It's beer in the Czech Republic, but it's coffee here," mused Stan. "That's how Sally and I approach our ministry with the youth. We have found ourselves pulling from our missiological reading and training as we share our lives and the gospel with these kids. Except for the fact that it's in English, it feels the same. But even their English and their youth culture create barriers to be crossed!"

"So, I need to be a missionary to my youth." Bill stretched his arms in mock exercise. "Okay, how do I start?"

Stan said, "I think you're ready for that article I mentioned to you earlier."

Bill reached under his notes and pulled out four stapled pages. "I've got it right here: 'The Viable Missionary: Learner, Trader, Story Teller,' by Donald N. Larson. Looks like a real page-turner!"

"LEARNER, TRADER, STORY TELLER"

Donald Larson's classic article (1978) seeks to reimagine the conception of the missionary role. Based on forty years of mission consultation, Larson notices that typically there is a gap between how missionaries conceive their role and how people in the local community perceive it. He suggests that locals tend to view missionaries, as they try to make sense of these outsiders, through three interpretive metaphors: school, market, and court. Locals often see missionaries as teachers who are there to communicate material to be learned. Or they view missionaries as sellers in the market, hawking their wares. Or they view missionaries as judges, establishing and executing certain standards.

Larson points out that a cultural outsider faces significant barriers when playing the roles of teacher, seller, and judge. Outsiders in these roles can be found irrelevant and dismissed easily. The way to become a valuable member of the community is to follow an important sequence. One should be learner before one becomes a teacher, "buyer before seller, accused before accuser" (158). Closing this perceptual gap requires missionaries intentionally to take on different roles within these interpretive metaphors—the roles of learner, trader, and story teller—in order to become acceptable and viable in the local context.

First, upon arriving at a locale, a missionary should be a learner, focusing primarily on the local language and culture. Taking language and culture learning seriously communicates to the local population that the missionary considers them worthy of time and effort. Putting oneself in the communication arena every day makes for good practice, to understand and be understood, and also provides opportunities to make new acquaintances and friends. A new language cannot be learned completely in a few months, but relationships can be initiated even with communication limitations.

Second, as the missionary continues to learn the local language and culture, one adds the role of trader. This role is aided if the missionary has "come with some recognizable commercial purpose" (160). The trader role is a kind of establishment phase, in which the missionary offers experiences, commodities, and/or insights that are interesting and valuable to the local community. In the process, one shares the joys and pains, the successes and problems, in how others live. Of course, language and culture learning progress, and the missionary becomes, hopefully, an established fixture in the community and a bridge to a "larger world" (160).

The missionary then is able to add a third role, that of story teller. One's knowledge of the local language and culture is used to translate the story of God. The story the missionary tells is "based on the wanderings of the people of Israel, the coming of Christ, the formation of God's new people, the movement of the Church into all the world and ultimately into this very community" (161). Along with this grand biblical narrative, the missionary tells his or her own story of coming to and walking with Christ.

Larson's suggestion that missionaries take on the roles of learner, trader, and story teller challenges the stereotype of missionaries as cultural imperialists. Larson explains:

> The learner role symbolizes a number of important things . . . in the communication of the gospel. The learner's dependence and vulnerability convey in some small way the message of identification and reconciliation that are explicit in the gospel. . . . The biblical mandate challenges the Christian to identify with those to whom he [sic] brings words of life. (163)

THINKING LIKE A MISSIONARY

Bill looked up from the article and smiled. "That Stan knows what he's doing," he thought. Bill considered Larson's description of a missionary as a learner, trader, and story teller. It dawned on him that those roles had a bit of congruency with his approach to youth ministry. While he and his youth all spoke English, there were times when he understood only about half of what they were saying. Also, there were a myriad of pop culture references that he missed, and he knew these things were shaping the perceptions and approach to life of his youth. There really was a youth culture, actually several youth cultures, for him to learn and know better if he was going to effectively translate the gospel story and communicate it to them to them. "Wow!" he thought. "I'm already starting to think like a missionary."

In processing these things, he recalled a youth ministry book he had read a few years back. He seemed to remember the author saying something about youth and mission. He searched his shelves and found it: *Almost Christian*, by Kenda Creasy Dean (2010).

YOUTH WORK IS MISSION WORK

In 2005 Christian Smith and Melinda Denton introduced to the public their seminal research of the National Study of Youth and Religion (NSYR) (2005), research that both rocked and affirmed what youth ministry practitioners understood about American youth. They concluded that American youth, in general, hold to a faith that Smith and Denton labeled Moralistic Therapeutic Deism (MTD). It is a faith that encourages people to be nice to each other and play fair. Its main purpose is to help people feel good about themselves. Yes, there is a God, but one that can be relegated to the fringes of life.

Dean (2010) published her compelling treatise on how the church should respond to the findings of the NSYR. What can be done to engage youth who exhibit a lackadaisical faith that only marginally connects to the historic, orthodox Christian faith? Indeed, what can be done when, as Dean pointedly tells pastors, parents, and youth workers, "we're responsible" (2010, 3)? What can be done when it is realized that this isn't just a youth ministry problem—it's a church problem?

Dean focuses on the 8 percent from Smith and Denton's study whom they identify as "highly devoted." These youth "possess articulate and integrated theologies" and "faith stories" that "influence their decisions, actions, and attitudes" (Dean 2010, 47). Borrowing from sociologist Ann Swidler, Dean proposes a "Christian cultural toolkit" that vital churches employ and that youth benefit from in the process of becoming formed like Christ. These include, first, claiming a creed. Christian creeds typically refer to historic declarations of faith, like the Apostles Creed or the Nicene Creed. Dean broadens the concept to include what youth think and say about God. Highly devoted youth communicate belief in both the transcendence of God (respect and grandeur for the Creator) and the immanence of God (as exemplified in God's desire for personal relationship through Jesus Christ). A second "tool" is a relational and authoritative connection to a faith community, particularly with available adults. A clear sense of calling is a third item in the toolkit. Dedicated youth express and live out a purpose and a moral responsibility to participate in God's work in the world. Hope is a fourth, though a bit less developed, tool demonstrated by faithful youth. Still, the highly devoted showed a greater propensity than MTD youth to put into practice "Christian hope as a generalized trust that God has the future under control" (Dean 2010, 78).

For Dean, operationalizing this Christian cultural toolkit is the antidote to the apathy of MTD. However, these tools are effective only as they are empowered by and point to Jesus. Dean explains, "Our creed, our communities, our sense of call and hope are useful only if they reflect Christ's Light into the dark places of the world" (2010, 84). This is done as churches recover their "missional imagination" (Dean 2010, 85).

"Every church is called to be a 'missional church,'" she writes, one that "ratchet[s] up expectations by consciously striving to point out, interpret, and embody the excessive nature of God's love" (Dean 2010, 85). She notes that recovering the core biblical, missional identity of the church makes sense in our current cultural climate: "American young people's experience of religious culture is less like the overarching Christendom of the Roman Empire, dominated by one religious perspective to the point of rendering most other religions invisible, and more like the Hellenistic pluralism of the New Testament, or the multireligious world of ancient Israel" (2010, 91–92).

Beyond the pragmatic analysis that we currently share a similar multireligious context with the first-century church—hinting that we might share similar ministry methodologies—is a central truth that God sends his people, his church, as a sign, symbol, and sacrament of the sacrificial love demonstrated in the work of Jesus Christ. This indicates that mission is foundational to the identity of the church. Further, mission is symbiotically tied to the incarnation. God sends himself to his creation in the person of Jesus Christ, who is fully human and fully divine.

Drawing significantly from missiologists Lesslie Newbigin, Lamin Sanneh, and Andrew Walls, Dean presents a big vision for youth ministry as mission that moves beyond the idea that mission is merely a one-week summer trip. Yes, the incarnation is a doctrine of Christian belief, and it is also a "template for the church's missional life" (Dean 2010, 91). It is the evidence of God's interest and engagement with the world. God takes definitive action in this world, and he calls/sends us to do likewise. The incarnation is the "perfect translation," and we continue the witness as "*re*translations" of the original (Dean 2010, 97). Dean summarizes, "Mission simply means translating God's love in human form, putting every cultural tool—stories, symbols, attitudes, language, practices, patterns of life—at the gospel's disposal. To be 'little Christs' means allowing God to become Incarnate in our own lives as we smuggle divine grace into the world" (2010, 98).

Dean suggests that the translatability of the gospel to the peoples of the world is the same kind of translatability that it takes to transmit the gospel to new believers of emerging generations. So mission is more than the geographic expansion of Christianity, for Christians are sent across every human-formed boundary—geographic, linguistic, cultural, and generational. "Parents, youth ministers, and congregations embody the church's missional imagination by transmitting the gospel across generations as well as cultures, translating God's self-giving love for young people through the medium of our own lives—lives that are remembered by Christ every time we remember him" (Dean 2010, 99).

Dean's remedy for the malaise of Moralistic Therapeutic Deism among American youth is a missional embodiment by parents and those who work with youth to translate the life-giving good news to the next generation. Youth work is mission work!

Incarnational philosophies and strategies, particularly among parachurch youth ministries like Young Life, became prominent in the mid-twentieth century,[2] notes Dean. However, the "language of mission field faded" (2010, 232–33) by the end of the century. She surmises that the strategy often shifts from the primary goal of pointing youth to Jesus to lesser, secondary goals of youth group attendance and denominational behaviors and identity. Youth ministries, in one sense, do recognize that a kind of cross-cultural mission is appropriate for the communication of the gospel to teenagers. Talk of learning the pop-cultural world of teenagers for the sake of the gospel pervades the conversations and thoughts of youth ministers across the nation. Without consistent and meaningful congregational/denominational support in training and volunteers, though, it is easy for youth ministers to succumb to the numbers and behavioral game. "Still," Dean asserts, "youth ministry offers the American church a well-stocked laboratory for experimenting with incarnational missiology at home, as we seek to follow Jesus into the developmental and cultural spaces of adolescence" (2010, 93).

TAKE A CHANCE

Bill sat back and thought, a bit wistfully, about reading *Almost Christian* for the first time. Was it really a decade ago? He had been so fired up! He had plans to incarnationally engage the youth of his church and the wider

---

2.   For example, see Mark H. Senter III's *When God Shows Up: A History of Protestant Youth Ministry in America* (Grand Rapids: Baker Academic, 2010).

community with the gospel of Jesus Christ. And there were moments when he seemed effective. He just could never seem to sustain it. The pressures of the church bureaucracy to report on attendance and budget (important stuff that needs to done), coupled with his own inability to clearly communicate and implement a missional strategy for his youth ministry, left him feeling inadequate. He decided to give Stan a call.

"Part of me is just saying, 'Quit your whining!'" Bill had arrived at the end of his long explanation about what he had learned from the Larson article and his rereading of Dean. "But another part of me is saying, 'You've got to take a chance!'"

"What do you mean?" asked Stan.

"I mean what I've been missing in my efforts of youth ministry is using the lessons of missiology. To use a really bad metaphor, it's like youth ministry and mission are two people who know and like each other, but only as 'friends.'" Bill used air quotes with his hands, even though Stan couldn't see him. Bill continued, "But now youth ministry is kind of looking differently at missiology and missiology is noticing and thinking youth ministry is kind of cute. And they decide to take their relationship to the next level, then they get married and make a life together!"

"And they save the whole world together!" Stan was laughing out loud at Bill's enthusiasm and questionable use of analogy. "You're right, that is a bad metaphor."

"Thanks a lot," Bill pretended to mope.

"Your explanation is quirky, but I think you're on to something," Stan said. "You know, people are always asking Sally and me what we are doing now that we are no longer missionaries. I try not to be too snarky when I tell them that we still are missionaries. We are missionaries to our neighborhood, to the larger community, and to the youth. All the things we did in the Czech Republic, we do here. We live among the people, we learn their language and culture, we craft ways to translate the gospel, and we find creative ways to articulate and embody the gospel that makes sense in this context where God has called and sent us."

"Yeah, people are always saying that you don't have to be a missionary to follow God. That statement has really started to bug me."

"Me, too," responded Stan. "The reality is you do have to be a missionary, one who participates in the story of God's mission, to paraphrase Mr. Goheen."

After a pause in which both Bill and Stan reflected on what had been discussed, Stan said, "Bill, I want to give you the rest of my answer to your question—'What is a missionary?' When we were trying to decide what neighborhood to live in after moving back from the Czech Republic, I came across a book by John Perkins (2001), *Restoring At-Risk Communities*. Mr. Perkins is an African American who grew up in Mississippi and experienced quite harsh racism during his life. He came to Christ in a powerful way, and God called him back to Mississippi to work among the poor and disenfranchised. Serving missionally among people means identifying with them in the name of Christ. Mr. Perkins quotes a Chinese proverb that concisely and eloquently describes the life of a missionary. It reads in part: 'Go to the people / Live among them / Learn from them / Start with what they know / Build on what they have'" (2001, 18).

"Thanks, Stan. That's beautiful," said Bill. "Now, I think I know what my next step needs to be."

"What's that?" asked Stan.

"These definitions of mission and missionary have given me an appetite for a better understanding of a theology of mission. If this is what God has called me to, then I want to be able to know it and apply it purposively," said Bill.

"I can help you with that!" promised Stan.

QUESTIONS FOR REFLECTION

1. In this chapter, Bill recalls a time when he heard a call from God. Think about a time when God called you. What were the circumstances? How did you respond? Who were the people in your life who affirmed the call? What actions did you take as a result of God's call?

2. Look over the "Defining Mission" section of the chapter. What are the common words or phrases that each author uses? What is the key idea that each author is trying to convey? Using the inspiration of this section, write your own definition of mission as you understand it at this point.

3. Which missionary role—learner, trader, story teller—do you resonate with most? Why? In which role are you most effective? In which role do you need the most improvement?

4. Why is youth work like mission work?

5. Since youth work is like mission work, what adaptations might this suggest for the way you approach youth ministry, church, and mission?

3

WHY MISSION?

SOPHIA SAT AT THE TABLE with her vanilla soy milk latte in front of her mouth, like she was about to take a drink. She had been like this for several minutes, her eyes open but not really focused on Bill.

He finally said, "If you keep sitting there like a statue, birds are going to perch on your shoulders, and then you'll have to clean up the mess they leave behind."

Sophia broke out of her trance, and she smiled a bit sheepishly. "I just got deep into my thoughts for a minute, but I was really tracking with you."

"Really?" asked Bill.

"Yes!" responded Sophia. "Thanks for sharing your journey with me. I can hardly wait to meet Stan. He sounds like a jewel. The way he helped you process the idea of mission and that youth ministry is like being a missionary clearly had a big impact on you."

"It sure did, and I'm still trying to figure out all the implications."

"Me, too," piped Sophia. "I'm supposed to be in mission to my youth, at least in how you've just described it, right?"

Bill nodded while taking a sip of his large black coffee.

"Well, then, why mission?" asked Sophia.

"What do you mean?"

Sophia thought for a moment. "I mean, I've never really heard it explained like that, at least not in depth. So, is it something that has a biblical justification, or is it just a clever use of words? If I start talking like this to my senior pastor and church board, then they're going to want to know if the Bible backs it up."

Bill replied, "That's a fair question, and one that I had too, after my initial discussions with Stan. I wanted a better understanding of a biblical theology of mission, and I think that's what you're asking."

"I guess that's why you suggested I read Newbigin's *The Gospel in a Pluralist Society*?" queried Sophia.

"In a sense, but that book speaks more to context. There's some biblical and theological development that helps make sense of Newbigin. If you want to meet up again, I could share with you some ideas that Stan walked me through," suggested Bill.

"I would love to!" exclaimed Sophia. "This stuff makes me think hard, but it's also nurturing in a way. Do you want to meet back here at The Daily Grind?"

"Sure," answered Bill. "I'm always up for some overpriced hipster coffee."

One week later, Sophia and Bill returned to The Daily Grind, ordered their drinks, took over the corner booth, and dove into the world of missional theology.

DEVELOPING A MISSIONAL HERMENEUTIC

Michael Goheen (2014) points out that, not so long ago, teaching on the biblical foundations of mission primarily consisted of gleaning mission texts from the Bible and stringing them together. There would be a few nuggets in the Old Testament, in places like Jonah and the last part of Isaiah. But, let's face it, Jonah is not exactly the poster child for pristine mission work!

Of course, the New Testament offers more in the way of mission texts, with Jesus's commands, the story of the apostles, and the example of Paul. Even in this wealth of material, there is the tendency to justify mission activity on the basis of a few favorite, significant texts.

That is not to say that this kind of mission apologetic work is unenlightening. William Carey's 1792 treatise on the requirement for Christians to use means to proclaim the gospel in non-Christian lands has become a proven landmark in the history of mission. Carey, "the father of modern Protestant missions" (Moreau, Corwin, and McGee 2015, 43), bases his argument on what is now known as the Great Commission, Matthew 28:18–20. Jesus's postresurrection command to "go and make disciples of all nations," Carey insists, is still valid. Along with the Anabaptist, Pietist, and Moravian efforts that predated him, Carey's premise carried the day, launching the great Protestant mission advance of the 1800s.

While Christopher Wright (2006) acknowledges there is much to laud about Carey's work, the choice of a single text "leaves the biblical case vulnerably thin" (34). Wright commends Carey for making a case in his context but laments that it was not further developed, particularly as the missionary edifice grew. Goheen (2014) suggests that, at least in the evangelical tradition, we became seduced by our own assumptions. "We knew what mission was, and we could not imagine anything but being committed to it. All we needed was a biblical foundation to justify it" (Goheen 2014, 15), no matter how narrow.

Wright (2006) offers one of the more thorough efforts to broaden the biblical basis for mission. He says a defense of mission cannot be satisfied with a search for additional biblical texts "to show that Matthew has indeed captured an essential element of the witness of Scripture" (2006, 35). This often amounts to a kind of proof texting, which is susceptible to merely corroborating our presuppositions, to the point where "we are likely to find what we brought with us—our own conceptions of mission, now comfortingly festooned with biblical luggage tags" (2006, 37). These are strong words, and it should be highlighted here that Wright is not disparaging this kind of "legitimate and essential" (2006, 37) work. Rather, he is attempting to offer more—a missional hermeneutic of the Bible.

Perhaps it takes an Old Testament scholar like Wright to really bring the Old Testament into the conversation about mission. For Wright, mission is the interpretive coherence, that "orienting point" (2006, 40) from which we read the whole Bible. "Mission is what the Bible is all about" (2006, 29), he asserts.

He justifies this audacious statement by appealing to Luke 24. In this postresurrection story, Jesus appears to two disciples on the road to Emmaus. The unnamed disciples do not recognize Jesus at first. After telling Jesus about his own crucifixion (there is a comedic element here!), Jesus responds: "'Did not the Christ have to suffer these things and then enter his glory?' And beginning with Moses and all the prophets, he explained to them what was said in all the Scriptures concerning himself" (Luke 24:26–27). Later in Luke 24, Jesus appears to the Eleven and others with them and has a similar conversation (Luke 24:33–49). In each scenario, Jesus's own words place him as the messianic focus of the whole Old Testament. Wright indicates that, in general, Christians throughout history have embraced the "messianic reading of the Old Testament" (2006, 30).

The crucial element, though, for this discussion, Wright contends, is that Jesus goes "beyond the *messianic* centering of the Old Testament Scriptures to the *missional* thrust as well" (2006, 29). In both conversations, Jesus makes his case from "all the Scriptures," the Law, the Prophets, and the Wisdom literature (Luke 24:27, 44). Not only is Jesus's messiahship in view here but also, as he declares to his followers, "repentance and forgiveness of sins will be preached in [the Messiah's] name to all nations, beginning at Jerusalem. You shall be witnesses of these things" (Luke 24:47–48). So, as Wright insists, "The proper way for disciples of the crucified and risen Jesus to read their Scriptures is *messianically* and *missionally*" (30). Importantly, this view is carried on in Paul's writings and his apostolic ministry. Wright points to Paul's testimony to Festus in Acts 26:22–23: "I am saying nothing beyond what the prophets and Moses said would happen—that the Christ would suffer and, as the first to rise from the dead, would proclaim light to his own people and to the Gentiles."

Another way of saying this is that the Messiah has "*missional* significance" (C. J. H. Wright 2006, 30). He is the anointed one of God who is king, deliverer, and priest, and he is the embodiment of the "mission of Israel" (C. J. H. Wright 2006, 31). What is this mission? It is nothing less than blessing the nations of the world. The mission hearkens back to God's covenant with Abraham, the father of Israel. Out of the clamorous confusion of fallen humanity, God calls Abraham. He promises Abraham greatness, nationhood, and blessing. God's blessing, he tells Abraham, will be extended to "all peoples on earth" through him (Gen. 12:1–3). It is the Messiah Jesus, in his life, death, and resurrection, through whom the blessing to the nations is made possible. Wright explains: "The full meaning of recognizing Jesus as Messiah then lies in recognizing also his role in relation to God's mission for Israel for the blessing of the nations" (2006, 31). Thus, a messianic reading of Scripture that keeps Jesus in central view also demands a missional reading of the biblical text.

A MISSIONAL READING OF SCRIPTURE

What might a missional reading of the Bible look like? Several scholars have offered versions of the narrative arc of Scripture in recent years.[1] Let's look at Michael Goheen's offering in *Introducing Christian Mission Today*.

---

1. Some examples include Bartholomew and Goheen, *The Drama of Scripture: Finding Our Place in the Biblical Story*; Moreau, *Introducing World Missions*; Dyrness, *Let the Earth Rejoice*.

Goheen (2014) claims the biblical story is true for all people, in all times, in all places. The main theme in this narrative is "God's mission to restore the world and its people" (Goheen 2014, 38). A divine restoration is needed because of the "destructive power of sin" that is brought into God's creation by human rebellion against God. It results in alienation from God, creation, other people, and ourselves. The consequences of sin infect and affect every inch of the earth and every person for all generations. Therefore, a holistic restoration is needed. God announces his plan to crush evil in Genesis 3:15. From this proclamation, "the story of God's mission is the path he follows to make this good news known to the ends of the earth"(Goheen 2014, 39). The summary of this story can be stated in the following words: "Israel, Jesus, church" (Goheen 2014, 40).

ISRAEL

Goheen encourages a reading of Scripture that recognizes the movement of God's mission "from the particular to the universal" (39). Thus, God elects one people, Israel, to initiate his redemptive purposes. Goheen notes that the choice of Israel is not limited to privilege. Israel's election always has universal implications. It also comes with obligations and, in times of rebellion, judgment. Ultimately, though, the choice of Israel is a sign of God's grace for both Israel and all others.

As mentioned above, Israel's election starts with the call and blessing of Abraham (Gen. 12:1–3). This singular act, though, is set amidst the "universal backdrop" (Goheen 2014, 40) of Genesis 1–11. Key themes emerge in the opening account, which are central to the biblical story. The God who calls Abraham is the creator of the universe. This God is not a limited, regional god but the Sovereign of all nations—indeed, the whole earth. Humanity is created in the image of this God, but all peoples rebel against him in thought, word, and deed. All come under the judgment of God, but at the same time he enacts his redemptive plan for the restoration of all his creation. Into this wide scope comes the call to one man, to one family, to bring God's promise to the whole world.

The family grows, and through a mixture of both faithfulness and faithlessness, the Hebrew people become enslaved. God intervenes with miraculous, liberating acts. In doing so, God chooses Israel "in God's redemptive purpose" (Goheen 2014, 42), to be a display people. He calls them "my treasured possession . . . a kingdom of priests and a holy nation" (Exod. 19:5–6). As a nation set apart, "Israel is summoned to be a model of what God intends for human life" (Goheen 2014, 42). The goal is that Israel's life in special relation-ship with God will be so attractive that other nations will desire a close bond with God too. This universal intention of their covenantal relationship is a central expectation, and reminders come in both stories (Jonah) and worship (Psalms), but Israel finds it difficult to maintain fidelity to God's mission.

God gives a land to Israel from which they live in view of the nations. Unfortunately, they enter into cycles of apostasy and recovery, and the people cry out for the stability of a king. Though this is an affront to God's rule of Israel, he grants their request but "incorporates the kingship into his cove-nantal and missional purposes" (Goheen 2014, 47). In the Davidic covenant, God promises an everlasting kingdom that "becomes the universal horizon of God's redemptive purposes" (Goheen 2014, 47). Still, Israel's covenantal rebellion continues until God's judgment comes as the northern kingdom is obliterated and the southern kingdom is defeated by Babylon.

God is not done with Israel yet. Though they play the harlot and chase after other gods, God redemptively loves them back into his fold (Hosea 1–3; Ezekiel 16). The prophets speak of a future hope, a time when God's mission through Israel will be fulfilled. They also speak of a Messiah, one who is both king and servant, and one who will bring God's mission to fruition.

Goheen mentions three terms in relation to God's mission through Israel: universal, centripetal, and eschatological. Israel's covenant with God came with the universal intent to bless all the nations. Centripetally, Israel is in focus as a showcase people, who in their worship of the one, true God point others to him. Ultimate fulfillment, though, waits for that eschatologi-cal moment "when God will break into history in an unusually powerful way through the Messiah and by the Spirit" (Goheen 2014, 49).

JESUS

Goheen highlights the recovery of Israel's mission in the coming of the Messiah, Jesus. The kingdom mission of Jesus is a time of gathering. Guests gather at a banquet (Luke 14:15–24); a harvest is gathered (Matt. 9:37–38); a shepherd gathers lost sheep (John 10:1–18). Jesus initiates this mission by gathering and restoring Israel, according to prophetic expectations. Jesus calls his people to the good life, characterized by "love, reconciliation, peace, joy, justice, compassion, and solidarity with the poor and marginal-ized" (56). In fellowship with the Father and Son and empowered by the Spirit, such a life is a participation with God to work transformation in the world (John 14–16).

If one wants to extract the essence of Christian mission, Goheen suggests, then one must look at how Jesus lived out his kingdom mission. First, Jesus's central message consists of an announcement of the arrival of the kingdom of God. "Jesus went into Galilee proclaiming the good news of God. 'The time has come,' he said. 'The kingdom of God is near. Repent and believe the good news'" (Mark 1:14–15). This announcement came with an invitation and the expectation of a choice. The decision to receive the gift of the kingdom and enter into it invokes urgency (Luke 9:57–62) and costliness (Luke 14:25–33). The blessings of the kingdom, though, bring forgiveness, relationship with God, and joy.

A second element of the kingdom mission of Jesus is authentication by deeds. Jesus's life is an inventory of demonstrations of the arrival of God's kingdom. From his Trinitarian relationship with the Father and the Spirit (Luke 3:22) and his commitment to prayer (Luke 5:16; Mark 1:35; John 17), to his teaching to both the few and the many in various social contexts (John 3; Matt. 5) and his acts of healing and forgiveness (Luke 21–23; Mark 2:1–12), Jesus enacts God's kingdom mission to restore creation to its original beauty.

Third, this missional life of Jesus, then, becomes a model of mission for his followers. In short, disciples of Jesus are called to mission the Jesus way. The gathered and discipled community does not exist for itself. It gives itself, like Jesus, in service to others. Such sacrificial service requires a life commitment for the sake and the salvation of the world. Moreover, it meets the challenges of various contexts "in the pattern of Jesus with imagination and creativity" (Goheen 2014, 59).

Participation in the missional life of Jesus requires the sustaining power of two cataclysmic events: crucifixion and resurrection. As Goheen explains, "these two events constitute the turning point of universal history" (2014, 60), as the old age passes away and the age to come arrives. The regathered Israel now has access to the liberating power over the darkness of Satan, sin, and death and can truly become light to the world. "The cross accomplishes the salvation of the entire creation and all nations; the resurrection is the dawning of the renewed creation. On the basis of these events Jesus draws his disciples together and commissions them to take the good news to all nations, even to the ends of the earth" (Goheen 2014, 60–61). As Wright would say, the Messiah has "missional significance" (C. J. H. Wright 2006, 30).

CHURCH

Two more events serve to launch the church (*ekklesia*—the assembled or gathered) into God's mission. First, Jesus ascends and is exalted. In Jesus's ascension, his rule over the world is proclaimed. Second, his presence with his people is assured through the coming of the Spirit. The new community is formed in the Spirit and begins to experience a life in the Spirit that is attractive, powerful, and nurturing.

In the midst of early growth, roadblocks to expanding God's mission rise up in Jerusalem and Israel in the forms of rejection of the gospel message and persecution. "Yet the time has also come for Gentiles who believe the gospel to be grafted on like wild shoots," writes Goheen (2014, 64). Beginning with the ministry of Peter among the Samaritans and with Cornelius (Acts 8:14–17, 10:1–11:18), and then spreading because of persecution, the gospel is extended beyond Jerusalem. It is in Antioch, in the gathered community of believers from both Gentile and Jewish backgrounds, where God's Spirit intentionally operationalizes the cross-cultural communication of the gospel. Moved by the Spirit in worship and prayer, the multicultural leadership of the Antiochian church send out Paul and Barnabas to spread the gospel to Asia Minor (Acts 13:1–3).

In the mission of Paul, a new aspect of God's mission blossoms. Paul plants gathered communities of Christ followers in new places and encourages them to "be mission" in their locale. He nurtures them with periodic visits and letters of chastisement and instruction. This method is significant, as it introduces a centrifugal direction in mission. However, the movement of sending out and gathering in are best held together in creative tension. Both serve the other and are needed for effectiveness in God's mission.

The expansion of these early Christian communities into new areas creates a disturbance. The simultaneous breaking out of the Hebrew/Aramaic Jewish world and breaking into the Greek/Latin Hellenistic world begin to raise important practical and theological questions (Sanneh 1989). Jewish opposition arises and a meeting of Christian leaders is called (Acts 15). The decision from this Jerusalem Council is that God's mission is not held captive by Jewish culture: "from now on the mission of God's people will involve a missionary encounter with all cultures, embracing the priceless treasures and opposing the destructive idolatries of all cultures" (Goheen 2014, 67).

This kind of reading of the biblical text reveals the "missional thrust" of the whole Bible, both Old and New Testaments. Missionary activity, then, becomes more than mere obedience by a few mission professionals to Jesus's last command. Rather, it demonstrates participation in God's mission to bless the nations as central to the identity of the church and of each disciple of Christ.

DEVELOPING A TRINITARIAN FRAMEWORK

Recognizing the core missional narrative of Scripture is a helpful and essential aspect of a vital missiology. Reading Scripture with an eye for the coherent story of God creating and then wooing his creation back into fellowship is compelling and inspirational. An additional way to look at mission is to focus on the main character of the missional story, God himself. Who is this God who creates, initiates, calls, blesses, forgives, returns, and restores?

Timothy Tennent suggests that "missions should never be conceptualized apart from the *missio dei*" (2010, 59). Recalling the exposition of the definition of mission in chapter 1, *missio dei* refers to God's initiative agency in expanding his kingdom. Since "mission is far more about God and who he is than about us and what we do," then "understanding mission through the lens of the *missio dei* is fundamentally sound" (2010, 59), asserts Tennent. He laments that much of evangelical teaching and training tends to disconnect God's agency from everyday missions practice. His remedy is "a Trinitarian framework for missions."

The God of Christianity is the triune God, who comes to us as Father, Son, and Holy Spirit. This is the way he is revealed in the scriptural narrative explored above, and it is the way the early church describes him in the historic creeds. Often the doctrine of the Trinity is seen as cold, irrelevant, and problematic, according to Michael Reeves (2012). Reeves contends, though, that exploring the knowledge of God as triune is to see his beauty. The love of God that is expressed in the eternal relationship of Father, Son, and Holy Spirit overflows into creation, redemption, and restoration. Reeves insists that knowledge and experience of the triune nature of God transforms life.

In the stream of that idea, Tennent makes the case that good missiology "flows out of a Trinitarian framework" (2010, 74). He delves into four themes for each person of the Trinity to construct the framework.

GOD THE FATHER

First, God the Father is the initiative force of missions. Too often in the history of mission, God has been presented and perceived as the possession of a particular culture or people. This tends to put the emphasis on human agency and relegate God to something akin to a wrapped present or a precious jewel in a treasure chest. When mission is described primarily as human activity, then it is easily entangled with colonialism and imperialism. "Thus, rooting missions in God the Father as the source and originator of mission delivers all past, present, and future agents of the gospel from a sense of triumphalism" (Tennent 2010, 76).

Second, God the Father is the sending source of missions. It is typical to present Jesus Christ as the primary sender. This is not wrong in the sense that Jesus, indeed, utters send directives. For example, see John 20:21: "Again Jesus said, 'Peace be with you! As the Father has sent me, I am sending you'" (NIV). And in the Great Commission passage of Matthew 28:19, Jesus instructs the disciples to "Go." Tennent points out, though, that Jesus is acting on granted authority from the Father. When this is underemphasized or missed, then mission becomes a New Testament addition, rather than a core aspect of the biblical story from the beginning.

The continuity of mission in the biblical story leads to the third theme related to God the Father: "human history is the stage upon which the divine drama unfolds" (Tennent 2010, 77). The calling and covenant of Abraham, the incarnation and crucifixion and resurrection of Jesus, the mission work of Paul and the early church, and the two-millennia expansion of the Christian movement around the globe all are rooted in historical accounts. Andrew Walls corroborates this idea when he says, "Christian salvation depends on a historical event: Christ suffered under Pontius Pilate" (2009, 72). This singular event, though pointedly significant, is connected to the historical process that precedes it and follows it. The implication, Tennent suggests, is that this grounding in history, from creation until now, indicates that God the Father is more than merely a metaphysical idea. God the Father purposively initiates and interacts with human history, which puts God's plan in the realm of public truth.

The fourth theme related to God the Father that Tennent develops is focused on the relational, holy love of God. In a world that tends to be skeptical of truth claims and other declarations of objectivity, the relational nature of the Trinity, which is the source of all human relationships, is a rich reservoir. Michael Reeves (2012) stresses that God as Father is foundational to his identity. God's fatherliness implies relationship to things he begets (the Son) and the things he creates (this earth and its inhabitants). Therefore, God's key quality is love, as reflected in these associations. Another foundational characteristic of God is holiness. "There is no relationship with God apart from holiness. The redeemed community is to be a holy community" (Tennent 2010, 80). This pushes the goal of missionary practice beyond individual conversions to a "renewed emphasis on holiness, intensive discipleship, and learning to live counter to the culture" as "a community that reflects the colloquy of the triune God" (Tennent 2010, 80–81).

GOD THE SON, THE INCARNATE ONE

God became human in the person of Jesus Christ. This simple statement has significant implications, as Jesus is not merely the carrier of a godly message. Jesus is the full embodiment and entry of God into the created order. The church, in order to live out God's mission, has more than a message to proclaim. It has a mission to live. Four themes highlight God the Son's embodiment of the *missio dei*.

First, the incarnation doubles down on the idea that this world and its history is the stage for the drama of the *missio dei*. The triune God, in the divine/human person of Jesus Christ, "intersects with human history to accomplish His redemptive plans" (82). Jesus, then, is the "archetypal missionary" (Tennent 2010, 81), who crossed the ultimate divide between humanity and divinity to bring life-giving news. So, the crossing of geographic, linguistic, cultural, and generational barriers in the past, present, and future by faithful missionaries, both professional and lay, "represents countless reenactments of the Incarnation on a small scale" (Tennent 2010, 84).

Second, Tennent, like Kenda Creasy Dean (see chap. 1), turns to Andrew Walls to emphasize the translatability of the gospel as depicted in the incarnation. Certainly the fact that the New Testament documents were written down in a common form of Greek, and that those documents are the primary witness of Jesus, the Incarnate One, shows that the gospel is translatable linguistically. This fact laid the theological foundation for the translation of the Bible to be a key method in the history of mission practice. Moreover, the incarnation shows that the gospel is translatable culturally. As mentioned above, the early church at the Jerusalem Council (Acts 15) determined that no one culture, not even Jewish culture, should hold the gospel captive. Even when humans are reticent, God boldly moves forward (Acts 15:6–11). "Thus, the Incarnation effectively throws open the door for all the strategic, missiological reflections on contextualization and how the gospel maintains its universal qualities even when it is embodied within a potentially infinite array of cultural particularities" (Tennent 2010, 86).

Tennent turns again to Walls for the development of a third theme related to the incarnation. In what Walls calls the "Ephesians moment" (2009), Paul declares that a key component of the church is its ethnic diversity united in the body of Christ (see Eph. 2). Or, as Tennent says, "The church was to be as diverse as the human race but still one in Jesus Christ" (2010, 87). Mission, then, is an outflow of this new human community and "should be the greatest force for racial and ethnic reconciliation" (Tennent 2010, 88). An additional outcome is that mission flows both ways, in that missionary activity has the power to transform both the receiver and the sender. Peter's encounter with Cornelius in Acts 10 demonstrates this reality, as both were changed by the cross-cultural encounter. Every time the gospel crosses a barrier, a more rich, robust, and full understanding of God is in view.

A fourth theme is "the holistic ministry of Jesus as a model for Christian engagement in the world" (Tennent 2010, 92). Tennent draws attention to gospel descriptions of Jesus's ministry that emphasize both proclamation and healing (Matt. 9:35; Luke 9:2) as models for mission practice. The kingdom of God, as exemplified by the Incarnate One, is concerned for and transforms both body and soul. Mission in light of the incarnation encompasses individuals and the systems they live in, calling for a full witness of the church that embodies evangelism, service, and justice (Snyder 1996).

GOD THE HOLY SPIRIT

While Tennent notes that the recognition of the work of the Holy Spirit in the Trinitarian understanding of God historically has not garnered the same attention as that of the Father and the Son, recent developments in the rise of Pentecostalism and in the writings of key twentieth-century theologians have brought attention to the Third Person of the Trinity.

The first theme Tennent mentions is the Spirit's empowerment for witness. He notes, "At Pentecost the church was equipped to be the community of proclamation that embodies in word and deed the inbreaking of God's reign" (2010, 95). This coincides with what we heard earlier from Goheen regarding the presence of the Spirit enlivening the church for an attractive and powerful communal life. Pentecost, occurring as it did in the midst of linguistic diversity, indicates that this empowerment is central to the cross-cultural communication of the gospel.

Second, Tennent says, "The Holy Spirit is the divinely appointed catechist for the church" (2010, 96). The passing on of the basic teachings of the Christian faith to emerging generations and to new cultural communities through both formal and informal instruction always has been an important part of the missional process. Every extension of the kingdom of God into new hearts and new places is a reminder of the Holy Spirit's role as teacher.

A third thematic development related to God the Spirit, according to Tennent, is sustaining power when faced with suffering and persecution. Suffering for the sake of the gospel, at least for most of the history of the church in the West, has been limited to those "professional" missionaries when facing rejection and sometimes death when advancing the gospel into new lands. For the "common" Western Christian at home, suffering and persecution are not typical experiences or topics for discussion. As the missional nature of the church is embraced and as a post-Christian context takes hold in the West, the voices and experiences of the church in the Majority World will be instructive. Guidance and empowerment of the Holy Spirit is crucial for these lessons from the Majority World to be learned and applied.

Finally, Tennent emphasizes that missions is the joyous overflow of life in the Spirit, moving it beyond merely obedience to a command. Understanding missions as an extension of the Holy Spirit's work in the life of the church has the potential to free missionary activity from overreliance on human agency. This directs the missional church to the goal of partnering with the Holy Spirit to usher in the new creation, so "we become heralds who embody the inbreaking of the New Creation" (Tennent 2010, 101).

RESHAPING MINISTRY

A month later, Sophia and Bill wrapped up their fourth weekly meeting. The table was strewn with books and papers and the ever-present reservoirs of caffeine. Bill now regularly ordered the bottomless cup of coffee. He even started bringing his own mug. Sophia, for her part, was feeling like she spent most of her salary on soy lattes.

Stan joined them this time. Like a "real" European, he sipped on a double espresso. He was impressed with Bill's explanations of missional theology and with Sophia's astute questions. He felt like a proud papa.

Sophia sat back and addressed Bill and Stan, "I want to thank you for all of this," she said as she spread her hands over the table. "As I soak in all of it, I think it has the potential to reshape my ministry."

"Well, you've been great. It's so nice to talk about this stuff with someone who is so interested," said Bill. "These sessions have also helped me. Talking about this stuff has caused me to refine some points and to affirm others."

Stan looked to Sophia, and asked, "Sophia, I'd be interested in how you think your youth ministry will be affected. I know it's early in the process, but what would you say is your launching point for reshaping your ministry?"

"Oh my!" exclaimed Sophia. She smiled, started to say something a couple of times, and then just looked at the other two with both delight and vexation. She began to talk with hesitancy and then picked up her pace. "Well, it's not that I haven't been thinking about the impact of missional theology on my ministry, because I have. But I haven't really said it out loud yet. I guess the launching point, as you call it, for my ministry is changing. When I got started in youth ministry, my main thing was to help the youth navigate the pitfalls of adolescence, and I thought Jesus was their best bet to do it. That's not a bad motivation, but I see now it is fairly limited. For example, what about when they graduate high school? Am I guiding them into something that will mold their whole life or just provide a fix for high school?"

Sophia was on a roll now. "However, reading Scripture with a missional hermeneutic shows me that the goal is wider and more intimate. It's wider in the sense that we are invited to participate in God's ongoing redemption of the world. It's more intimate in the sense that to accept that invitation means a total reorientation of one's life. It requires a total commitment that can only happen as we open our lives to the outgoing love of the Father, Son, and Holy Spirit."

Sophia giggled. "Listen to me. I'm starting to sound like a theology professor. But this stuff has real applications. If I am working with God's agenda, then my goal is not just fixing kids. What I'm inviting them into is life-altering. That means I have to meet them where they are, learn their lives, language, and culture. And I'm not just reaching individual kids. I need to help form them into a missional community. I need to think and act like a missionary!"

Stan replied, "I'm quite impressed. You're saying things that took me a few years to figure out."

"Thanks, Stan," said Sophia. "Now I know I can talk about it. I'm still trying to figure out how to do it." She turned to Bill and asked, "Is that why you had me read Newbigin?"

"Yes, it is," said Bill. "Newbigin, with his years of mission work experience in India, was able to turn his expertise toward the post-Christian West. He was one of the first to see that the West is a mission field, too. His book is a bit heady, but I find his ideas extremely valuable for the youth ministry context."

"I'd like to get together and talk through those ideas," said Sophia.

"Same time, next week?" asked Bill.

"Can I tag along again?" inquired Stan.

Sophia replied, "I can't imagine doing it without you!"

THE NEWBIGIN CHALLENGE

God's mission clearly has a spatial dimension. The mission works toward completion as people are gathered from across cultural and linguistic barriers into one body, worshiping together in one place. For example, Ephesians 2 indicates that "the dividing wall of hostility" (v. 14) has been torn down between Jews and Gentiles and that they have been made into one body. They now are "fellow citizens" and "members of God's household" (v. 19). Paul's ecclesial description here shows the early church working out what it meant to "make disciples of all nations" (Matt. 28:19).

Andrew Walls (1996) expounds on this spatial dimension of God's mission, but he also points to the temporal aspect. Rather than collapsing various salvific events together such as incarnation, crucifixion, resurrection, and second coming, God patiently is waiting for his mission to be completed. Walls says, "The work of salvation is a historical process that stretches out to the end of the age" (1996, 73). The implication is that not only are all peoples of various ethnicities gathered together. It is also true that "salvation is complete only when all the generations of God's people are gathered together" (1996, 74). Since the "work of salvation is cross-generational" (74, 75), no one generation has a monopoly on Christian expression. Social and cultural realities must be taken into consideration for effective extension of God's mission.

Lesslie Newbigin (1989) steps into the social and cultural reality of the current age with *The Gospel in a Pluralist Society*. Newbigin's long, distinguished career as a pastor, missionary evangelist, and theologian prepared him to turn his missiological insights on his own Western culture. In doing so, he develops what some call a domestic missiology for the West.

Newbigin challenges the church to a new way of functioning by encouraging it to live out the "plausibility structure" of the gospel in order to provide a quality witness to the reigning culture. He attacks the false dualism that reached fruition during the seventeenth-century Enlightenment. Christianity's failure to critique the rise of reason and empiricism as the sole basis of knowledge allowed a separation between the world of facts and values. By questioning the assumptions of this prevailing plausibility structure, Newbigin shows how Christians can confidently assert the truth claims of the gospel. We are called as Christians to live within both the biblical tradition and our Western cultural tradition.

The Christian tradition, or story, which flows from the heart of God's mission to restore creation is grounded in the "happenedness" of the biblical record and includes the experiences of Christian communities as they have struggled through the ages to live gospel truths. The Christian church in the West today also lives squarely in the reigning Western tradition. Newbigin's call, which every Christian should heed, is to enter both traditions. As members of contemporary society, we share in the reigning plausibility structure. Though it is not the "home" tradition of Christians, we know what it feels like to live in it. We internalize the debate. A healthy participation in the Christian tradition/story, then, prepares the church for a faithful witness. Newbigin writes,

There is room only for faithful witness to the one in whom the whole picture of God for cosmic history has been revealed and effected, the crucified, risen, and regnant Christ. So the logic of mission is this: the true meaning of the human story has been disclosed. Because it is the truth, it must be shared universally. . . . The gospel calls us back again and again to the real clue . . . that history is given its meaning by what God has done in Jesus Christ and by what he has promised to do; and that the true horizon is not at the successful end of our projects but in his coming to reign. (1989, 125–26)

This is particularly true as the modern project based in Enlightenment thinking crumbled in the twentieth century. In our current postmodern world, in which "facts" can be manipulated and faked, the Enlightenment is now seen as a spent force, and a moral consensus cannot be developed based on reason alone. Science and education, apparently, cannot bring inevitable progress, as actions and reactions to the COVID-19 pandemic have shown. As George Hunter notes, this crumbling of "intellectual foundations" has left "Western humanity without a consensus worldview" (1996, 22).

Newbigin's call to the Western church to embrace its missional nature, then, is even more essential today than when he initially made it. In taking up Newbigin's challenge, the Western church needs to rediscover the mission frontier at the church's front door—or even the church's pews, as the case may be.

THE CHURCH AS GOSPEL HERMENEUTIC

It is in this vein that, as it participates in God's mission, the church is the hermeneutic of the gospel. It is the living interpretation of the gospel by word and deed. Newbigin notes that Jesus did not come to write a book but to form a community. This community, the church, when it is true to its calling, should reflect the character of Jesus as it shapes its members to live out God's mission. He identifies six characteristics of the church as a missional community. First, the church counters the mood of the general society by being a community of praise. In a time when leaders and facts continually are held in suspicion, and when trust is broken between the people and key institutions of society, then well-placed reverence for the one, true God offers people a recovery of their worth and dignity. The praise of God is marked by thanksgiving, recognizing that "we have been given everything and forgiven everything and promised everything" (Newbigin 1989, 228). The church's response is an overflow of gratitude that pours into care for others.

Second, church is a community of truth that lives and proclaims the plausibility structure of the gospel and is skeptical of the messages of general society. This should not be seen as a retreat from a media-soaked world. Rather, through the remembrance and proclamation of the true gospel story, the church community is able to present truth to its environment with "the modesty, the sobriety, and the realism which are proper for a disciple of Jesus" (Newbigin 1989, 229).

A third characteristic is that the church "is God's embassy in a specific place" (229). This implies a vital connection to both God and neighborhood. The church is an agent of the mercy and judgment of God as it facilitates the relationship between people and God. Also, the church's neighborhood is squarely in view, and the church knows the needs of its environment so well that "good news overflows in good action" (Newbigin 1989, 229).

Fourth, the church is a community of priests. Here, Newbigin speaks of the New Testament doctrine of the priesthood of all believers that the Protestant Reformers highlighted. A priest mediates the relationship between God and people. Jesus does this in the ultimate sense in his salvific and sanctifying work through the incarnation. In turn, "the Church is sent into the world to continue that which [Jesus] came to do, in the power of the Spirit, reconciling people to God" (Newbigin 1989, 230). Regular worship by the church community is a reminder of its participation and "sentness" in regard to Jesus's ministry, and the world is the realm where the church's priesthood is manifest. Newbigin indicates that sustaining this kind of priestly ministry requires a kind of "missionary training" (1989, 231) that is nourished by the preaching and teaching in the local church. Also, the church should be open to a diversity of gifting and service in support of the priestly function.

Newbigin's fifth characteristic of the church as hermeneutic of the gospel is that it is a community of mutual responsibility. This is a direct challenge to the radical individualism promoted by Western society. The church is "a foretaste of a different social order" (Newbigin 1989, 231) that recognizes that human identity is found in relationship with others. Only by living in accountability to each other can the church viably call the prevailing culture into account.

Finally, sixth, Newbigin characterizes the church as a community of hope. Once again, this gospel of hope confronts Western life, which places much of its trust in technological advance. The result, unfortunately, has not been enhanced social relationships. The very technological advances that promise so much often result in despair and separation and an inability to really listen to each other. Each social media app that is launched is an example of this alienation. The church is sent into such communal dysfunction as a sign of hope. But, Newbigin proclaims, this hope will only be known:

By movements that begin with the local congregation in which the reality of the new creation is present, known, and experienced, and from which men and women will go into every sector of public life to claim it for Christ, to unmask the illusions which have remained hidden and to expose all areas of public life to the illumination of the gospel. (Newbigin 1989, 232–33)

BOSCH'S MISSIONAL ECCLESIOLOGY

An excellent complement to Newbigin is the work of the world-renowned South African missiologist David Bosch (1991). In his epic tome *Transforming Mission*, he describes various biblical and historical paradigms that have formed the Christian understanding of mission. He identifies two aspects of a missional ecclesiology as the church lays claim to its mission nature in a postmodern world.

First is the recognition of a new relationship between the church and the world. Rather than setting church and world in direct conflict, Bosch shows how many now see the two more in solidarity. Bosch suggests a coexistence that sees mission as church-with-others. In this way the church truly can be salt, light, and servant to the world. "Just as one could not speak of the church without speaking of its *mission*, it was impossible to think of the church without thinking, in the same breath, of the *world* to which it is sent" (Bosch 1991, 386, author's emphasis).

Bosch submits, second, that two views should be held together for effective mission. One view sees the church owning the exclusive realm of salvation. The other views the church as a sign of God's interaction with the world. Bosch suggests that the two views need not be mutually exclusive. Rather, he advances a perception of the church with a dual focus held in "creative tension" (Bosch 1991, 390–98). The church's gathering together in worship and prayer sustains its involvement in the world. He writes:

> One may, therefore, perceive the church as an ellipse with two foci. In and around the first it acknowledges and enjoys the source of its life; this is where worship and prayer are emphasized. From and through the second focus the church engages and challenges the world. This is a forth-going and self-spending focus, where service, mission and evangelism are stressed. . . . The church's *identity* sustains its *relevance* and *involvement*. (Bosch 1991, 395)

BACK AT THE GRIND

"You know, Newbigin and Bosch use some terminology and concepts that stretch my mind," said Sophia, "but these discussions really got me to see applications for youth ministry."

Sophia, Bill, and Stan were sitting in their corner booth, which they now called "The Bunker."

"Stan, I've really appreciated your applications from a European context. They seem to be a few years ahead of America in their post-Christian context. Hearing about your ministry, particularly with university students, helps me see how to minister to my own kids," remarked Sophia.

"Sally and I essentially do the same thing here that we did in Europe," replied Stan. "We're still doing missions!"

Bill jumped in, "And that brings us back to your original question, Sophia. Why mission? Do you think you have an answer yet?"

"Okay, I knew you were going to ask me that. So, here it goes." Sophia took a deep breath and proceeded, "I think the answer has two facets: a panoramic view and a more focused view. The wide view is that mission initiates in the life of God, who is Father, Son, and Holy Spirit. The vibrant love of the Trinitarian community overflows into the creative act and, in the face of sinful rebellion, extends into redemption and restoration. The scriptural record is the story of how God sends himself to Israel; in the incarnation, crucifixion, and resurrection of Jesus Christ; and in the sustaining power of the Holy Spirit. The church, then, gets to participate in the mission of the triune God as it is the embodiment of God's mission for the world. Why mission? Because it is a joining with God's mission."

Stan and Bill erupted with cheers, and the three share high-fives in The Bunker.

Sophia continued, "The focused view tells me that my current context is in need of mission. It's in need of the kind of ministry that willingly and intentionally seeks to cross barriers of language, culture, and worldview. My context, and the context of my youth, speaks and lives a dialect that is different and even opposed to the gospel story. So, with my knowledge and experience of the current pluralistic context, along with my knowledge and experience of living the gospel of Jesus, I am called to embody and translate the gospel story in the world where I live. That means I am a missionary sent to this place, here and now. Why mission? Because my local context requires it for the gospel to be cross-generational."

"I couldn't have said it better myself," said Bill. "No really, I have never said it better." Bill looked at Stan. "The student has surpassed the teachers!"

"Then, I think it's time for us to get out of The Bunker and get back out there!" piped Stan.

"Let's go!" yelled Bill and Sophia.

QUESTIONS FOR REFLECTION

1. What are the implications for developing a missional hermeneutic for the reading of Scripture?

2. If mission is the "orienting point" of the biblical story, as Christopher Wright suggests, then what is the relationship between a messianic and a missional reading of Scripture?

3. Develop your own outline of the biblical narrative, similar to Michael Goheen's.

4. Since God initiates mission, how does knowing God as Father, Son, and Holy Spirit enhance your understanding of mission?

5. Lesslie Newbigin challenges the church to embrace its missional nature. How would leaning into the six characteristics he outlines for the church as missional community begin to change and form your own local church and youth ministry?

4

THE IMPACT OF
THE INCARNATION

SOPHIA AND BILL CONNECTED over coffee the following month. After they shared a little bit about families and ministry busyness, they got back into the conversation about mission and youth ministry.

"Okay, Bill. I get that what we are doing is God's mission. I get that in being a missionary we are 'learners, traders, and story tellers.' It is energizing, freeing, and humbling to realize that we are part of something much bigger than ourselves. It is also pretty awesome to think of the God we serve as a God who loves in that kind of way. But I have a much more practical question for you."

"What's that, Sophia?" Bill responded.

"How does God's mission to make himself known show up today? I understand that God desires to be known by all of creation. But it seems like the middle school boys who come to youth group on Wednesday night are much more interested in the newest game on their phone than knowing God. How does God show up in their lives? I believe he does, but I sometimes have a hard time seeing it. I also have a hard time explaining that to some of the other adult youth leaders in my church. They often want to *make* the youth 'get in line' so they can learn the right information. While I do think respect is important, it feels awkward when we seem to push all our mission activity into a classroom-like setting. Doesn't God show up in more than just our instructional style teaching?"

Bill smiled broadly at this. Sophia feigned throwing her coffee at him. "What are you laughing at? This may seem obvious to you, but it is not to me."

"I am not laughing at you or because this is easy. I am smiling because you just described me and my approach the first ten years of my ministry. I know the impulse your adults are experiencing. I am also impressed by your intuitive understanding that this is not the best way."

"So, what changed?" Sophia prompted.

"Everything," Bill calmly stated. "Everything, but it was so subtle that most people did not even realize the shift. I started focusing on relationships and stopped trying to fix people. We still did weekly programs, monthly programs, annual programs, and so on. But my focus, and then the focus of our youth ministry, shifted."

"I am not sure I really understand the shift. I am also not sure what this has to do with God showing up in people's lives."

"It started with a lot of failure on my part. That and reading a great book by Andrew Root, *Revisiting Relational Youth Ministry*." Bill continued, "It was failure because while I was doing a good job getting a lot of youth to come to youth group—quite a few of whom were 'making decisions for Jesus'—and I had a high approval rating among parents and the elders, we were not doing such a good job producing real disciples of Jesus."

"So how did this book help? Is it another mission text?" Sophia wondered.

"Nope. In fact, I am not sure he even uses the word 'mission' one time in the whole thing. But it changed everything for me because it pointed me to the incarnation. While Root does not specifically name his theological exploration of the incarnation as missional or missiological, it clearly seeks to connect God's people, specifically youth workers, with God's mission as exemplified in the incarnation. His book got me interested in reading more about incarnational ministry, and then I found this great little book from Darrell Guder called *The Incarnation and the Church's Witness*."

"Tell me more!" Sophia prompted.

WHAT THEY FOUND

In youth ministry there has been an emphasis on relational ministry and relational evangelism. This usually means that the youth leaders should be willing to go to where youth are, try to share with them the good news, and then expect a specific response that fits the church's criteria. Root calls this building "connections," which are different from real relationships.

When youth leaders approach people through connections, this is an ideological approach. It starts with a search for a common belief, like being fans of the same team, liking the same kinds of music, or believing the correct way about Jesus. If there is not a common belief, then the goal is to convert the other person to the ideology of the youth leader. An ideology is a system of ideas and ideals that is the basis for one's actions.

In the case of Christian youth workers, when operating from an ideological approach, there is an attempt to convert youth to an ideology of how a good Christian looks and lives. This is often an easy trap to fall into because it appears easy to measure. For example, before meeting the youth pastor and attending the youth ministry, Johnny did not know Jesus, swore all the time, disobeyed his parents, and went to drinking parties. Now that Johnny has met the youth pastor and visited the youth ministry, Johnny has realized the errors of his life and has said the right prayer, no longer swears, obeys his parents, and goes to youth group events instead of drinking parties. His ideology has been changed from the previous incorrect one to the one that is correct.

The difficulty in this approach to relational ministry is that youth workers start their relationship with youth with an agenda: changing the youth's ideology. It turns out that youth, and most people, do not want a relationship with someone whose big desire is to "fix" them. Youth can sense this agenda and do not want to be a part of that kind of relationship.

In a way, the youth leader is cheapening the relationship with their agenda to change ideology instead of just caring for the person. What happens to the relationship between Johnny and the youth leader if Johnny does not change his ideology? Those youth rarely stay around because the youth leader can get frustrated with Johnny's "lack of obedience to God" (as the youth leader defined it) and throw up his or her hands and say, "I did my part, but Johnny did not change." Then the youth leader would move on to a relationship with another youth. This makes Johnny feel like his only value comes if and when he changes his ideology to match that of the youth pastor and youth ministry.

While approaching youth relationships with an agenda can seem very self-defeating, it is important to note that most youth leaders are reaching out to youth because of a good heart. They desire young people, like Johnny, to come to know God! The youth leader knows it is really a transforming experience. The problem is that when a youth leader, youth group, or church is focused on changing ideology and behavior, they appear less and less like

Jesus. They appear to care only about new relationships when the new person is willing to become like the youth leader, youth group, and church.

THE INCARNATION IS AN EXTENSION OF GOD'S MISSION

When youth leaders are asked to define the word "incarnation," they often respond, "the Word made flesh," quoting John 1:14 (NIV). This is a great start to the definition. Bill mentioned a really small book, not even sixty small pages, called *The Incarnation and the Church's Witness* by Darrell Guder, that is really helpful for deepening an understanding of the incarnation. Here is how Guder defines the incarnation in a way that connects it to God's mission:

> When we use the term *incarnation*, then, we are referring to the specific and historical event in which God's mission reaches its central point and its fullest disclosure. We are also emphasizing the fundamental character of movement and purpose that God's action reveals: "into the flesh" testifies to the fact that God is active and sending within human history. The God of both testaments engages the history of his creation, speaks in such a way that his voice can be heard, and calls people not only to respond to his voice but to become part of his mission. In sending Jesus as the Christ, God draws all of salvation history together, as witnessed to in the Old Testament, and simultaneously opens it up for proclamation to the entire world. (2004, 3)

This definition helps youth ministry connect with the incarnation as a relational move by God that starts with love. It is an act of grace. It is not earned, and it is not a response to right ideology.

What can be discovered through Root and through some of the mission literature is that God is extending his mission through the incarnation. Christopher Wright says, "So all our missional efforts to make God known must be set within the prior framework of God's own will to be known. We are seeking to accomplish what God himself wills to happen. That is both humbling and reassuring" (2006, 129). The incarnation of Jesus demonstrates the very mission of God. God came to us. God reconciled the world to himself. God is not like any other god. God is the wholly other God who brings truly good news for all people (C. J. H. Wright 2006, 126–35). This is God choosing to act, to come to humanity.

What many youth leaders want for youth is an encounter with Jesus, which is important. However, the youth leaders have been so focused on the reality of sin and the power of the cross and the resurrection that they have focused everything there. They sometimes have missed the modeling that happens in Jesus's life. Some of the literature refers to this narrow focus in terms of approaching the Gospels as "passion histories with extensive introductions" (Bosch 1991, 513)—an approach that misses out on much of the story of Jesus.

THE INCARNATION IS RELATIONAL

Focusing on the cross and the resurrection is important. Please do not misunderstand the point. The literature on the incarnation is not discounting that at all. Darrell Guder describes the fullness of the incarnation, that

> begins at Christmas and leads all the way to Pentecost. Every chapter in the earthly life and ministry of Jesus is essential to his sending, and to ours. We err if we leap to the event of Holy Week and ignore the earthly ministry of Jesus. We err just as much if we make Jesus into a moral teacher and leave aside the suffering, cross, and resurrection as ancient myths that can no longer speak to "modern humans." (Guder 2004, 11)

When youth leaders miss the fullness of Jesus's incarnation, they miss an important framework for the cross and resurrection—and unfortunately, so do the youth they are attempting to reach. It is like trying to put together a puzzle with only part of the lid available. When you cannot see the full picture on the lid, it is difficult to put the puzzle together.

Humanity did not have to do anything for God to send his only Son. There was not a sacrifice that was the "correct" one that God was waiting for. There was not a specific prayer that was the "key." God sent Jesus out of an ongoing love for us. When youth leaders approach relationships with an agenda, are they being like God? It is right for them to want to go to where youth are who do not know God. This is part of the incarnation for sure. Jesus came to earth, Jesus took on human form, and Jesus came to humanity. Youth leaders are often trying to do that too, but when they approach relationships ideologically, they are going to youth with an agenda that Jesus did not have. They are doing it only if people will change. If the youth do not change after a little while, then youth leaders just move on. Jesus does not move on from us because it is part of his mission to be known, out of his love (John 3:16). Jesus stays with us and continues to love us even if we do not make the choice to love him back or even to acknowledge his reality. Jesus's love and desire for relationship endures.

Youth leaders are not the only ones to approach ministry with an agenda. Cross-cultural missionaries have historically done this as well at times. Guder critiques many of the missionary methods of the past because he says they "have contradicted both the teaching and actions of Jesus as he trained his disciples to continue his ministry. The message may have been the gospel, but the way the message was made known was often not congruent with the gospel" (2004, xii). This should cause churches and youth ministries to evaluate their own approach to relational, incarnational youth ministry.

Root articulates that Jesus is present in and helps form our relationships. As we are fully present to others, not connecting to them for the sake of an ideology, we can truly see them as other. When we see them in this way, we move past "fixing them" to being our true selves with them. This type of relationship is where Jesus is present! In the midst of that relationship Jesus is making himself known to both the youth leader and to the other person.

If that's true, then Christ can be seen in the other person. That means that the youth worker is not the only one teaching, sharing, or giving. When the youth leader steps into the relationship without an agenda, and is present to the whole of the person, then Christ can be found. It's in that type of relationship where a youth leader hears and joins in someone's suffering and pain—not to fix it, but to be with them—that one finds transformation truly happening. The relationship has to happen for the relationship's sake, with the only agenda being love. Relationship is the end goal, not a means to an end. The youth worker is not the only one ministering here. The youth leader can be ministered to through the relationship as well. It is a true relationship.

This can be one of the hardest things for youth leaders to wrestle through. They are so used to being the people in a power position, coming to help these poor pagan teenagers who need God. They are well intentioned, but youth could tell it was not real relationship. When a youth leader "targeted" youth for mission, the youth leader was just like those colonial missionaries.

Approaching young people out of a desire for relationship spins everything around so that now all are working together to reach the world around them, and each other, with God's grace through relationship. This approach acknowledges the power in God's Spirit, who is at work in all of us, teenagers and adults alike, to join in God's mission.

INCARNATION IS EMBODIED IN OUR WITNESS
A robust understanding of the incarnation reveals that God is motivated by love. Guder adds, "What the mission of the church is called and

empowered to incarnate is God's love in Christ. This is the heart of the matter. Jesus forms this community to carry out its witness as the continuing and expanding embodying of God's love for the world" (2004, 39). So, youth leaders join in God's mission as they step into true relationship (not just connections) with teens. True relational ministry is just that: relational. The relationship is the end goal, not the means to an end. When youth leaders accept people as they are, the type of community that starts to form is quite remarkable.

There are many divisions in the world today. The kinds of divisions may depend on where someone lives, but the divisions are real. When a youth group follows the true incarnational model of loving people as their primary agenda, then there is a freedom for people to express themselves in ways that are authentic and come out of their hearts. This means that some of those expressions might be new to the youth group or church. Some of the heart language of people might very well stretch the youth group to listen, to see, and to feel God's love and work in new ways.

There is a danger here that is worth noting: cultural isolation. The youth ministry must be careful not to reduce their relationships only to relationships with people who are like them. It is possible for a youth ministry to step into relationships without an agenda, but to only seek out those relationships with people who culturally act and think like the people currently in the youth group. This would be a shift back to relationship by ideology. Guder says it this way:

> What we see in the event of the incarnation, that is, in the earthly life and ministry of Jesus, is a remarkable and unsettling cultural freedom. . . . That means that one will not have to become a practicing Jew in order to follow him. The word will continue to become flesh in all the diverse ways in which humanity forms itself into distinctive cultures. The story will be told in every tongue, which is what began at Pentecost. (2004, 50)

Youth groups seeking to love in an incarnational way need to reach across cultural divides as well.

In spite of the many divisions in the world today, imagine what a witness to the power of God's love it is when the youth group and church forms these communities of different types of people, all with the cultural freedom to know God in their own unique and wonderful way. This is what made the early church so remarkable. This is a true expression of the kingdom of God.

THE INCARNATION IS EMBODIED IN SOLIDARITY

Sophia asked Bill at the beginning of the chapter, "How does God's mission to make himself known show up today?" God is made known in the midst of following God's model of relationship in the incarnation. Youth ministry is called to step into relationships for the sake of relationship, with the only agenda to love—no matter what the person decides to do or say, or how they may choose to change or not.

This kind of incarnational living should sound like it is difficult . . . because it is. When the church lives in incarnational relationships and gives people freedom to truly be themselves, then communities start to form that include people who are different. There will be people who have different cultures, different experiences, and different ways of seeing the world.

This type of true relationship means the youth group is willing to take on one another's suffering. They are willing to "place-share" with the other.[1] Think about what Jesus did and continues to do for everyone. He is with us all in the midst of our suffering. God's promise is that he will be with us.

God is with us in the suffering and takes that suffering on. Jesus's presence with people in the suffering has some radical implications for what true relationships look like lived out in youth ministry. It is more than just not running away when Johnny does not change his behavior and start coming to church every week. It is knowing Johnny well enough to know the suffering and pain in his life. It is about being with Johnny in the middle of that suffering and pain.

Sometimes adolescents who are in the midst of deep pain want to lash out at others in response to their suffering. This can make them difficult to love and to know. Youth leaders who love youth in the midst of suffering can become targets of this lashing out, not because the youth leader has done anything to deserve this aggression but because the youth knows that the youth leader may be the only safe person to release their frustration and anger upon. This is not to advocate for accepting any kind of physical violence, but it is a recognition that youth may verbally and relationally be unkind at times because of their pain. While they may not be aware of why they are doing it, they are in many ways asking the question, "Do you really love me?" The youth who need the most love can sometimes be the hardest to love and maintain relationship with.

---

1.   Andrew Root develops this concept of place-sharing very well in part 2 of his book *Revisiting Relational Youth Ministry*.

A young lady, Jordan, had experienced unspeakable abuse at the hands of her mother and stepfather. Jordan had been removed from the home and lived with her grandparents. Her grandparents—strong, committed Christians—took her to church and youth group. The youth pastor at the church, Lakisha, reached out to Jordan, and they developed a pretty good relationship. It did not take Lakisha long to hear some of the stories from Jordan's childhood and to realize how much emotional pain Jordan was in. Lakisha did her best to be there for Jordan and stand by her. One Sunday morning at church Lakisha, Jordan, and several other youths were standing together in the lobby of the church talking. The day before, Jordan had received a rare visit from her mother. Jordan turned her attention to Lakisha and started criticizing Lakisha's outfit. Jordan started saying all kinds of unkind things about how the colors did not go together and how no one should ever wear that pattern. Lakisha, of course, was hurt by this verbal attack. But Lakisha was also able to understand the deeper things going on in Jordan's life and realize that the attack was Jordan's way of letting go of the pain and suffering that she could not safely let go of elsewhere. This did not make what Jordan did okay, but it did help Lakisha realize what was really going on and to accept that suffering with Jordan for a short time. Lakisha wisely changed the topic of the conversation, and later made sure that Jordan knew that Lakisha was still committed to loving Jordan and standing with her.

It is also true that youth leaders can be suffering, and youth can stand with them. Opening up to this incarnational kind of love has to go both ways. Youth leaders need to practice this kind of incarnational relationship and must be willing to receive it as well. Youth leaders are often uncomfortable with this, because they do not like being vulnerable to youth and because they do not like being ministered to. True incarnational relationship means that youth leaders do not see youth as a lower species or incapable of being used by God to extend his love in the world.

Youth ministries join in God's mission as embodied in Jesus's incarnation by stepping into true relationship, by embodying these kinds of diverse and healthy relationships with people who are much different, and through place-sharing with others. This is why Jesus is so beloved by the poor and despised by those in power. Jesus calls the church to stand in solidarity especially with those who are experiencing so much injustice and pain.

Teens are often asking questions about why the church has not joined those who are hurting the most or who are most oppressed in the community.

They see that Jesus did that. They are joining in that but are wondering why the church and youth ministries sometimes are not.

It appears that many young people are sensing this disconnect in the inaction of the church in social and political arenas. It seems that the more young people know about Jesus and his love for the poor, his presence among the marginalized, and his compassion for the victimized, the more they feel like the church is not being who it is called to be. On one hand, the church needs its young people to stand up and hold it accountable. On the other hand, if the church is not willing to listen and change, then perhaps it largely will miss out on a generation of young people looking for the good news of love for those most hurting and in need.

Embracing the incarnation is freeing, humbling, and overwhelming. Youth leaders get to be in real relationships. They do not have to perform and try to get youth to do what they want (behavior modification). This is freeing. Youth leaders also get to experience Christ in the midst of these relationships, which is humbling because it means that God chooses to work through them and chooses to speak to them through others. It is overwhelming because it feels like there is a lot of work to do. Youth leaders may need to shift some of the ways they approach relationships. They also may need to shift what they are inviting other adults and teens into. But if youth ministries could do this, it could be truly transformational. It feels more like Jesus, more like good news.

What if youth leaders, youth workers, and teens had permission to be honest about their own faith and to truly be themselves? What if youth leaders changed their posture from the older expert who is going to help you change a teen's ideology to a co-pilgrim who is willing to journey together with young people?

INCARNATIONAL CONNECTION

That God appreciates the diversity of cultures is, perhaps, best seen in what Christian anthropologist Darrell Whiteman, in his book *Anthropology and Mission*, calls the "incarnational connection" (2003, 407–9). It is significant to note that God came to a particular culture in a specific time, taking on all the limitations of the imperfect first-century Jewish culture. The early church embraced this reality, as seen in Paul's letter to the Philippians:

> Let the same mind be in you that was in Christ Jesus,
> who, though he was in the form of God,

did not regard equality with God
as something to be exploited,
but emptied himself,
taking the form of a slave,
being born in human likeness.
And being found in human form,
he humbled himself
and became obedient to the point of death—
even death on a cross. (2:5–8 NRSV)

When one truly takes on the attitude of Jesus, as these verses command, then the incarnation becomes more than a statement of belief. It also becomes a model for the Christian witness.

God calls Christians to cross barriers and build bridges. Out of love, he crossed the ultimate barrier when he became human in a particular culture to bring the message of reconciliation. Likewise, in our time we must be willing to enter other cultures, living and proclaiming the gospel in ways that are authentic to that culture, learn from that culture, and in all ways point to Christ.

Cultural relativism, the idea that one cannot judge another culture based on criteria outside of that culture, suggests that Christian witness is a dubious enterprise, whether across cultural boundaries or within a multicultural society. Cultural relativism says that since all cultural customs and values are valid and should be respected and tolerated, any proposal that people should change the way they behave and believe is wrong and insensitive.

Is it possible to remain sensitive to other cultural values and still be an effective Christian witness? It is, when we incarnationally enter another person's world with an appreciation for the diversity of cultures and a value for people, while still holding out the possibility that transformation and reconciliation to God is necessary for a complete life. Whiteman notes the importance of anthropological understanding when he writes, "I submit that without the insights of anthropology that help us to understand and appreciate cultural differences, we will automatically revert to our ethnocentric mode of interpretation and behavior" (2003, 408). Staying grounded in Christ, while engaging many cultures, is a tall order, but there is a way forward. Whiteman offers several practices for incarnational witness that are revised in the four following points (2003, 409).

First, we must become vulnerable, not relative. There are parts of all cultures that are helpful for the gospel, harmful for the gospel, and neutral to the gospel. There is no power in the mere acceptance and tolerance of other cultures. Neither is there power in shutting off ourselves from other cultures by creating homogenized Christian enclaves. There is power, though, by allowing ourselves to be vulnerable to the diversity of cultures while at the same time calling ourselves and others to transformation in Jesus. Mathias Zahniser declares that these "close encounters of the vulnerable kind" require "dialogical proclamation" in the context of intimate relationships. When we become vulnerable in relationships, then God's Spirit has opportunity to engage us and our partners "in dialogue in the painful but liberating process of conviction" (1994, 77).

Second, we should start where people are, taking their culture and context seriously. We can do this by discerning appropriate anthropological insights that will help our witness. For example, we can enter another person's world as a participant-observer. When we do, we will see how that person perceives life through both the limitations and the opportunities that the person's worldview offers. Then we will hear the questions one is asking. Most importantly, by closely observing and participating in another reality, we will be able to discern where God's prevenient grace is already at work in the culture.[2] Rather than coming with our preset formulas, we will let God set the agenda.

Third, it is crucial that we walk with another person in humility, realizing that we are outsiders with much to learn. In the not-so-distant past, the missionary enterprise was closely tied to the colonial power structure. Given the technological advancement of Western societies, at least in the mechanistic sense, Christian missionaries entered other cultures draped with prestige, power, and at times, domination. In the brief review of the development of cultural relativism,[3] we can see that the supposed superiority of Western culture is an outgrowth of ethnocentrism. This cannot be a part of authentic Christian witness.

Fourth, the previous points highlight the need for us to have our identities tied to the kingdom of God, which will free us to live among, learn from, and love people from any culture. The goal is not to make them become like

---

2. Prevenient grace is a helpful Wesleyan understanding of the work of the Holy Spirit in people's lives prior to justification through events and circumstances that draw people back to God. See Steve Harper's (1983, 37–46) *John Wesley's Message for Today* for a concise description. Zahniser points out that "given this prevenient gracious activity of God's spirit that goes on everywhere, it is foolish to proclaim the Gospel without first being sensitive to that activity among the people, or in the person, to whom we direct our witness" (1994, 75).

3. We look more at cultural relativism and engaging culture in the next two chapters.

us but to value and love them and in so doing encourage them to become like Christ. So when every knee bows and every tongue confesses Jesus as Lord (Phil. 2:10–11), there will be representatives "from every nation, tribe, people and language" (Rev. 7:9 NIV).

LEARNING TOGETHER

As Bill and Sophia shared their insights, Sophia wondered, "This sounds great on a lot of levels. But it does seem like it requires something more from us."

"What's that?" Bill asked.

"It seems like we are going to have to really try to learn about our youth. To learn who they are, what they care about, what they do, what they like, because we love them and care about them. We are also going to have to learn about their world *with* them so we can reach it together. This requires those 'close encounters of the vulnerable kind.'"

"You got it. I think this might be one of the most important things we can help each other do: learn culture so we can help connect to people. One more quick quote from Guder since I have the book open: 'To practice incarnational witness means learning the cultures into which we are sent: learning what they think and how they think, what it feels like to be part of their world, and how to communicate on their terms' (2004, 54). This willingness to learn will change us as the church and challenge us to change the ways we express our faithfulness.

"Guder acknowledges that this kind of incarnational witness will continue to convert the church as it recognizes its own cultural arrogance and seeks God's forgiveness. For me, seeing the incarnation this way has been a big transition. I used to think that approaching youth ministry as a missionary meant that all of youth were the 'mission field' and I was the 'missionary.' But now I realize that relationships are the end goal. I am also beginning to see that many of the youth in my ministry and community are in fact relational missionaries too. They are just as much contributors to what God is doing in our midst. Our role together is to learn who people are, what they care about, and how they approach the world so that we can love them in ways that point to Jesus's love. That sounds like some good news to me!"

"Learning youth culture is pretty easy for me." Sophia noted.

"Well, this is going to be really important for us. Because old people like me do not always understand what is going on! I look forward to finding some ways we can learn culture and teach others to learn culture out of love," Bill said as he stood. "Now I have to go to a staff meeting."

"Now that can be another culture!" Sophia laughed as they stood to leave.

QUESTIONS FOR REFLECTION

1. What is the difference between "connections" and "relationships," according to Andrew Root? How have you seen both of these in your own life?

2. How is the incarnation an extension of God's mission?

3. How does the view of incarnational relationships articulated here differ from and/or align with some of the ways you have experienced youth ministry in the past?

4. What do you think are some barriers to moving past the cultural isolation that many youth groups seem to face? What are some steps you might be able to take to help your youth ministry move beyond those barriers?

5. What is one way you could practice a "close encounter of the vulnerable kind" this week?

5

THE TRANSLATABILITY
OF THE GOSPEL

SOPHIA SURVEYED HER OFFICE. The floor was littered with the aftermath of various youth group activities—balls, nets, water guns. Her desk was a collection of folders and loose papers, with parental permission forms and information sheets sticking out here and there. Used coffee mugs were stacked precipitously on a corner of her desk. Sophia dared not look into the cups, as the hardened leftovers of sugar and cream were not particularly appetizing.

Just in front of her computer dock were two Bibles, a commentary, some random youth ministry curricula, and her notepad. In the midst of the clutter, Sophia was trying to organize her teaching plan for the upcoming year. She looked at her notepad, and nothing on it seemed to point to any coherence. She felt her frustration rise as she thought about next week's meeting with her parent youth council, when she was supposed to present her plan. Right now, though, she just felt stuck. She picked up her phone and shot a text to Bill.

Sophia: I need HELP!
Bill: What's up?
Sophia: Trying to do some planning, but it's going nowhere.
Bill: I've been there many times. Happy to help. How about a coffee break?

Sophia: Don't have time today. Maybe a Zoom call later this afternoon?
Bill: Sure! I can do it at 3:30.
Sophia: Can you see if Stan can join in? I've got another mission question for him.

Sophia logged into the Zoom call at 3:35, and Bill and Stan were already talking to each other. Greetings were shared, and Sophia got right down to business.

"Here's the deal," Sophia declared. "I am drowning trying to develop a teaching plan for my youth. This is usually exciting for me, as I imagine all the great things I get to teach about. This time, though, I feel stymied. I can't help but wonder if I am really teaching in a way that connects to them. I mean, are they hearing what I'm saying? And even if they are hearing me, does it really matter to them?"

Sophia hesitated for a moment, then proceeded, "I am reluctant to say it, but here it goes: Does the gospel really relate in any meaningful way to youth today? Is it possible that the Christian life and words of Scripture can't really connect with today's postmodern, secular culture? Okay, I said it. Don't shoot me!"

"Hey! There are no arrows coming your way from us," said Bill.

"That's right," said Stan. "In fact, I asked similar kinds of questions when we were missionaries to the Czech Republic."

"I'd be interested to hear about that," said Sophia.

Stan replied, "Well, in many ways the cultural context of the Czech Republic is similar to American youth. It was definitely secular, probably more so than here. And the lack of a firm foundation for ethics gave the culture a real postmodern bent. The difference, though, is that the historical experiences of the Czechs came with heavy doses of oppression from Nazism and communism, along with a long track record of religious wars dating back to the Reformation. The result is a real lack of trust in the institution of the church and the documents of Christianity, including the Bible. It's not just a question of whether Christianity is true; many Czechs don't even see it as good."

"How did you approach your mission work in such a context?" asked Sophia.

"Good question. We had to ask ourselves a foundational question: Is the gospel translatable for this context?" replied Stan.

Bill jumped in, "I guess you were asking if the gospel really was viable for all people, in all times, and in all places. If it is, then translatability is a key characteristic of the gospel."

"That's right," said Stan.

"You know, Dean talks about mission and translation in her book," said Bill. "Let's get together and look at her discussion with some of your mission literature."

"Sounds like it's time to schedule a session in The Bunker!" exclaimed Stan.

"I've got to get back to my planning," said Sophia. "This conversation has given me some ideas. I want to have this translation discussion too, but it's got to come after my parents meeting. See you in eight days?"

"It's a date," Bill and Stan said in unison.

Sophia, Bill, and Stan gathered eight days later at The Daily Grind. With books, notepads, and computers littered about The Bunker, they launched into a discussion on the translatability of the gospel and its relation to youth ministry.

THE IMPACT OF TRANSLATION ON THE GOSPEL

The fact that the Christian gospel has crossed numerous linguistic and cultural frontiers is clearly evidenced by history and current demographics. In *Translating the Message*, Lamin Sanneh (2009) moves beyond the fact of gospel translation to how the motivation and impact of translation shapes Christianity itself.

The Jewish context of early Christianity is clear. Jesus's pedigree is assuredly Jewish, as is his disciples' ethnicity, and each lived within the confines of a Jewish religious structure and culture. While there were several instances of pushing the boundaries of the status quo (eventually leading to Jesus's execution) and several instances of reaching beyond the strict confines of the Jewish world (e.g., the Gerasene demoniac and the Samaritan woman at the well), Jesus generally is presented as a wise, though a bit edgy, Jewish rabbi. This Jewish legacy proved to be a rich trove: "Christian opposition to idolatry, the commitment to the oneness of God, and [dedication] to the towering sovereignty of the moral and ethical code demonstrated the continuity of key elements of Jewish religious teaching" (Sanneh 2009, 21).

There is a decided change with the advent of Jesus's death and resurrection. While still keeping within the traditional understanding of Jewish ethics and monotheistic theology, Jesus fully takes on his messianic role. For the apostles, "the earthly Jesus was the promised Messiah," and this title now had revolutionary impact (Sanneh 2009, 18). Drawing on Adolph Harnack, Sanneh shows how the Jewish "uncompromising worship of one God" was affirmed in early gospel proclamation, while incorporating the crucified and resurrected Jesus as the Son of God, Judge, and Lord. This enlarged the "inherited boundaries of Jewish ritual fellowship," making faith in Jesus, rather than genealogy, the key factor for entry into God's kingdom. Thus, while building on Jewish foundations, it made possible the "Gentile breakthrough" (Sanneh 2009, 19).

The spread of Christianity in the Gentile world was propelled by several external factors. One was the geographic spread of the Jewish communities across the Roman Empire, known as the Jewish Diaspora. In the several generations of intermingling with Greek ideas and culture, Jewish synagogue communities had developed sophisticated apologetics, which included a translation of the Hebrew Bible into Greek (the Septuagint) and the adoption of Greek philosophical terms, such as *logos*, to "bridge the gulf" between Jewish and Greek understandings of divinity. In addition, the Roman Empire provided several cultural and structural advantages. These included a common language (Greek), administrative unity across the empire, a climate of commercial and intellectual exchange, and a reasonably open religious policy. Overall, "wrapping itself round its Judaic roots and taking shelter under the liberal climate of Roman imperial administration, the Christian missionary movement thrived from a double advantage" (Sanneh 2009, 26).

Clearly, the seminal figure in the translation of the gospel message for the Gentile world was Paul. His efforts to form and nurture communities of Jesus followers throughout the empire put him in creative tension as he experienced the reality of God's presence outside his home culture. For Paul and the early Christians, Sanneh suggests there were two paths. One is mission by diffusion. It relies on the original religious culture and language to be the singular vehicle of transmission.[1] A second way is mission by translation. It assumes the recipient culture (and its people) is a worthy receptacle. In translation, the originating culture holds no linguistic or devotional sway over the receiving culture.

Sanneh declares that "mission as translation is the vintage mark of Christianity" (2009, 34). The transcendent reality of the presence of God was and should be validated through multicultural expressions. Various local idioms and practices are seen as equally sanctified mediums for appropriate Christian worship and gospel proclamation. The use of local vernacular and indigenous practices and artifacts pushed for contextual theologies to develop, as

---

1.   Islam is a prime example of mission by diffusion, as it essentially considers Arabic a sacred language for the communication of its sacred text, the Quran, and for devotion (Sanneh 2009, 33); also see Winfried Corduan, *Neighboring Faiths: A Christian Introduction to World Religions* (2012).

varied experiences elicited new questions. Each required local theological inquiry. What became clear, and this is key, is that the Christian gospel cannot and should not be encased in any kind of monocultural captivity: "No one culture is God's favorite. . . . God is not an abstract notion bounded by cultural restrictions" (Sanneh 2009, 35).

Sanneh notes three implications of mission by translation. First is the deferential role of the originating language. Indeed, the originating language is insufficient for the communicative task at hand! The act of translation distinguishes the meaning of the message from the medium of the message. This "challenge[s] believers to uphold the primacy of the message against its cultural packaging" (Sanneh 2009, 36). Second, with the emergence of Greek as the language of gospel proclamation in the early church and the subsequent diminution of Aramaic and Hebrew, the languages of Jesus, a natural "cultural decentralization" took place (Sanneh 2009, 36). Third, mission as translation affirms that cultures receiving the gospel are worthy beneficiaries of God's grace. It is a pronouncement that the promise of the *missio dei* has arrived at this particular place.

Sanneh discusses a number of examples of mission as translation throughout the history of the expansion of the Christian movement. He demonstrates how the translatability of the Christian gospel is central to the Christian faith. Moreover, he documents how the pursuit of translating Scripture into the vernacular served to revitalize local communities, with impact beyond the religious sphere into economic and educational realms. While not absent of theological impact, Sanneh's treatment of mission as translation primarily explores historical and sociological implications. Let's return to Kenda Creasy Dean and Andrew Walls for more theological underpinnings.

THE PERFECT TRANSLATION
OF THE INCARNATION

Chapter 2 introduced the idea that youth work is mission work, and, according to Kenda Creasy Dean and the missiologists she references (Lesslie Newbigin, Lamin Sanneh, Andrew Walls), mission work is translation work. In words, actions, and attitudes, we are called to convey the love of God across cultural and generational barriers in fresh, relevant, and understandable ways. Translation work is incarnational work, and chapter 3, with particular insight from Andrew Root and Darrell Guder, deepened and expanded the understanding of the incarnation as both a motivator and a model for effective youth ministry and mission. Remember, the incarnation—God becoming human in the person of Jesus—is the "perfect translation" (Dean 2010, 97; Walls 1996, 26). It is worth one more look at the incarnation and its implications for the translatability of the gospel.

In a succinct and thought-provoking paragraph, Andrew Walls crucially identifies the relationship between incarnation and translation:

> Incarnation is translation. When God in Christ became man, Divinity was trans-
> lated into humanity, as though humanity were a receptor language. Here was a
> clear statement of what would otherwise be veiled in obscurity or uncertainty,
> the statement "This is what God is like." (1996, 27)

This concise yet grand theological declaration is the basis for all subsequent gospel translation work. Where Sanneh explored more of the historical and sociological impulses of Christian translation, Walls highlights this central Christian article of faith (incarnation) as the root of translation and therefore mission. Indeed, Walls indicates that this previous act of divine translation, referencing John 1:14, provides confidence that the Bible itself can be translated at all. "There is a history of the translation of the Bible because there was a translation of the Word into flesh" (Walls 1996, 28). Thus, this initial act of translation incarnate provides impetus for all future missional acts of crossing cultural barriers and retranslating the gospel in new areas for new people.

Walls further connects the act of translation to conversion. As God was fully translated and embodied in human history, a new, full, and complete understanding of what it means to be human was revealed in Jesus. Embracing this reality requires conversion, in which one's whole human experience, identity, and web of relationships conform "to the new meaning, to the expression of Christ" (Walls 1996, 28). Translation, then, is "both a reflection of the central act on which the Christian faith depends and a concretization of the commission which Christ gave the disciples. Perhaps no other activity more clearly represents the mission of the Church" (Walls 1996, 28).

MISSIONARY PRINCIPLES OF TRANSLATION

We live in a world where multicultural and multireligious contexts are on constant display. As a result, for many it is unrealistic, maybe even a bit crazy, to ascribe to any kind of universal truth. Is there really anything, any idea, any reality that is true and applicable for all people, in all times, and in all places? To insist there is could risk one being called oppressive or bigoted. Yet the translatability of the gospel declares one God who is Father, Son, and

Holy Spirit. This God has created all things, has offered grace in response to sin, and has personally and lovingly entered the human experience to bring redemption, restoration, and fullness of life to all people.

How then can one navigate the varieties of language and culture in view of good news that is meant for all nations? Once again, Andrew Walls offers keen insight in his 1982 article "The Gospel as Prisoner and Liberator of Culture," later reprinted in his book *The Missionary Movement in Christian History: Studies in the Transmission of Faith*.[2] In order to illustrate how Christian forms of spirituality have changed through history, he creatively asks the reader to imagine that a space-alien researcher in interplanetary religions periodically visits earth to observe Christians.

The space alien's initial visit is to the first Christians in Jerusalem around the year 37. He notices that these Christians actually function as a sect of Judaism, worshipping in the temple and obeying the law. Their distinguishing feature is their belief that the Messiah is Jesus of Nazareth.

The space alien researcher's next visit comes in the 300s at the Council of Nicea. Their issues differ from the earlier Christians. While they use the Jewish law books, they also hold in high esteem a later set of writings. Their concern about metaphysics and theology causes the space alien to wonder about their connection with the Jewish Christians he first visited.

The alien researcher then visits sixth-century Ireland and finds monks putting themselves through rigorous exercise, apparently striving for holiness through austerity. These monks seem driven to tell others about a heavenly kingdom. They travel extensively carrying with them intricate, artful manuscripts of the same writings revered by earlier Christians.

The researching space alien returns in 1840 to London's Exeter Hall and witnesses a meeting promoting the sending of missionaries to Africa. Many speak against slavery and petition the British government for support. Once again, they read from the same book the other Christians used, but this time in an English translation.

The diligent space researcher comes again in 1980 to Lagos, Nigeria. Here, he witnesses a vibrant outdoor service featuring singing and dancing. They read the same book the others do. Their focus, however, is on the power of God revealed to people through preaching, healing, and visions.

2.	This summary of Andrew Walls's article/chapter also appears in my dissertation, *The Challenge of Generation X: Unchurched Xers and the Churches That Reach Them* (Mays 1999).

The space researcher discovers several points of continuity between these divergent examples of Christianity. He finds a historical connection, as each group is conscious of their connection with the other. The person of Jesus Christ is regarded with ultimate significance among each group. Also, each constituency holds to the same sacred writings, though in different languages. Walls suggests, then, that this alien observer recognizes the essential continuity in Christianity. Nonetheless, these continuities always are clothed in a particular environment.

With this intriguing introduction, Walls launches into a discussion of two opposing, yet gospel-inspired, tendencies that should help us understand our Christian past but also our present and future. First, the "indigenizing principle" (Walls 1996, 7–8) emphasizes that God comes to us in our culture. God does not seek to turn us into Westerners or Easterners. God does not force us to adopt a Northern Hemisphere mindset if the Southern Hemisphere is our home. God takes us as we are, sinners, in the culture where we live with all our relations and "dis-relations." The possibility to live as Christians and remain in our culture as fully functioning members of society is based in the incarnation. That God became human in the person of Jesus Christ in a particular place at a particular time embracing good and rejecting evil opens up the possibility for Jesus to continue doing this across space and time in the lives of believers.

> The fact is, then, that "if any man is in Christ he is a new creation" does not mean that one starts or continues one's life in a vacuum, or that one's mind is a blank table. It is formed by one's own culture and history, and since God has accepted each of us as we are, our Christian minds will continue to be influenced by what was in them before. And this is as true for groups as persons. All churches are culture churches—including our own. (Walls 1996, 8)

The second tendency Walls calls the "pilgrim principle" (Walls 1996, 8–9). The "pilgrim principle" emphasizes that to be Christian puts one in conflict with the prevailing culture as God calls for the transformation of all people and all cultures. This principle tells the Christian "that he has no abiding city and warns him that to be faithful to Christ will put him out of step with society; for that society never existed, in East or West, ancient time or modern, which could absorb the word of Christ painlessly into its system" (Walls 1996, 8). Being a Christian pilgrim will put us at dis-ease with our culture, but at the same time it provides continuity with Christians in other cultures, to Christians in other times, and, somewhat surprisingly, to the whole history of Israel.

Through history, as gospel communicators have crossed linguistic and cultural borders, a kind of dance has ensued with these two principles. The incarnation exclaims that God has come to us and meets us where we are, loving us in our context. The incarnation of God in the person of Jesus Christ, though, also points to the transformative work of the cross and the resurrection that follows. This reality bellows that our true identity is now ultimately tied to the kingdom of God. Both the indigenizing and pilgrim principles need to be fully embraced in mission as translation.

MISSION, TRANSLATION, AND YOUTH MINISTRY

In *Almost Christian*, Dean (2010) contends that effective youth ministry necessitates embracing these two incarnational principles in the mission-as-translation work that is youth ministry. Certainly, the words and ideas we speak and write need to be accurate, clear, and natural. Both history and theology indicate this is possible in the translatability of the gospel. The Christian gospel, though, is more than words and ideas; it is life itself. And life is meant to be lived.

In this vein, Dean calls for youth workers to be living translations of the gospel. Borrowing heavily from Walter Brueggemann, Dean asserts this is done by "nurturing a bilingual faith" (2010, 112). This is illustrated in the story of the Assyrian siege of Jerusalem recorded in 2 Kings 18–19. With the fate of Jerusalem and its people at stake, the Assyrian official attempts a negotiated settlement at the city's walls: essentially, surrender or die. As the distraught people of Jerusalem gathered behind the city walls to discuss their options, they remembered, with the help of Isaiah, who they were as people of God. Deliverance was in the hands of God, not the king of Assyria. The conversation behind the wall fueled the engagement at the wall.

Both mission as translation and youth ministry require the desire and the ability to converse behind the wall, in the reality of God's presence; and the church's expression of that presence, and to engage at the wall, in the public discourse and assumptions of the prevailing culture. To be sure, "the controlling conversation, however, is the one behind the wall" (Dean 2010, 114). In the midst of God's reality, "we gain cultural tools that critique the dominant culture's view of reality" (Dean 2010, 114). And this behind-the-wall conversation can, and should, propel robust public interactions at the wall. After all, the gospel is innately translatable, as the examples of Christian history have shown.

HERE'S WHAT I NEED!

Sophia cried out, "I need someone to translate more caffeine into my body, right now!"

"Wow! That seems a bit overdramatic," chided Bill.

"If you call me a drama queen, then you may feel my cup on the side of your head," teased Sophia. "I guess I just need a moment to collect my thoughts."

"That's fair," chimed in Stan.

After a resupply of caffeine and a bio break, the three returned to The Bunker.

"Okay," said Bill. "A significant point is that the gospel is translatable. This is seen in the earliest days of Christianity when the good news of Jesus broke into the Gentile world. Early on, the church was dealing in multiple languages and multiple cultural contexts. I appreciate how Sanneh shows that translatability is a hallmark of Christianity, and I love how Walls anchors it in the incarnation, which is the ultimate translation."

Sophia added, "And I totally get when Dean says that youth ministry demands this kind of translation work."

"You know," Bill said, "in my head, I always thought that what I was doing as a youth minister was really translation. I just never said it aloud. I guess I thought it sounded a bit presumptuous. Me, a translator? I barely speak one language! But translating is what I constantly do. When I prep and teach Bible studies, when I try to explain certain theological ideas, when I try to show the relevance of Jesus for life in this crazy world, it's all translation work. Sometimes I do it well, and other times not so well."

"Here's what I need," declared Sophia.

Bill and Stan looked at her expectantly.

"I would like a guide for translation. I really don't have the desire or the linguistic knowledge and skills to be a 'real' Bible translator," she said, using air quotes. "But I do want to nurture the kind of bilingual faith that Dean describes. So, is there some kind of accessible guide for this mission as translation stuff?"

Stan piped up, "I think I can help you there!"

STAGES OF CROSS-CULTURAL GOSPEL COMMUNICATION

Missiological anthropologist Darrell Whiteman presents a user-friendly model for the cross-cultural communication of the gospel in his article published in *Missiology*, "Effective Communication of the Gospel amid

Cultural Diversity" (1984). Whiteman concisely identifies the dilemma of cross-cultural ministry, which is our "attempt to communicate our under-standing of the universal meaning of Christianity through cultural forms that are bound by time and space" (1984, 275). His description of the problem is what Sophia, Bill, and all youth leaders face in their ministries on a regular basis. Whiteman points out that the nature of Christianity is absolute and universal; however, the learning and relearning of the Christian message through cultural and generational forms brings various nuances of meaning to different people. This seems problematic, but Whiteman offers assurance:

> Our present understanding is only partial and limited, but the full meaning of this absolute and universal truth will be known at the Parousia. Meanwhile there is no cause for despair, for the Christian message continues to become incarnate in many situations with all the limitations, as well as all the possibilities, of life here and now. (1984, 276)

Effectively translating and communicating the gospel across cultural barriers, Whiteman suggests, involves a three-stage process:

> Stage 1. *Discovering* the original biblical *meanings* conveyed in the cultural forms of the Hebrew, Greek and Roman societies

> Stage II. *Distinguishing* the original biblical meanings from the contemporary forms we use to express those meanings in our own society

> Stage III. *Communicating* the biblical meanings in ways that will ensure the maximum transfer of meaning across linguistic and cultural boundaries (1984, 276)[3]

DISCOVERING

Above, it was seen in the work of Lamin Sanneh and Andrew Walls that the entry of the gospel into the Gentile world, and all subsequent cultures throughout Christian history, both experientially and theologically, confirm

---

3. Whiteman's stages are similar to a typical exegetical, inductive study of Scripture. For example, see *Grasping God's Word: A Hands-On Approach to Reading, Interpreting, and Applying the Bible*, by J. Scott Duvall and J. Daniel Hays (2005), and *Inductive Bible Study: A Comprehensive Guide to the Practice of Hermeneutics*, by David R. Bauer and Robert Traina (2011). As a missiological anthropologist, though, Whiteman's contribution is that he pays close attention to "the cultural aspects of communicating the Christian Gospel" (1984, 275).

what Whiteman declares: "*All* cultural systems are essentially useable by God" (1984, 276, author's emphasis). So, though God chose the Hebrews, the people and their culture, to reveal himself, it was not because of their perfection. Hence, the language and cultural forms used to convey God's truth to the Hebrews hold no particular sacredness. Likewise, with the expansion of God's revelation in the historic incarnation of Christ and the early church's missionary efforts, the language and forms used to express devotion to God took on a Greco-Roman flavor. Whiteman rightly points out that the Jerusalem Council, recorded in Acts 15, lays out the way to understand this cultural dynamic: "The issue was resolved by the declaration that one could follow Christ at the *meaning* level, and still remain within one's culture at the formal level" (1984, 277, author's emphasis). Gentiles did not need to become Jewish in order to follow Christ!

This clean break from the cultural captivity of Christianity, then, means that each culture and each generation has the theologizing task to extract eternal meaning from both the biblical and the Christian historical contexts and answer the question: What does it mean to follow Christ in our context, our place, our language, our culture? When this takes place, then real conversion and real discipleship is possible (Whiteman 1984, 276).

When the process of discovering original biblical meanings is done poorly, then meaningless cultural forms can coerce people's discipleship goals. Whiteman asserts, "Unfortunately, we have had to relearn this lesson in every period of the Church's history, for it has been easier to insist that *they* become like *us*, if they want to become Christian" (1984, 277, author's emphasis). If discovering biblical meaning is done rightly, then God's truth will penetrate mind, body, and soul. We see in Whiteman's assertion strong affirmations of Root's differentiation between ideology and relationship, as discussed in chapter 4.

DISTINGUISHING

Whiteman then highlights the need to differentiate the discovered "biblical meanings from the contemporary cultural forms we use to express those meanings in our own society" (1984, 278). Christ followers in every culture swim in their own cultural waters. They get to know these waters in such an intimate way that it is easy to equate cultural expressions of truth with the truth itself: "that is, in our minds, the cultural forms we employ *are the same thing* as the meaning they are intended to convey" (Whiteman 1984, 278). Whiteman employs a number of examples of missionary failures, where

Western missionaries, inculcated with Western values, insisted that non-Western indigenes embrace these values. Essentially, they equated certain expressions of Western values with the gospel itself. So, things like modesty in dress, avoidance of smoking and chewing betel nut, avoidance of dancing and other indigenous art forms, and affirmation of private property rights were given primary significance to the detriment of clear gospel communication and Christian discipleship.

Likewise, in youth ministry, it is often easy to settle for inadequate discipleship goals that are caught up in cultural forms. George Hunter identifies several inadequate goals that quench apostolic communication in the church. Goals such as we want people to "behave like us," "be religious," or "share our politics" "do not sufficiently reflect essential Christianity" (Hunter 1996, 36–42). However, churches are often satisfied with these kind of insufficient objectives for themselves and for youth. The remedy is discovering biblical meanings and distinguishing them from our everyday cultural expressions of them. Once again, the attempt to convert to ideology, as discussed in chapter 4, comes into view.

COMMUNICATING

Communicating the discovered biblical meanings while distinguishing them from contemporary cultural forms is complex. Whiteman describes it as going through a two-filter process. The initial filter belongs to missionary communicators. Their experience, culture, personality, and denomination all influence what they perceive and communicate as the essential Christian message. A second filter is employed by the non-Christian receivers in their indigenous cultural context, who interpret the message according to their cultural perception of reality. When done well, the meaning that the missionaries intended is received by the indigenes even after being processed through the two filters. Whiteman says it is then that the communication is "truly Christian [and] the indigenes will see Jesus and not simply the missionaries and their requirements" (1984, 280).

The process does not end with this initial communication. Missionary communicators must examine what meanings Christian converts have attached to various forms. Importantly, indigenes should be encouraged in the practical theology of contextualization to explore what local forms and expressions best convey Christian meaning within their own culture. This kind of work by the local hermeneutical community is needed, Whiteman insists, to avoid nominalism which comes from clinging to meaningless forms (1984, 281).

A MODEL OF DYNAMIC EQUIVALENCE

To accomplish this kind of gospel communication, Whiteman calls for following a process of "dynamic equivalence." The interest in equivalence in gospel translation and communication, in contrast to formal correspondence, is often credited to Eugene Nida in his linguistic work with the American Bible Society. Nida asserts that the goal of Bible translation is to arrive at "the closest natural equivalent, first in meaning and secondly in style" (1960, 194). The objective of meaning over form pushes the gospel communicator to prioritize the local forms of the receptor to achieve a translated communication that is accurate, clear, and natural to the receivers. Charles Kraft expounds on dynamic equivalence this way: "*The central aim is communication, not mere literalness* for its own sake. . . . The biblical writers, however, intended to be understood, not to be admired or to have their writings so highly thought of that they would be transmitted in unintelligible or misleading forms" (Kraft and Wisley 1979, 272, author's emphasis).

To illustrate the concept, Whiteman offers a helpful diagram.

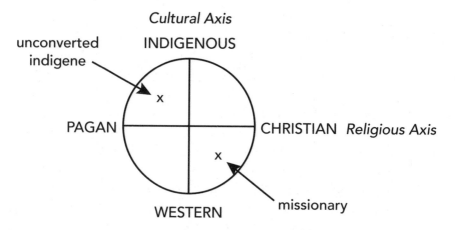

**Figure 5.1. Religious-Cultural Matrix in
Missionary-Indigene Interaction (after Whiteman 1984, 282)**

This model shows two kinds of processes at work in translating and communicating the gospel. One axis points to a religious dynamic, moving from Christian to pagan; and the other axis represents the cultural dynamic, ranging from Western to indigenous (or non-Western). Speaking primarily to Western, American missionaries, Whiteman's model shows that the goal is to move the unconverted indigene from the top left quadrant to the top right quadrant, from the Indigenous-Pagan quadrant to the Indigenous-Christian quadrant. This requires "a heightened sense of cross-cultural awareness and sensitivity" (Whiteman 1984, 282) on the part of the Western missionary to incarnationally enter the indigenous-pagan context and communicate the central meaning of the gospel in words and actions. It is unnecessary, and extremely problematic, to expect a non-Western, non-Christian person to move down the cultural axis toward Western culture.

With a few adaptations, the model can be applied to the kind of cross-cultural translation and communication that takes place in incarnational youth ministry.

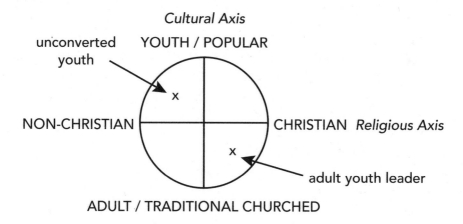

Figure 5.2. Religious-Cultural Matrix in Adult Youth-Worker
Interaction (after Whiteman 1984, 282)

Though admittedly a bit generalized and somewhat imperfect, this adapted model still effectively illustrates the issue at hand. In order to embrace both the pilgrim and indigenizing principles of mission as translation, and in order to be living translations of the gospel, youth workers must meet unconverted youth in their non-Christian, popular-culture world. In forms that they will relate to and understand, the gospel must be translated and communicated so that the biblical meaning will become accurate, clear, and natural to youth. The result can be real, deep conversions to Christ. Whiteman says, "Becoming Christ-like is a process that occurs in a cultural context" (1984, 285). We want converted youth who can speak powerfully and radically in their popular-culture "heart language." The translatability of the gospel makes this possible.

MUSIC TO MY EARS

Stan looked up from his sketch of the diagram. "I don't know that I love all my labels on my diagram, but it does remind me what my goal is for these kids. Just like I wanted my Czech students to be fully devoted followers of Christ in their Czech culture, I want the youth I work with to become fully devoted followers of Christ in their expression of American popular culture. The lessons of Scripture and church history and my own experience in the Czech Republic tell me this is possible."

"Well, I asked, and you provided," remarked Sophia. "The stages of discovering, distinguishing, and communicating are going to be great guides in my curriculum plan for the year. And it's a great reminder of what the overall goal of my youth ministry should be. I really think this could impact my teaching and general communication with my youth."

"I think you're right, Sophia," said Bill. "All this reminds me of the story about Bible translation that you told me, Stan. Why don't you share it now?"

Stan leaned back and began to reminisce. "Well, all right. After Sally and I returned from the Czech Republic, a friend of mine who works with a Bible translation organization contacted me about the possibility of being a volunteer Bible translation consultant in Nigeria. At first, I wasn't sure I'd be a good fit. After all, I was a missionary to Europe, not Africa, and I was not a trained linguist. My friend assured me I would do just fine with my graduate studies in theology and missiology. So I found myself in rural Nigeria at a translation camp for three weeks."

Stan paused and smiled as he remembered. "Now, there are more than five hundred languages in Nigeria, and though many of the language groups have a vital Christian presence, many of the peoples still do not have a Bible in their own language. So, in order to enhance the translation process, translations are done from an English text, since English is an official language of Nigeria from its colonial days. The organization I worked with used indigenous translators, who were fluent in English, to create a phonetic alphabet for their previously unwritten tribal language. Within a fairly short period, these indigenous translators were able to begin translating the Bible from English into their native tongue.

"I arrived at a translation camp to work with a tribal group's first attempt at translating the Bible into their language. The passage we worked on was the good Samaritan story in Luke 10. They started with an oral translation, refined it, tested it with each other, and began to work toward a more polished version. My role was to ask key exegetical and cultural questions, to help them have an accurate and clear translation. Their role was to take the accurate and clear meaning and put it into a linguistic form their people could readily understand."

As Stan continued with the story, his voice took on more emotion. "After all our work, it was time to make a recording on an old cassette player. They were going to take this recording back to their local churches to test the translation. The elder of the group, everyone called him Baba, was chosen to read for the recording. After he finished, I asked the team what they thought. One member of the translation team was a young widow woman who was a song leader in her church. Her face lit up and she exclaimed, 'Hearing Baba read these words in our language was music to my ears.'"

Bill and Sophia were captivated, as tears welled up in Stan's eyes. "I realized I was witnessing a holy moment. This was the first time that this woman had heard Scripture in her own language. It spoke to her in a way that nothing else ever had."

Stan paused, and then continued, "That's what I want for these youth. I want to translate the gospel so well into their culture that it becomes music to their ears. Then, I want them to take that gospel music and impact their culture."

"Amen!" exclaimed Sophia and Bill.

QUESTIONS FOR REFLECTION

1. What are the implications that mission work is translation work? For your understanding of Scripture? For your church? For your youth ministry?

2. Andrew Walls describes two missionary principles—indigenizing and pilgrim. What happens in youth ministries when the indigenizing principle is overemphasized? What if the pilgrim principle is overemphasized? What are some positive examples that you know where the principles are held in creative tension?

3. Use Darrell Whiteman's model to analyze various aspects of your youth ministry.

4. What would an indigenous Christian youth look like, in your context?

5. When has the gospel become music to your ears? When has the gospel become music to the ears of your youth?

6

ENGAGING CULTURE

SOPHIA ENTERED THROUGH THE DOORS of The Daily Grind, and the aroma of ground coffee and slightly burnt milk brought a smile to her face. She was beginning to associate these familiar smells with intense missiological discussions. "Weird," she thought. After she placed her regular order—which the barista now knew by heart—of a vanilla soy milk latte, Sophia sat down in The Bunker.

Sophia noticed Bill rushing from the parking lot. He barged through the door, headed to the counter, and ordered his standard—a large black coffee. "With no fancy stuff!" he reminded the millennial behind the counter.

Chuckles began to erupt from Sophia as Bill plopped down at the table.

"What?" asked Bill, with his arms raised in a symbolic plea.

"No, I'm not going to tell you. It won't sound right."

"Oh, come on. I can take anything you have to dish out. After all, I'm a youth minister." Bill offered a goofy grin to make his point.

"Okay, okay, but don't hate me."

"I'm waiting."

Sophia took a breath, sighed, and began, "Now, don't take this the wrong way, but I don't see you as a youth minister." She quickly continued, "I don't mean that you aren't good or dedicated, It's just that . . .". She hesitated.

"It's just that I'm an old guy whose body has never been covered by a pair of skinny jeans—not that any would fit me—and it probably seems a little creepy to some people that a guy my age likes to hang out with teenagers."

"Well, yeah," Sophia said, relieved and surprised at the same time.

"And the fact that I want to talk about Jesus to these youth probably puts me on the loony list in many people's eyes."

"That's the part I think is great. That's why I love these conversations so much. I feel like they are giving me new eyes to see my youth. You've been such a big help."

"Thanks, Sophia. These conversations have been a big help to me as well. I want to ask for your help now."

"Sure, if I can."

Bill looked out the window for a second. Turning to Sophia with a plaintive look in his eyes, he said, "I have always thought of myself as a decent communicator. When I started in youth ministry, people often mentioned my lessons as one of the reasons they came back to youth group. But now . . .". Bill's words tailed off.

He looked out the window again, and collected his thoughts, "Now, I often feel like I am saying words they know, but they do not understand. More important, to me, is that the news I am sharing seems like it is less and less 'good' news." He turned to Sophia, "It just feels like it's noise.

"And one more thing I have been noticing—forgive my rant—is how hard it is to get the group to feel like one big group. There are so many smaller groups within the large group. We have dealt with cliques before, but this somehow feels different."

Sophia nodded and quickly responded, "This reminds me of something that happened last week after Bible study. Chloe is a sixteen-year-old who is very thoughtful and bright. She comes from a rough home and has to spend a lot of time making it on her own. I think she was even homeless for a while. She started coming to youth group about a year ago. I think it started as a place to be. Lately, she has been asking a lot of good questions.

"Anyway, last week she grabbed me after Bible study and asked me, 'Does God speak my language? You say that God is at work everywhere, pursuing everyone. Well, what about us?' So I asked her, 'Who do you mean when you say "us"?' She responded, 'People like me—people who speak the language of the streets. I've been listening to all of you at this church for about a year now, and I think I like what you are saying. But I don't always understand what you are talking about because you use different words.' So I responded, 'Of course!

God loves everyone and speaks to everyone in their heart.' She replied, 'How do you know? How can I know? I want to hear.'

"I was not sure what to say at that moment, but God helped me. I said, 'I do believe that God speaks to us in our hearts because I have heard him there and know others who have as well. But alone, it is very hard. Together, it is much easier.'"

Bill nodded at the wisdom of Sophia's comments and asked, "Did she accept that?"

"Well, she asked me how we do that together. So I talked a little about Bible study and how that is one place that we do this together because God often uses the Bible to speak to people. She was looking for something more. Then I told her that God is speaking in everything because he is present in every situation, revealing truth in all situations. I was thinking of our earlier conversations about the incarnation and God in our midst.

"Then she started asking me about things like music and videos. I like to think that I am pretty in touch with what's current, but there were some things she mentioned that I have never heard of. She seems to be able to find some truth in those places. But she also has a lot of questions. We finished our conversation, and she committed to bringing up some of her questions at Bible study with the other girls. Later on, I kept thinking about how I know some youth culture, but other parts I miss because I am not naturally drawn to them." Sophia's eyes met Bill's for a beat.

"Wait until you are my *old* age!" Bill exclaimed, "Then you are naturally drawn to almost none of it!"

Their eruptive laughter caught the attention of several patrons. They tried to suppress their laughter, which turned into middle school–like giggles.

"It seems to me there are two parts to this journey," Sophia continued in a more serious tone. "First, there is the task of understanding other cultures, and second, there is the task of communicating in ways that another culture understands."

"That's a good way to break it down," Bill responded.

"In one of my undergraduate courses, we read about a tool that I think is pretty useful in helping us understand youth culture," said Sophia. "It's an acronym: LASTS."

A TOOL FOR LEARNING CULTURE: LASTS

Sophia already mentioned that the first step is understanding culture. One of the practical questions that a youth leader should be asking by now is

"How can I listen to culture?" and the connected question, "How can I teach others to listen to culture as well?"

Dean Blevins, professor of practical theology and Christian discipleship at Nazarene Theological Seminary, developed a great tool to listen to culture in his book *Discovering Discipleship*. While *Discovering Discipleship* is not a formal missiological text, the chapter "Paying Attention to People and Culture" does provide a good framework for investigating culture.

Blevins's tool is an acronym: LASTS—Language, Actions (and Actors), Space, Time, and Symbols. Blevins recommends using this tool to help discern key characteristics in cultures and subcultures (2010, 106–12).

Language refers to the words people use. This is not just English, Spanish, or another formal language. People may be speaking English, but they are not always using the words the same way. For example, someone who is familiar with a specific field or discipline, like mathematics or systematic theology, will use jargon related to that field. Another person may know the words and their meaning but does not understand what is being communicated. In addition, language is modified and enhanced by accents, slang, and other insider languages. These are ways members of cultures can accurately talk about things. They also are a way to quickly tell who is an "insider" and who does not belong. Teens do this too, of course.

Actions (and actors) refers to what people do (and who does these actions). These can be everything from a ritual event like shaking a hand in greeting to individual events that help us get through the day. Most youth study and learn at school. But what else do they do with their time? What actions are they involved in? Do they work a job? Where? How? With whom? What do they do for fun? We typically associate certain types of people with certain actions (gamers play video games, athletes play sports, academics study and read, etc.). Knowing what people *do* helps to see another part of the culture.

Space indicates where people are. What are different places and spaces where they spend their time? We know that most youth spend a lot of time at school. Where else do they go? Sometimes certain actions are associated with certain spaces (shopping at the mall, learning at school, prayer at church, etc.). This is an area of youth cultures that has changed quite a bit in the last few years. When I (Brian) was growing up, we wanted to be together, and so we physically went to the mall or stayed after school to hang out together. Now, with almost all teens having cell phones, internet access, and video game consoles, their connecting spaces are often virtual.

Time is how people spend their time. The use of time often demonstrates priorities and values. The issue is not just about the amount of time spent on things but the timing of the action. Simply looking at the amount of time someone spends doing an activity is not enough. The one category that people spend the most time on is probably sleeping. This does not mean it is the most valued activity for everyone. Rather, people usually give their *best* time to the things that matter most to them. For teens, this is usually when they have "free" time.

Do you know what an average day in the life of the teens in your group is like? What are key moments that are most important? If a youth leader's only interaction with youth is at the formal church program, then he or she is unlikely to learn that. However, investing in real incarnational relationship leads to learning the important times in someone's life. Every teen is unique and lives his or her own life, but it can be surprising how stressed-out many youth are about how busy their schedule is. They feel like their lives are so full and they have no space and little control.

The last one is symbols. Symbols often do not need an explanation but ignite feelings and imagination. Take the American flag, for example. Depending on where you are and who you are with, when an American flag is seen various emotional responses will be triggered. What are the symbols you see all around youth and their specific cultures?

For example, a new girl started attending a youth group. She had just begun sixth grade and was invited by her friend whose family were regular attendees. The two of them became good friends and seemed like sweet, innocent girls. The youth leader was very surprised when this new girl wore a shirt one day with a marijuana leaf on it. When the youth leader finally had some time with the two girls, she asked the new girl about what was on her shirt. It turns out she had no idea it was a marijuana leaf. For her, it was just a comfortable shirt that she borrowed from her older brother. When her youth leader explained it, the girl was embarrassed. She had missed the symbol that many others knew.

There is one more step that we would like to add to Blevins's model: Flow. (We know LASTSF does not quite sound as memorable!) Flow is asking the question: Where do all these things we observe in culture (LASTS) come from? For example, hip-hop culture is prevalent throughout the world. Hip-hop originated from the urban core among African Americans, who were trying to put a voice to their emotions of anger and frustration due to injustice. Hip-hop has at its core four elements: B-boying (break dancing), DJing (turntableing, aural), MCing (rapping, oral), and Graffiti (visual). These elements are meant to give voice to the disenfranchised who had no voice. When one understands where hip-hop comes from (flow), then the medium and the message begin to make more sense, and values emerge. When one knows these values, then it is easier to understand why youth of all economic classes gravitate to the underlying messages of naming oppression, calling for justice, and providing a voice to the suppressed. Where something originates is not always easy to discover, but if a youth ministry begins to understand cultural and symbolic origins, then they can also discern the values behind those cultural elements.

This grid of LASTSF helps people to be intentional. It can also help youth leaders talk with their adult and youth leaders about what they are seeing and hearing and to notice where several of these things overlap. For example, sometimes people say and do things only in certain spaces.

One example might be how people can use the Bible at church and nowhere else. But it is not just church that gets people "code-switching," the practice of shifting language or the way one expresses herself in conversations. It is all kinds of places. The more we are intentional about being around youth and trying to at least understand their world, the more we see the pressure and normalcy of acting in different ways in different places while with different people. It also opens our eyes to issues that might help us start to contextualize the gospel.

ADAPTING TO WHAT WE SEE

After Sophia walked through the LASTSF model, she continued to the second part.

"Okay, I have wondered about this," Sophia said. "If I know at least some things about a culture, how do I contextualize the message without being phony or manipulative?"

"Good word: contextualize. What does that mean to you?" Bill asked.

"It means taking a message and putting it in a way that your audience can understand."

"Great!" Bill affirmed. "This is another area of mission literature. Let's talk about this. This is where I was hoping we would go with this conversation when I asked my question earlier. It seems like the Bible models contextualization. The four Gospels are written to four different audiences. While they are trying to tell each of those groups about Jesus, they emphasize different parts of the story, use different words, and adapt things so that their audience can get an understanding of Jesus. How do we do that, but with the teenagers in our youth groups? And to make it even harder, some scholars say that youth culture changes every two to three years!"

"Wow, Bill! When you put it like that, I feel like this is a huge issue. Even if I know everything about youth culture, which I don't, if I can't do the work of helping youth in their culture understand who Jesus is, then I'm not that helpful."

Bill replied, "If we believe that God does speak to everyone in their own language as you have said to Chloe, then we need to wrestle with the kind of theology we are sharing and inviting our youth to participate in."

Sophia added, "We all use our own words and stories to make our understanding of God our own. I know I do, and I certainly have seen it from the church as a whole. Sometimes people say things that are meaningful to them, but they aren't meaningful to me at all."

"Let's get some help on this." Bill quickly texted his missionary friend, Stan, asking for some book recommendations.

"Bill, you may not know coffee culture or wear skinny jeans, but you at least know how to text," Sophia commented.

Bill shakes his head and mutters, "Ugh! Kids these days," with a smile.

Before departing, Bill divides Stan's list of books between the two of them. They leave ready to dive into the world of culture and contextual theology.

THE NEED FOR UNDERSTANDING CULTURES

Bill and Sophia have stumbled onto one of the most important reasons for exploring mission literature in youth ministry—developing a well-rounded approach to youth ministry that encompasses theology, adolescent development, *and* culture. In our experience, many youth ministries have some elementary understanding of one or two of these areas. Rarely have we found youth ministries that include all these approaches in their youth ministry in an intentional way.

As has already been discussed in earlier chapters, a biblical theology of mission can drive a youth ministry and church to engage as participants in God's activity in the world. This is a powerful shift toward proactively approaching the world looking for God's work already happening within it. It is a choice to listen to and value individuals and cultures as places where God is already at work. The temptation can be to see individuals and cultures as places to *fix*. A biblical theology of mission can drive a ministry to investigate where those individuals and cultures are valuable and affirmed and where there are places in need of transformation. This applies to looking at one's own culture as well. Then a ministry can see and join God in what he is already doing!

HUMAN DEVELOPMENT IN CULTURE

Youth ministry as it is found in most churches today was born out of an awareness of differing developmental needs for adolescents. Adolescents are clearly no longer children, as can be seen physiologically. Adolescents are also not yet adults, as can be seen by the search for identity and viability. This recognition that adolescents have different needs and expectations than either children or adults is an important part of youth ministry. But it is not the only part.

While youth ministry may be aware of and responsive to the developmental needs of adolescents, most ministries to youth in the United States are built on models that assume a uniform youth culture. The reality is that there is not one uniform youth culture in the United States, but many youth cultures. Missiology can inform this reality by understanding and engaging new cultures, by deepening understanding of God's revelation in people's lives, and by developing a hermeneutic community. Missiology has much to offer ministry with the globally connected adolescents of today.

The core issue is one of culture. In studying the dominant youth ministry literature, it seems there is some confusion between what is cultural and what is developmental. The fact that people change and have needs at different stages of development is not necessarily tied to culture. There are many areas of adolescent development to study: physical development, cognitive development, and faith/moral development, to name a few. These areas of development might be impacted by culture, but a healthy human will develop in these areas no matter the culture. For example, a child born in one country, adopted by a family from another, who moves and grows up in a third culture does not stop growing physically.

The one area of human development that is perhaps most affected by culture is that of identity development. H. Stephen Glenn and Jane Nelsen have noted that in the process of *habilitation* (2000) every person is looking for significance, meaning, and capability. Significance relates to the sense that the individual matters to others, that one will be missed if not present, and that one contributes to the social group. Meaning refers to the sense that each person has a purposeful role to play in life and that this role needs to be filled. Capability refers to the sense that not only does each individual have a role to play but that he or she can do that job well. Significance, meaning, and capability can be found as the developing person interacts with one's social group and culture.

LEVELS OF CULTURE

Culture is the human-formed aspects of our environment. Michael Rynkiewich articulates a definition of culture in *Soul, Self, and Society: A Postmodern Anthropology for Mission in a Postcolonial World* that is compelling:

> *Culture* is a more or less integrated *system* of knowledge, values and feelings that people use to *define* reality (worldview), *interpret* their experiences, and *generate* appropriate strategies for living; a system that people *learn* from other people around them and *share* with other people in a social setting; a system that people use to *adapt* to their spiritual, social and physical environments, and that people use to *innovate* in order to change themselves as their environments change. (Rynkiewich 2012, 19, emphasis added)

In contrast to many other descriptions of culture, Rynkiewich's definition is notable for not mentioning behaviors or artifacts. Rynkiewich would argue (and we agree) that behaviors and artifacts are products of culture. They are the results of culture interacting with the environment. This definition is helpful in that it recognizes that all people are participants in culture. So culture is not something that happens exclusively *to* someone, but is also something that happens *with* and *because of* someone.

Relying on this definition of culture, one first notices the broad, macro level of culture, which is the layer that is the most evident and most discussed when people refer to the word "culture." At the macro level, there are commonalities in the integrated system of knowledge, values, and feelings. People can define reality; interpret their experiences; generate appropriate strategies for living; adapt to their spiritual, social, and physical environments; and innovate in order to change themselves as their environments change. For much of the world, the ongoing shift from modernity to postmodernity would be a good case study for such a macro culture (see figure 1).

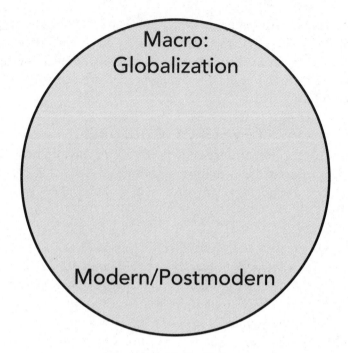

Figure 6.1: Macro Culture

Secondly, there is a local level of culture (see figure 6.2), where most people recognize something uniquely different from the global culture around them, although the local level of culture exists within the broader macro level of culture. This local level is where people identify themselves as unique in customs, ethnicity, language, religion, and family or tribal groups. While at first glance the distinctions between local cultures are not always obvious and clear-cut, when one looks deeper the importance of local cultural differences becomes discernable.[1] Even when the distinctiveness of each "local" culture is not readily clear, one should be able to see quite a bit of diversity in the local level of culture. The 2010 US Census discovered that more than 32 percent of young people (10–24) are non-white, representing up to 331 identifiable different population groups. A language other than English is spoken in 20 percent of American homes.

---

1.   For more on these ideas, see Jan Nederveen Pieterse, *Globalization and Culture: Global Melange*, 2nd ed. (New York: Rowman & Littlefield, 2009); and Richard R. Osmer and Kenda Creasy Dean, eds., *Youth Religion and Globalization: New Research in Practical Theology* (Wein: Lit Verlag, 2007), among others.

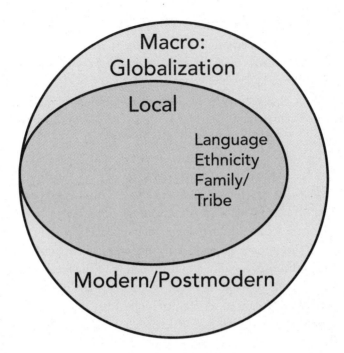

Figure 6.2: Local Culture

Thirdly, and most uniquely, there is a micro layer to culture (see figure 6.3). This is the layer of culture where our youth of today are distinctive in their cultural identity. Peer cluster theory tells us that beginning in mid-adolescence, youth begin to separate themselves into clusters of four to ten teenagers of the same gender with an integrated system of knowledge, values, and feelings. It is important to note that each of these youth, as they discover and integrate into these clusters, play a role in helping to shape the culture of that cluster. Chap Clark, in his book *Hurt* and the follow-up *Hurt 2.0*, does an excellent job highlighting this peer cluster theory. As he points out, youth at this level are in fact on their own (Clark argues, due to the abandonment of adults); define their reality; interpret their experiences; generate appropriate strategies for living; adapt to spiritual, social, and physical environments; and innovate in order to change themselves as their environment changes. "But," as Clark says, "what gives a cluster its power is a common, almost tribalistic bond and unifying social narrative (a grand story that gives meaning and cohesiveness to the cluster and defines who is in and who is not). This bond is the hallmark of the social group that nearly all mid-adolescents will rely on throughout their high school life" (2011, 61). It is in these peer clusters where youth embrace their identity. Clark further explains:

While a cluster is being developed, a subtle, almost imperceptible negotiation goes on among the members. The necessary rules, norms, values, and even narratives of the cluster that serve to bind the members together are all worked out prior to the cluster's ultimate formation. After these have been negotiated and established . . . the members of the cluster tend to subordinate their own personal convictions, loyalties, and norms to the will of the collective whole. (2011, 66)

In short, they are a culture unto themselves.

What makes this development of peer clusters important to note is that it marks a different layer of culture, one that does not seem to have been there before. In the past when adults were actively engaged in the lives of young people through this period of adolescent development, the young people were able to find significance, meaning, and capability at the local level of culture in which they actively participated. As Clark notes, "The striking thing is that the systems that are present to serve mid-adolescents are typically locked into servicing a more or less cohesive adolescent community" (2011, 72). The reality is that there are many adolescent micro cultures.

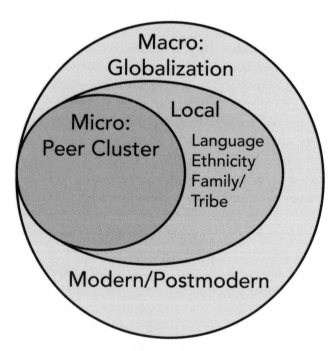

Figure 6.3: Micro Culture

Regarding culture, it should also be addressed that this micro youth culture does not fit the theories of "subcultures" in that these peer clusters are not operating solely in reaction to a dominant culture.[2] Rather they are much more aligned with the definition of a true culture themselves. Remember Bill's observation about the smaller groups? This is what Bill has been sensing.

There is a problem in the current models of youth ministry that do not acknowledge differing cultures. I reviewed the leading youth ministry books in 2008[3] and discovered a widespread acceptance of the reality of the developmental issues of adolescence. Twenty-one of the twenty-four books mentioned development issues. Regarding culture, only four of the books did not use the word "culture" at all. Two-thirds at least referenced a macro "youth culture." Of those that did not reference the macro level of youth culture, it is probable they were assuming a uniform youth culture. Just over half (fourteen) at least referenced the reality of a local culture, but always with the assumption that those local cultures were homogeneous enough that the model put forward in the book was relevant in all of those contexts. There was not very much awareness of the micro culture issue, with only six of the twenty-four addressing it in some way. Not surprisingly, all those who discussed a micro youth culture also discussed culture at a local and global level (even if those specific labels were not used). To summarize, 75 percent of the leading youth ministry texts in 2008 were basing their youth ministry models on a uniform youth culture.

There is a disconnect among the dominant youth ministry literature (and, it would not be too much of a stretch to assume, percolating into local youth ministries). Most of the literature is blind to the reality of a multicultural adolescent world. The issue, then, is that there are many youth cultures but that the literature perpetuates, and ministries operate with, models that assume all youth culture is the same.

While it is vitally important to understand the development levels and stages of adolescents in youth ministry, it is also vital that those ministering to youth learn to see and understand the cultures of the youth they are seeking to engage (see figure 6.4). As a good theology of mission calls the church to discover where God is already at work, so then must each local church and

---

2. For more on this idea, see Pamela Erwin, *A Critical Approach to Youth Culture: Its Influence and Implications for Ministry* (Grand Rapids: Youth Specialties Academic, 2010).

3. This list comes from D. Andrew Zirschky, "Beyond Fakes and Phonies: Toward a Theological Understanding of Authenticity for Youth Ministry Leadership," presented at the Association of Youth Ministry Educators meeting, 2008.

youth ministry work to discover where God is already at work within the cultures present. This is not optional for ministries seeking to join God's missional work in the world.

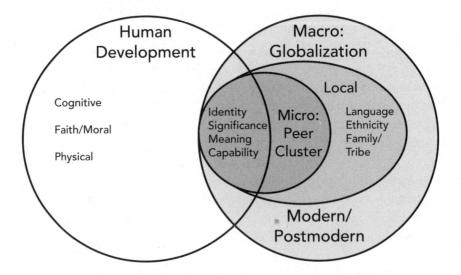

Figure 6.4: Identity Development

THE NEED FOR CONTEXTUALIZATION

As Sophia and Bill are discovering, there is a need to know people and their culture, and there is also a need to communicate in ways that people understand in their own context. Contextualization is the name of the process of finding appropriate ways to make the gospel understandable in a new context (Moreau, Corwin, and McGee 2015). As youth leaders engage cultures that are different from their own, they must adapt their communication of the good news of Jesus Christ. This is something that is done best at the local/micro level.

Ultimately, all theology is local, taking shape in a particular place and time. Missiology, as it draws understanding from both theology and anthropology, highlights the idea that everyone is a theologian. Missiologist Stephen Bevans says, "There is no such thing as 'theology'; there is only *contextual* theology" (2002, 3). Every person has a theology, whether it is concretely expressed or not. Every person, young and old, has a perspective of God or ultimate reality and is making sense of that perspective within his or her context. Therefore, everyone constructs his or her theology at a local level. Robert Schreiter, another key writer on contextual theology, calls this "constructing local theologies." Schreiter points out that not all theology is truly contextual, but he does believe that all theology is local, in that it happens within the local area, not from the outside (1985, 6–7). Schreiter warns that not all local theologies are effective in reaching and reflecting the context.

The more one realizes that others see and experience the world differently, the more necessary contextualization becomes. As a youth leader, like Bill, gets older, cultural distance increases. When a youth minister like Sophia encounters a youth like Chloe, whose micro culture seems strange, there is a divide. Macro- and micro-cultural divides occur on a regular basis. Youth leaders, then, must engage in contextual theology as they model and teach their youth how to navigate these differences.

When one starts by acknowledging that everyone is a theologian and that all are working it out together, then it helps youth leaders step into that conversation more intentionally. Dean Flemming says it well in *Contextualization in the New Testament*: "We have increasingly realized that it is not crosscultural missionaries alone who must grapple with these issues. Every church in every particular place and time must learn to do theology in a way that makes sense to its audience while challenging it at the deepest level" (2005, 14). Because we live in a cross-cultural world, everyone must learn to contextualize theology. Missiologists like Bevans, Schreiter, and Flemming are trying to help the church be more aware of the process of contextualization.

DEVELOPING A PRESENT CONTEXTUAL THEOLOGY

Missionaries have realized that sometimes their efforts to reach another culture with the gospel have produced a group of people who know the "right" answers, but who have not integrated these answers into everyday values and practices. Missionaries noticed that when they are in one specific context—in a church building during a discipleship class, for example—the people give them the "correct" answers about what Scriptures say. However, when certain events, particularly tragedies, occur, these same people often revert to past non-Christian behavior and rituals. This happens in youth ministry as well. Young people might cognitively know the right answers to questions in a small group setting, but they do not live these things out in their everyday lives at school or home.

Rachel is a fifteen-year-old member of her girls' small group at church. By all appearances, it is a strong group. They often have insightful conversations about Scripture and the need to make application in their daily lives.

Rachel grew up in the church and knows the Bible and theological language very well. One night, they were studying 1 Corinthians 12, about the body of Christ and the importance of each member.

During the discussion, the question was asked, "Do you think everyone is of equal value to Christ and in the church?" Rachel quickly answered, "Yes! As the passage says, we might all be different, but we all have a role. An ear can't be a nose. A musician shouldn't want to be a preacher. Both are important and valuable to the church, especially when they do their role."

Rachel's small group leaders affirmed the good response, and off the conversation went! Tiffany, a fourteen-year-old who is new to the church and her faith, joined the discussion. Once Tiffany started to answer the question, Rachel rolled her eyes, turned to her best friend who was sitting next to her, and started talking about something else. At school, Rachel never talks to Tiffany, despite having several classes together, because Tiffany is socially awkward, wears "stupid" clothes, and has "stupid" friends, so Rachel says. Immediately following small group, Tiffany anonymously posts a nasty message on Rachel's Instagram.

One way to view this typical scenario is to recognize that Rachel and Tiffany are early adolescents who, in their development, are searching for clarity in their identities and their social roles. Coupled with biological changes, erratic behavior is to be expected. Without discounting these important details, could there be more going on? Could Rachel's and Tiffany's disconnection between their faith and how they act be related to how they heard the gospel message?

Missiologist Paul Hiebert addresses this "split-level Christianity" in several articles and chapters (1982; Hiebert, Shaw, and Tienou 1999, 2000; Hiebert 2001). In short, split-level Christianity is a phenomenon that came about as missionaries from the West, highly influenced by the Enlightenment, engaged cultures that have a strong sense of the spirit world. The non-Western cultures received the message of the high God of Christianity, but they retained and relied on their belief of local ancestral spirits and gods for understanding disease, death, and fortune.

Split-level Christianity is the result of improper contextualization. The gospel message is not given, nor received, in a culturally relevant way at a local or micro level. Therefore, the "right" answers do not penetrate everyday lives and values. Hiebert notes that split-level Christianity is also common in Western churches, as people simultaneously live with two competing, dissonant views. One is a statement of faith that is claimed to order life, and the other is an underlying set of thoughts and customs for how the world works.

Another way to describe what Rachel and Tiffany demonstrate is referred to as "banked beliefs" by some missiologists. Banked beliefs are "beliefs that do not fit in with other beliefs. They are remembered or stored away but do not affect the way a person acts, except perhaps, when those beliefs need to be 'regurgitated'" (Hughes 1984, 251–58). In other words, these are beliefs that we learn and only recall when the setting is just right. Youth like Rachel and Tiffany learn the content of a set of beliefs, and they "bank" them away for use in the next Sunday school lesson or for the next time their parents quiz them on what they are learning at church. What they "learn" does not influence the way they live their everyday life. This can be contrasted with "actual beliefs"—the beliefs that influence a person's behaviors and actions. Often, people do not articulate these out loud (although they can). Rather, they emerge by observing how one interacts within a cultural setting.

Youth leaders desire that what young people learn moves from their heads to their hearts—from banked beliefs to actual beliefs. This can only happen when the message is communicated in a way that truly connects to a person at a micro-cultural level. It is affirmed when the person can exercise these beliefs in that same micro culture. These experiences—and sometimes these are experiences of failure—are prime opportunities for learning, adapting, and trying faith.

The journey to transformation requires an integrated approach to sharing the good news. Bevans says that "doing theology contextually means doing theology in a way that takes into account two things. First, it takes into account the faith experience of the *past* that is recorded in scriptures and kept alive, preserved, defended—and perhaps even neglected or suppressed—in tradition. . . . Second, contextual theology takes into account the experience of the present, the *context*" (2002, 5). The church can help young people engage both sides: the faith experience of the past, and the context young people live in right now. Contextual theology takes both seriously, and helps youth make their faith a present reality! Youth leaders are called to live in this incarnational, relational place *with* youth and to help them engage in this conversation.

MODELS OF CONTEXTUALIZATION

Schreiter identifies three different models of local theology: translation, adaptation, and contextualization. In the translation model, the missionary or minister takes scriptural or theological imagery and initially conceptualizes it.

Then the concept is put into an equivalent image in the local culture. This is sometimes referred to as the "kernel and the husk" theory. The husk is removed, and the kernel remains. The missionary/minister's job is to put the kernel into a different husk without damaging or changing the kernel.

We know one youth minister who was trying to translate the gospel well. At the time, the video game *Call of Duty* was really popular. The youth minister decided to do a teaching series by the same name, including graphics closely connected to the game in the promotional material. The teaching series involved an emphasis on the "call" of God on everyone's life and the "duty" to serve others. In this case, the youth minister took kernels of truth from Scripture about vocation and loving neighbor, removed them from the husks of the scriptural stories, and then placed them in new husks from popular culture.

While translation might be a good starting place, the dangers of utilizing this model are quite high. First, it often leads to a rapid translation that is not fully or adequately true. In the case of the youth minister using the *Call of Duty* video game, little reflection was given to the main theme of the video game: killing and conquering the opposition. As a result, the connection of people having a duty to serve one another in mercy and justice was blurred, at best. Second, Schreiter raises the question of whether something can be truly removed from its cultural medium without changing the meaning. Perhaps the husk and kernel cannot ever be separated (Schreiter 1985, 7–10).

Adaptation, the second model, involves missionaries or ministers taking an aspect of their understanding of the gospel and "planting it" in a local context. There, it interacts with and grows within that context, moving to maturity in an ideal situation.

Vincent Donovan's *Christianity Rediscovered* describes a great example of this working. Donovan was a missionary to the Masai[4] people of East Africa. In his first year there, he realized that the church up to that point had done a good job helping the Masai with educating their children and with health care, but they had not been successful in sharing the good news of Jesus Christ. None of the priests were actively involved in any of the teachings on Jesus. The little teaching offered was often incorrect. Donovan decided to leave the work of the school and health care to others so he could go directly to the Masai and

---

4.   Donovan uses the spelling "Masai" in his book so we have chosen to do so here as well. More recent spellings usually are "Maasai."

talk to them only about God. The results of his work were transformative for both Donovan and the Masai.

While that method did work for Donovan, the reality is that most cultures already have an existing perception of Christianity and/or Christian culture that influences the development of Christianity in that local context. Therefore, it is rarely a genuinely contextualized gospel (Schreiter 1985, 10–14). Even in Donovan's case, the Masai had never associated Christianity with anything that impacted their spiritual lives, and so there was an obstacle to overcome.

Another example of this is a story about my friend from seminary, Daryl, who came from another country. Daryl had been called by God to pastor. Daryl's family and friends raised the money to send him to seminary in America to be trained so he could return and be their pastor. Before he showed up, he bought several bow ties to wear because he thought all pastors wore bow ties. All the pastors he ever knew wore bow ties. After learning of Daryl's bow tie collection, we did the duty of good friends, playfully teasing him and asking him where he came up with that notion. One of the missionaries who started the work of the church among Daryl's people wore a bow tie. All the ministers who followed him wore bow ties to emulate him. The missionary never said, "All pastors wear bow ties." However, the people believed that the bow tie form was essential to Christianity, and they wanted to be good pastors.

The third of Schreiter's models of local theology, contextual theology, departs from the first two models by locating theology within the receiving culture. Thus, it begins with a problem or issue within the local context. Then Christian Scripture and tradition are engaged to help wrestle with the issue.

While this model takes the local culture seriously, there is the difficult and dangerous need to evaluate the values of the local culture. If theology begins with local culture, then a key question arises: At what point does the gospel message challenge the core values of that culture (Schreiter 1985, 14–18)?

Contextual theology done well, though, can have transformative effects. For example, there was a community in a small country in West Africa that was having a lot of trouble with their relationships. People would continually talk behind one another's back about their problems. This undercut many relationships within the community. A young missionary came to that area to help train pastors and assist discipleship. As he began to engage with this community, he continually heard the same complaints about people talking behind each other's backs. People were hoping their missionary pastor could help them! He led his community in a search for a different approach to relationships and conflict as stated by Jesus in Matthew 18, specifically verses

15–17. By starting with an issue within the culture, the young missionary was able to help the people discover a better kind of life as found in Scripture. When the people began to experiment with relationships according to Jesus's way, they found it was better and produced better relationships.

While Schreiter's description of contextual theology is the approach that most integrates theology into actual beliefs, Schreiter argues that most missionaries and ministers who take culture seriously go through all three stages. They start by translating and then move to some sort of adaptation. As they continue to evaluate their models, they move to a truer contextualization (Schreiter 1985, 25–33).

As one gains more understanding of culture and where God is at work there, the youth leader should be more able to start with the issues in people's lives and take seriously that God is present in the local cultures of youth. The validity of youth ministry requires youth leaders to initiate and guide a conversation between everyday issues that young people face and Christian Scripture and tradition.

It is helpful here to return to Dean Flemming, who points out the importance of the entire narrative of Scripture. He indicates that "focusing on the narrative of what God has done allows us to engage the gospel in a way that shapes our own context and stories" and "points the way to finding unity in the midst of our theological diversity" (2005, 301). For Flemming, the biblical narrative models this contextualization, while linking us to a bigger story. In other words, the more we know Scripture, the more we see the authors contextualizing their message to their specific audience, and the more we realize that these issues involve us in the grand narrative of God's activity in the world.

Questions and issues that people are facing have to be brought up together in our youth groups and churches. It allows space for people to help each other in this process, turning to Scripture together. Flemming continues, "Although we might say that the Holy Spirit is the *ultimate* agent of contextualization, the *visible* agent is the church. Wherever it happens to be situated, the church is a local, particular embodiment of the gospel story. Consequently, contextualization is inherently an *ecclesial* activity; it is done *by* the church *for* the church" (2005, 318, emphasis original). Helping our communities to contextualize the gospel is more than just a good suggestion—it is a mandate.

Flemming's statement has major implications for the church. First, it means that the youth group and local church have to do this together in community. A youth leader cannot do this alone in the office. Second, the goal should be helping the church to grow and be united. Unity should be a result, but the process will take time. Third, it leads the church to go out and find where God is at work. This also means listening to what people are saying in our communities. Fourth, it might start with conversation, but it has to move to action. As Flemming says, the Christian community should be "embodying the kingdom of God within its particular circumstance" (2005, 319). What a local church (and a youth peer cluster) believes and works out together should show up in the ways they live their lives. They must become actual beliefs.

IDENTIFYING SOME DANGERS

Again, contextualization is the conversation between the present issues people are facing and the truth revealed in the past through Scripture and Christian tradition. If we move too far in one direction or the other, we can get into some places that do not lead to transformation.

On one side, if we do not engage the present issues people face, ignoring our context and focusing solely on Scripture and Christian tradition, then we become sectarian. A sectarian church is so separated from culture that it has no real voice or impact on the culture. A sectarian church relies on banked beliefs, often communicating with jargon that is not listened to or understood by the prevailing culture.

This can be seen when missionaries locate in mission compounds, which tend to be havens of expatriate culture from which missionaries make forays into the indigenous culture. The missionaries then "go to work" during the day by stepping into another culture, complete with a different language, knowledge, values, and feelings, where they try to share the good news of Jesus. At the end of the day, they return to their compound and their exported home culture. The problem in this scenario is that the missionary never really engages the indigenous culture, because so much of life occurs behind the walls of the compound. This also can communicate with the host culture that the missionary does not see them or their culture as valuable enough to embrace. The gospel that tends to be communicated and received in that setting is characteristically sectarian: to be a real Christian, one must separate from the local culture.

Youth ministries practice this same kind of sectarian mission when they continually offer alternative activities at the same time as community youth events so that their youth will interact with the "world" as infrequently as possible. The youth leaders may then wonder why community youth and families never attend their events. Perhaps they have lost their voice by separating themselves from the culture.

There is also a danger in indiscriminately merging with the local culture. This can lead to syncretism, when the central elements of the gospel give way to non-Christian practices and/or beliefs (Moreau, Corwin, and McGee 2015, 18). The church and youth ministry cannot lose sight of Christian Scripture and tradition as a core of the conversation. Mission history is replete with misguided syncretistic results.

An example of this from the missionary field might be the missionary who not only learns a culture and its religion but begins to mix its religious practices with Christianity. One missionary working in Asia struggled to have his people truly integrate Jesus into their lives. The people loved the story about Jesus and wanted to believe it; however, they continued with their ancestor worship as well. Instead of challenging this practice, the missionary began to have his church pray to God and then also to the ancestors. His effort to connect to people became too intertwined with ancestor worship, and the Christian message was distorted.

I (Brian) know of a youth pastor who began to investigate the lyrics of Dave Matthews Band. He liked some of the songs with deep meaning and especially enjoyed the "Christmas Song," which tells the story of Jesus's life. The youth pastor began to use some of the lyrics and songs in his messages. He began to use Dave Matthews Band so much that he led a youth group trip to a concert. While there is nothing wrong for looking for truth in all situations and places, when the youth pastor began to get so wrapped up in this band and its lyrics, he lost his ability to critique it. His messages became too wrapped up in culture and lost its contrasting voice that pointed to Christ.

How does the church know if an expression of faith is truly Christian? Schreiter recognizes that as local churches and cultures participate in a local theology, their expressions of Christianity may differ. Just as there can be quite a few differences between cultures, so too can there be a wide variety of expressions of Christianity. The question then is, what are the criteria for Christian identity? What makes a people Christian? It has to be more than their Christian T-shirts! Schreiter lists five criteria that many missiologists have used effectively and seem to be widely agreed upon (Bevans 2002, 22–25; Flemming 2005, 302–5; Moreau, Corwin, and McGee 2015, 110–14):

1. Does the expression follow and flow within what the Christian tradition has done and believed in the past? This is more about attitude

and values than it is about exact forms. If something that claims to be Christian directly contradicts what has been Christian in the past, then there should be a lot of questions. However, it is also true that we cannot slavishly hold onto the forms of the past.[5]

2. Does the local expression of worship continue to point to Scripture as well as an encounter with the living Christ? The ways that people worship may very well take on different forms, but the worship needs to be faithful to Scripture, and there should be recognition that the living Jesus Christ is encountered. Worship should be more than just dead intellectual information or emotional highs. It should reflect a local cultural reflection of the people's heart for good news and their reaction to that good news.

3. Does the expression or practice of the church in everyday life show and reflect on the fruit of the Spirit? Communities in a relationship with Christ should bear this fruit within their culture as outlined in Galatians 5:22–23.

4. Does the local church welcome accountability from other Christian churches and communities? Is there an openness to invite others in to see what they are doing and a willingness to welcome critique on the basis of Scripture and Christian tradition? We see Paul model this in the New Testament when he welcomes accountability. He submits his case for the contextualization he is doing and submits to the authority of the larger Christian community as they hold him accountable (Acts 15:1–35).

5. Does the local church provide accountability to other Christian churches and communities? Paul is again a great example here. He is willing to ask Peter and others if what they are doing is in line with

---

5. There is a Jewish parable that helps illustrate this well: Long ago there was a rabbi who gathered his disciples every day in the afternoon at the synagogue to pray. While he and his disciples were praying, an old stray cat would come around each day yowling and screeching. After several days of this, the rabbi came early to the prayer time, caught the cat, and tied it to a tree outside the synagogue to avoid the distraction. Eventually, the rabbi passed away and the disciples continued to catch the cat and tie him up before prayer. After some time, the tree died, and the disciples planted a new tree in the same spot to tie the cat to. Eventually, the cat died, and the new disciples found another cat to tie to the tree every day. After many years, people wrote theological arguments for the purpose of catching the cat, of tying it up, and of the kind of tree that should be used. The ritual of catching a cat and tying it to a tree before prayer became an expectation. Obviously, this tale gets a bit silly as time goes on, but this is a good picture of some of the ways the church can hold on to practices that were once purposeful and useful but are no longer because of changes in culture or time.

Christ and Christ's teaching (Gal. 2:11–21). In youth ministry, this can be difficult, but it is important that youth learn that they too are a part of protecting and advancing the name of Christ. This should always be done in grace and love, and in ways that are appropriate. (Schreiter 1985, 117–21)

None of these criteria are related to style or form. Certain denominations, networks, and local churches will have their additional criteria for a group to meet their expression of Christianity. While denominational and other structures are important and serve a purpose, they are specific to the local places and are impossible to quantify here. That is why local youth leaders must be aware of them!

QUESTIONS FOR REFLECTION

1. Which aspect of the LASTS model of understanding culture is the hardest for you to see? Why? How might you be able to use this model within your current ministry?

2. Describe some ways you see peer clusters, as defined here, being a part of the mid-adolescent life. What are some ways you think might be effective at reaching peer clusters?

3. How have you personally tried to discern the best way to live between sectarianism and syncretism? How have the ministries that you know done this?

4. Which of the three models of contextualization as described by Schreiter (translation, adaptation, and contextualization) do you feel the youth ministry you know best is currently doing? Why? What could they do to take the next step toward contextualization?

5. Do you agree with Schreiter's criteria for Christian identity? Which one do you agree with the most? The least? Are there other criteria you feel should be included?

7

CULTURAL RELATIVISM

BUT WHAT ABOUT . . . ?

Bill yawned, stretched his arms into the air, and stared at the pile of books and notes on his desk. He was intrigued by all that he had learned about culture and contextualization. But there was a nagging thought tugging at his brain.

"All this contextual stuff sounds so . . . so . . . relativistic," he said to himself.

He thought about his conservative, evangelical church and shook his head as he imagined the worried looks he would receive if he gave any indication that Christianity somehow did not have a universal expression. He recalled a recent hallway inquisition from a church elder who questioned Bill's use of popular music in his teaching at youth group—never mind that the ultimate point was to teach the youth how to use discernment in their entertainment choices.

Bill knew that any talk of engaging culture would likely bring cries of "slippery slope" and "cultural relativism" from several key church members.

Bill called his lifeline, Stan, and explained his dilemma: "As the youth minister, it's like navigating a minefield. Going one way, I encounter concerned parents and church leaders who speak and worry about the plight of youth in a relativistic culture. To suggest to them that the demise of 'absolute truth' is not the source of everything that is wrong with society is to risk an explosive response of severe proportions. On the other hand, some whole churches and denominations basically fail to provide real distinction to the Christian life.

For example, I grew up in a mainline denomination and have witnessed innumerable situations in which a lack of thoughtful discernment has led to an undermining of the Christian heritage. A step either way brings an explosion! It's like walking through a minefield."

"Listen," said Stan, "our mission organization had to walk through this exact issue. It's an important question: How do you remain faithful to the Bible and still engage with culture effectively? After a lot of study, prayer, discussion, and discernment, here's where we landed."

MISSIOLOGICAL INSIGHTS ON CULTURAL RELATIVISM

WHAT IS CULTURAL RELATIVISM?

The relationship between anthropology and Christian missiology is a symbiotic relationship of mutual and competing interests. On the one hand, anthropology is the study of humans and their interactions. It is a purely humanistic study that avoids prescribing what humans could be but only describes how humans are. In anthropological study, religion and any appeal to the supernatural are considered a creative function of humanity.

On the other hand, missiology is an interdisciplinary field that studies the nature, goal, and methods of Christian mission. It begins with the reality of God who is reaching out to a lost humanity. It recognizes where humans are and hopes to reconcile them to God so that they can be all that God created them to be.

In spite of the obvious differences, anthropology and missiology have benefited from each other's presence. Anthropology emerged as a discipline in the nineteenth century when social philosophers began to speculate on the nature of human culture. Much of this speculation was fueled not by firsthand study but by reports from world travelers, many of whom were missionaries. Just as anthropologists benefited from missionary data, the study of mission is indebted to anthropological insights in developing appropriate methods to communicate the Christian gospel across cultural barriers. Despite this mutuality, there exists significant distrust and conflict between the anthropological and missiological communities (Whiteman 2003).

For Christians who are concerned with the communication of the gospel, how is it possible to balance the exclusive claims of Christianity in the face of cultural diversity and the resulting relativistic stance that anthropologists claim as necessary? Is it even appropriate for Christians to borrow insights from a discipline that seems opposed to it? The answer to this dilemma not only affects Christian missiologists but any Christian witness (including youth ministry).

Darwinian ideals and the hope of inevitable human progress dominated early anthropological development in the 1800s. As thinkers searched for a scientific explanation for the cultural diversity found in exotic venues, an evolutionary paradigm began to emerge. It was postulated that cultures, like organisms, move from the simple to the complex. Models were developed using these assumptions, placing cultures on a hierarchy moving from savages to barbarians and, ultimately, to civilized. Many anthropologists believed that when "savage" cultures were introduced to rational thought, they would leave primitive superstitions behind and move up the culture ladder, eventually achieving civilization status (Whiteman 2003). Predictably, civilization to these early anthropologists looked like enlightened Western culture.

By the turn of the century, some anthropologists began to question the ethnocentrism inherent in this scheme, particularly the notion that Western culture was naturally superior. For example, W. G. Sumner discussed the concept of ethnocentrism, describing it as "the technical name for this view of things in which one's own group is the center of everything, and all others are scaled and rated with reference to it" (1906, 13). He not only applied the concept to primitive tribal units but also to modern states: "Each state now regards itself as the leader of civilization, the best, the freest, and the wisest, and all others inferior" (1906, 14).

Other anthropologists raised objections to the assumption of Western cultural superiority. Franz Boas stood out as a leading voice, setting the agenda for what became the doctrine of cultural relativism. Boas (1911) helped introduce a new concept of culture and race through his research and writing. In *The Mind of Primitive Man*, he used scientific inquiry to indicate that there is no fundamental difference between civilized and primitive humans. Rather, Boas proposed, differences in physiology and personality largely were due to environmental factors. Not satisfied with localized study, Boas pushed for the application of his anthropological insights to the sweeping contemporary issues of his time, such as racism in America and the Nazi regime in Germany. In *Anthropology and Modern Life*, Boas concluded that other cultures "are so different that the valuations given by them to human behavior are not comparable. What is considered good by one is considered bad by another" (1929, 204). For Boas, then, the recognition that customs are relative to context and, moreover, are meaningful only in their home context, was central in his teaching. This idea became the dominant stance in anthropology.

Boas is remembered not only for his innovative scholarship but also for his students who continued to interpret and extend his original ideas. Chief among them was Ruth Benedict, whose comparative study of three distinct cultures in *Patterns of Culture* (1934) provided what many consider to be the prototypical treatise on cultural relativism. Benedict pointed out the need to move beyond thinking that one's own culture is universal and see that cultures naturally develop diversity in adapting to particular circumstances. As Benedict delineated her understanding of this study, she arrived at the following conclusions. Because of varying contexts, one cannot bring judgment on another culture. In other words, evaluations of a culture can be made based only on that particular culture's criteria. Since individuals are shaped by the institutional forces of the society in which they are raised, one must be able to move beyond absolute definitions of morality based on one's own culture. The imperative, then, is to embrace cultural relativism, which will cause discomfort but will be the basis for tolerance and coexistence.

The impact of cultural relativism on cultural anthropology was significant. As anthropologists explored the implications of cultural relativism, some, like Melville J. Herskovits (1970, 50–51), recognized that there were serious philosophical implications to the facts of cultural relativism and critiqued efforts to separate the reality of cultural differences from value judgements. Even though he claimed that relativism required the withholding of judgment on such "customs as repugnant to [one's] personal experience as infanticide, head-hunting, various 'unpleasant' dietary and sanitary habits, and the like" (1958, 67), Herskovits did not call for behavioral anarchy. However, others pushed for a radical relativism, which asserts that cultures cannot even be compared and, in fact, that a culture can only be understood by someone enculturated in that culture. By insisting that cultures are incommensurable, this view moves beyond the questioning of absolutes and further suggests that there are no universals that can be applied cross-culturally (Edgerton 1992, 26).

From this brief historical review of the development of the anthropological doctrine of cultural relativism, four points emerge that shape the concept:

1. Societies' customs and values must be understood in the context of that culture.
2. There are no absolute standards for judging customs.

3. All cultures and cultural values are of equal value and dignity.
4. We, therefore, should have tolerance and respect for cultural aspects different from our own, even if they are considered evil by our cultural standards.

BENEFITS AND CRITIQUES

There is much to commend in cultural relativism. As a central doctrine in anthropology, it provides an effective counterbalance to the evolution-ary ideas that affected earlier studies in human diversity, which saw cultures evolving up a ladder of progress. It calls into question the assumed superiority of Western culture over less technologically advanced and primitive cultures, opening the possibility for seeing diverse cultures on their own terms and revealing beauty and harmony in various societal systems. In many ways, cultural relativism put understanding, respect, and tolerance on the agenda of Western powers (and many Western missionary efforts) in place of coloni-zation, subjugation, and oppression.

Even so, cultural relativism is not without its problems. Cultural relativ-ism rests on two conclusions: (1) all cultural values are equally valid; (2) all cultural values are worthy of acceptance and tolerance. However, some argue it is possible to evaluate cultures based on how they affect the people who live within them, looking at how many and who benefit from the accepted beliefs and customs. While one certainly wants to avoid labeling a whole culture as bad, specific practices within a culture can be evaluated.

In his groundbreaking book *Sick Societies*, anthropologist Robert Edger-ton goes even further when he says, "All societies are sick, but some are sicker than others" (1992, 1). Edgerton contends that anthropologists have failed to see the maladaptations of cultures because the constriction of rela-tivism caused anthropologists to romanticize their ethnographies, explain-ing away or even ignoring dark aspects of culture. Edgerton meticulously documents various maladaptive cultural practices that endanger people's health, happiness, and survival. By making all values relative, except toler-ance, anthropologists have avoided scrutiny and evaluative analysis in favor of uncritical assumption. Edgerton's critique is noteworthy and an impor-tant reminder to all that the concept of cultural relativism must be applied carefully. However, he presupposes rationality to be better than irrational-ity, putting superstitions, witchcraft, and most religious beliefs in the irra-tional category. In Edgerton's view of the world, there still is no place for the reality of the supernatural.

SOME CONCLUSIONS

For those who are trying to put Christ first, Edgerton's suggestion of cultural maladaptations provides a helpful insight, but his insistence on rationality to the exclusion of religion is unacceptable. What insights are gained from the biblical perspective? First, the biblical witness agrees with Edgerton that all societies are sick and are in need of transformation. God's concern for how a society treats its people, for example, is seen in his condemnation through Amos's prophecies of the corrupt practices of Israel and its neighbors—practices that included mistreatment of the poor, profane religious rituals, and oppression through violence. What God desires, instead, is to "let justice roll on like a river, righteousness like a never-failing stream" (Amos 5:24 NIV). The things that God desires become clearer in Jesus's delineation of kingdom values in the Sermon on the Mount (Matthew 5–7). God's kingdom is noted for its spiritual thirst, comfort in sorrow, meekness, mercy, purity, and peace. These are the values by which individuals and societies are judged.

Second, the biblical perspective shows an appreciation for the diversity and acceptance of a variety of cultural expressions. True, God did choose one group, Israel, for a special purpose. But this purpose was not for all the nations to adopt the culture of Israel, but that through Israel all nations would be blessed. The realization of the blessing of all nations was initiated in Abraham and found fulfillment in Jesus, the Jewish Messiah *and* the Savior of the world. The Jerusalem Council in Acts 15 made this clear when it decided that Gentiles did not have to become Jewish (through the sign of circumcision) before being reconciled to God through Christ. This decision opened up the possibility that Christianity would be a truly universal religion in which people could be restored to God and worship God in their own culture. As missiologist Lamin Sanneh writes in summarizing Paul's ministry, " . . . God does not absolutize any one culture." Sanneh indicates that "all cultures have cast upon them the breath of God's favor, thus cleansing them from all stigma of inferiority and untouchability" (2009, 54). This is not done on the basis of diversity or rationality, but because "faith, as the absolute gift of a loving God, is the relativizing leaven of culture" (Sanneh 2009, 54).

As mentioned in the chapter on the incarnation, Christians should be present with others, valuing their culture, while at the same time claiming an identity in God's kingdom above all else. Jesus models more than a claim on beliefs. He calls his followers to live in this way of love. Valuing the other puts the Christian in a place of vulnerability, being willing to be transparent and transformed by Christ in the midst of the relationship.

"JOIN ME ON THE JOURNEY"

Bill had listened to Stan's explanation and critique of cultural relativism for thirty minutes, taking notes and jotting down questions. When Stan finished his last point, Bill slowly said, "A lot of what you say makes sense. Did this approach to cultural relativism help your mission organization?"

"It did," replied Stan. "We had a way to train our missionaries in how to engage culture without losing biblical fidelity, and we were able to develop a way to evaluate issues that arose in various contexts."

"So what does it look like in real life?" wondered Bill.

"Let me answer you by telling you a story. In my first significant cross-cultural exposure, I experienced a little of what it means to be an incarnational witness across cultural barriers. Thirty years ago, my wife and I spent the summer as English teachers in a small Japanese church on the outskirts of Tokyo. Because of our short time in Japan, we were able to learn only snippets of the language, just enough to shop and travel."

Stan continued, "One night I was returning to our small village from Tokyo by train. I got off the train at my station, and the ticket clerk checked to see that I had purchased the appropriate ticket. As I handed him my ticket, he said something to me that I did not understand. I somehow figured out that I had bought the wrong ticket and that I owed more money. I could also see that he was telling me how much I owed, but in my limited Japanese I could not understand the exact amount. My heart began to pound and sweat began to emerge on my forehead. Finally, I did the only thing that I could think of. I reached into my pocket and retrieved all of my change, which made up a good portion of my small weekly stipend. With my hand open exposing all my money, I nodded to the clerk. He dug through the coins, found what he needed, and I was free to go."

"Sounds like you had to trust the guy," noted Bill.

"Yes," said Stan. "When I consider the implications of incarnational ministry, I am reminded of this incident. When we enter another person's world, we should come with an open hand. We come with an openness to learn from other views of life and with a willingness to see where God is already at work. Also, we come with an open-handed invitation for others to join the journey to life in Christ. It's risky and sometimes even scary. But it shows our willingness to appreciate cultural diversity, and it reveals the concern that God has for people of every culture."

Bill began to tap his pencil lead on the paper faster and faster. Finally, the lead broke and Bill almost shouted, "Yes!"

"What?" asked Stan.

"I have been in youth ministry quite a few years, and I love it. But one thing has always bothered me. It seems parents, church boards, and senior pastors often expect me, the youth minister, to serve as the moral police for the youth. They are happiest when I am addressing external behaviors of youth, like drinking, sex, and stuff like that. It's gotten to the point where I think youth ministry exists to serve the adults by easing their worry about their kids' behavior. The easy thing is to get youth to act a certain way, at least in the short term. We can train them to give the right answers. The hard part is walking with them in their turbulence. You know, it's really a struggle for adolescents to figure out who they are with all the competing cultural voices. And I'm tired of trying to be some superhero answer man, who says, 'I have all the answers you will need.' Sometimes I'm not even sure what their questions are. I'd rather be seen as a fellow traveler, who invites others to join me on the journey."

"Well, I know one thing," replied Stan.

"What's that?"

"Nobody will ever confuse you for a superhero," Stan said, as he burst into laughter.

"I think it's time to pray," said Bill.

SAFE AND BRAVE SPACES

Where does all this leave us? It can feel so complicated and so difficult that we might want to throw our hands up and say, "Let's just get back to the gaga ball and pizza parties."

Let's summarize what has been discovered so far. At the core, all of this talk about understanding culture, contextualizing the gospel, and reaching the core identity level of transformation is one simple reality and one strong call to action. The reality is that it is God who transforms people, not a youth leader or anyone else. This reality is important because youth leaders do need to do their part in creating environments where people can listen to, experience, encounter, and respond to the living Jesus Christ. But the true transformation only comes through the power of God's Spirit. This is good news to youth leaders, because that means it is not all up to them. It is also good news because the best thing is to be in relationship and point people to Jesus. That it is God who transforms is also humbling news, because it means youth leaders are not the ones who do the transforming.

The call to action is to create spaces and places where young people can express who they are, experience love, ask the hard questions, and find co-pilgrims on the journey. Creating these places means making them safe. Our churches and youth groups need to be safe from physical, emotional, mental, and spiritual harm. No one who sets up a youth ministry has the goal of creating an unsafe place. But when a youth leader does not do the hard work of protecting spaces, then those spaces can become unintentionally harmful. Youth leaders must be wise and careful about not allowing anyone (including themselves) to make fun of other people or their opinions. It is important to see doubts and questions as steps on the journey rather than as threats. These steps help both teens and youth leaders know that there is a commitment to truth. By receiving these doubts and questions, youth leaders create a culture that permits youth to ask out loud what many are already asking and exploring in their heads and hearts. By making the church and youth group the spaces where these kinds of questions are welcomed, valued, and seriously considered together, youth leaders are allowing people, young and old alike, to participate in true contextual theology.

The call to action is to create brave spaces[1]—spaces where people know that when they bring things up, they will be invited into a community that is going to help them try to live a flourishing life. These are spaces of vulnerability and humility. The community may hold someone accountable for actions and words that are harmful to themselves and others. The teenager too must hold others in the community accountable for actions that lead away from truth and Jesus. A true contextual theology starts with the issues of the people, and a true Christian response to those issues goes deep.

FORGIVENESS HITS THE STREETS

Six weeks later, Bill and Sophia sipped their drinks in The Bunker at The Daily Grind.

Sophia confessed, "I didn't get some of that contextual theology stuff at first. But then something happened in my girls' Bible study that made it real for me."

"What's that?" asked Bill.

---

1.   The term "brave spaces" was first developed by Brian Arao and Kristi Clemens (2013) in their chapter "From Safe Spaces to Brave Spaces," in the book *The Art of Effective Facilitation: Reflections from Social Justice Educators*, in an effort to address the realities that "safe spaces," as they have been defined and operated, largely benefited those with privileged identities. Brave spaces are places of safety, but they also include challenge. While we are not talking specifically or exclusively about social justice issues here, the idea of spaces that include safety and challenge is helpful to our discussion.

"I have a great example of how we try to live this out. Remember the girl Chloe I told you about?"

"Sure I do," said Bill.

"Well, she has been coming and engaging relationally in the group. She has also been trying to learn as much as possible in our times together. A couple of weeks ago, we were studying John 8:1–11, the story of the woman caught in adultery. As we were reading, I could see that Chloe was really processing through some things intellectually, emotionally, and spiritually."

"What was going on?" Bill asked.

"I was explaining some historical background on the laws during Jesus's day about adultery. Chloe had a lot of questions about this. Then it all got very real and personal." Sophia paused for a moment then looks at Bill. "She began to tell us about when her family had no money and they were living in their car. . . ."

Sophia's pause began to make Bill anxious to hear the story. "Come on, Sophia, what happened?"

With a pained look in her eyes, Sophia continued, "Bill, Chloe told us right there that her mom began prostituting in order to get money."

"Wow!" said Bill, as he slumped back in his chair.

Like water gushing from a fire hydrant, the story began to spew out of Sophia. "Chloe started verbally processing through this story. She started by admitting the shame she felt about this part of her mom's past. She also shared that she sometimes judged her own mom for doing this. On the one hand, Chloe thought what her mom did was wrong. On the other hand, she knew her mom was desperate and needed money for Chloe's family. Chloe just laid the whole mess right out there in front of the whole group. At this point, all of us were pretty speechless and a lot of the girls were crying.

"Then Chloe started asking questions about Jesus. 'Do you think Jesus would forgive my mom? Do you think my mom would be accepted by Jesus? Do you think my mom could ever know Jesus?'

"As I was listening to her share, I was trying to hear the heart of what she was saying. I asked a question that I thought got to the bigger issue. 'Does God forgive everyone?' The group paused and seemed to catch their breath, and then all the girls started nodding 'yes,' that they believe that God does forgive everyone.

"Chloe sat in stunned silence that only grace can bring, and then she said, 'So I guess if God does forgive me, then God is willing to forgive my mom too. Despite all the ugly things she has done, Jesus loves her too and stands up for her . . . and me . . . and all of us. This is helping me to see Jesus's love is real and that I need to forgive my mom too.' Chloe was saying this through tears and a smile all at the same time. Then she got this surprised look on her face and said, 'Now I hear and feel Jesus speaking to me!'"

"Wow! That is really powerful and beautiful," Bill interjected.

"Yeah, I wanted to say something, but I was in tears. Then one of the other girls started to share how she was struggling to forgive someone in her family. Then another girl started to share her own doubts about Jesus's love for her personally."

"What a powerful night!" Bill shook his head side to side in a "can you believe it?" look of astonishment at both the story and at Sophia's excitement.

Sophia continued, "I wanted to help the girls move from just talking about this to doing something too. I asked them what they thought forgiveness looked like. They thought for a while and Chloe said, 'I know I need to tell my mom I forgive her and that Jesus has forgiven her.' Chloe also said that she told her mom that she understood her desperation and appreciated her desire to help her family. Another of the girls talked about telling her family member that she forgave them. They made some commitments to have some hard conversations in the next week.

"That's when they developed a plan for doing something together. They began to commit to helping each other have these hard conversations over the next couple of weeks. They began to plot out where and when one or two of the other girls could join someone in their forgiveness talk. I gave them a few ideas and suggestions for how they might best start these conversations and how to stay humble in the midst of them, recognizing that they had some things to ask forgiveness for as well.

"The last couple of weeks have been amazing. These girls are experiencing and sharing a new kind of freedom! There have been some really difficult conversations to be sure, but the girls have stayed committed to loving their friends and family no matter what. Some of the people did not receive it particularly well, but they all sensed there was something genuine and real in the girls' forgiveness. Others, like Chloe's mom, were blown away by this act of love and grace. The girls have had a lot of powerful and important conversations, with more to follow."

Bill asked, "What's happening with Chloe's mom?"

"Oh, man!" exclaimed Sophia, "That's another crazy thing. Chloe wanted to bring her mother to church, but she was wondering if the people would accept her mom if they found out about her past. I'm going to be talking with my senior minister later this week about that. Chloe and the girls have already said that they plan to sit with her mom and introduce her to the other parents. They are on a mission."

"That is good contextualization for sure," Bill noted. "They started with real issues, valuing the people and the relationships, while also allowing God to challenge and change them with his love. You were able to understand their issues and help them work through them in their own ways."

Sophia said, "I know that God is helping me with this, and I am learning so much. It's fun to see how what we are learning together makes an impact on ministry. I know that Scripture is a big part of what helped us work through this issue. And it opens the door for a deeper understanding about forgiveness, as well as repentance. But this is a really good start."

Bill nodded as he finished his black coffee. "Well, you did a great job with this situation. If the conversation is between current experiences and Scripture, I know youth know their current situations and culture, but how do I get them into *the* story, Scripture? More and more of the youth who come to my youth group know very little about what the Bible actually says. If contextualization calls for Scripture to be one of the conversation partners, how do I get youth to engage it and present it in a way that starts to connect to their lives?

"What I like about this idea of a conversation is that it takes seriously theology, Scripture, and tradition, as well as the present context. This is one of the things that I have personally struggled with in youth ministry. Sometimes I feel like I tell students to only look to Scripture or listen to what the church tells them, but when I do that too much, it feels like I might be ignoring their current situations and reality—or at least not connecting the two."

"I think I have our next book to read!" exclaimed Sophia. "My pastor and I were talking a bit about this journey I am on in thinking missionally about youth ministry. The next day he gave me one of the books he had that brought together both a an appreciation of the whole biblical story and mission. He said it was helpful for him in thinking about preaching. It's called *The Drama of Scripture: Finding Our Place in the Biblical Story*—let's read it and see if it helps."

Bill and Sophia sat in silence for a few moments, trying to put all the pieces together in their heads and their hearts. Sophia wrapped up their time with a prayer: "God help us as we seek to recognize God's presence in our midst, surrender control to him who truly can transform, and open ourselves up to love that does not allow us to stay put."

QUESTIONS FOR REFLECTION

1. How is cultural relativism defined? What are some benefits of it? What are some weaknesses? How do you think Christians should engage in an incarnational way?

2. What is a "brave space," and how might it help to create such spaces in youth ministry? What are the challenges or obstacles in creating these spaces?

3. Thinking about the community or town you know best, what are some things they value that are helpful to the gospel? What are some things they value that work against the gospel?

8

DEVELOPING A DISCERNING COMMUNITY

WHEN THEY SHOWED UP for their coffee time the next month, Sophia handed Bill a book. "*African Proverbs Reveal Christianity in Culture*," Bill read, "by W. Jay Moon. What is this?"

"Remember the girl Chloe I told you about?" asked Sophia.

"Sure," said Bill. "She's the one who is pretty sharp and asking some good questions, right?"

Sophia nodded affirmation, "Well, she came to me again this week a real mess. One of her friends, Isabella, was recently killed. Chloe and her friends are having to do a lot of the funeral arrangements because her family is pretty absent. I could tell Chloe wanted to ask me something pretty big, but she kept hesitating. Finally I just asked her what she was wanting to talk about. 'Sophia, would you be willing to be the pastor at the funeral?'

"I was flattered and shocked she asked me because I had never met Isabella. I told her that I would be honored to, and then I asked why she had hesitated to ask me.

"She replied, 'Well, my friends and I want to play this Tupac song, "Changes,"[1] at the funeral. I know you and the church don't swear and Tupac

---

1. Tupac Shakur was a rapper and is considered one of the best hip-hop artists of all time

swears a lot. I also know Tupac talks about some things you all do not agree with. Do you think we could still play that song at the funeral?"

Bill encouraged Sophia, "What an honor and blessing to be invited into this! This really shows how much you mean to Chloe and how much she means to you. But this is a tough issue to be brought into. What did you say to her?"

"We have been growing closer together in our Bible study group, and I knew what I should do. I knew that the small group would want to be a part of the funeral and asked her if we could bring up the issue of using the song with the group."

"That's a great idea!" said Bill. "But that also seems tricky to lead that kind of a conversation."

"I doubt I would have thought of turning to the group if it weren't for the book *African Proverbs Reveal Christianity in Culture*, because it talks about developing a true discerning community."

"Well, I can't wait to hear how it goes with the group," said Bill.

COMMUNITY AND THE GOSPEL

The poetic text from Genesis 1:26–27 reads, "Then God said, 'Let us make mankind in our image, in our likeness, so that they may rule over the fish in the sea and the birds in the sky, over the livestock and all the wild animals, and over all the creatures that move along the ground.' So God created mankind in his own image, in the image of God he created them; male and female he created them" (NIV).

These verses point to the community of God in the plural language of "us" and "our." The text points to the Trinity in its perfect community: God the Father, God the Son, and God the Spirit—each different, living in perfect loving community, serving each other. Out of this perfect community, humanity is created. Humanity is created from perfect community for perfect community. This is why each person has a deep longing for community!

Not only does the Bible speak about humanity's communal nature in Genesis 1, it models that same communal nature by the way it was put together and has been used for most of human history. The Bible was written to communities. It was written with groups of people in mind. Paul's

---

in part because of the way he brought social issues into his music. His song "Changes" references many of the social issues for African American youth and calls for change in the ways people treat one another.

letters were written to churches, the Torah was written for God's people, the words of the prophets were written for specific people groups, and the teachings of Jesus were to groups of people. For most of the life of Scripture, it was read together by people in community. Before the majority of the world had access to education that enabled everyone to read and write, and before there was the printing press, there were groups of people who gathered together to read the handwritten text aloud to each other. It was in the midst of these readings and discussions by communities that God called and moved people.

One of the consequences of the era of modernity and its focus on the individual was a move away from community. This showed up everywhere in culture, including the church and its leadership. No longer, the church was taught, did God give vision to people in community but rather to an individual leader who would then become the voice of God for all the people. The single leader of the church was the one to whom all big decisions would fall. Instead of the community looking to God to guide them, it seems the community wanted a "king."

If it is true, as we have previously articulated, that being Christian is to embrace mission, and if youth ministry must be a part of that mission, then it is also true that youth ministry happens in context with people, in conversation with Scripture, and in relationship with God through Jesus Christ. All of those elements are *dynamic*! This means that involving the community in the process of discernment is both necessary and complicated! There is no "one size fits all" program, nor is there a "silver bullet" that will solve all the problems a youth ministry community is facing. What works for one youth ministry in one context may not work at all for another youth ministry in another context. This is what makes youth ministry at the same time both difficult and rewarding. Each local church is called to engage youth ministry together as community.

Missiology is calling the church back to the roots of the gospel, back to discerning God's vision and will in the context of community. This is a good thing, but a hard thing. For those who have been trained up in the way of modernity, these lessons are almost foreign. Despite this contrast, it is exciting to see so many people yearning for a communal kind of approach and seeking to live differently in today's youth ministry culture. Thankfully, missiology has been in the depths of this conversation for a long time and has much to offer youth ministry leadership in moving back into a model of discerning together.

MISSIOLOGY TEXTS

David J. Bosch, in his seminal work *Transforming Mission: Paradigm Shifts in Theology of Mission*, begins by naming the "pluriverse of missiology" (1991, 7–8),[2] which reflects the complexities and necessity of engaging in God's mission together. Bosch is referring to the many ways that missiology has been defined and practiced over the years. His argument is that the church must bring into conversation as many of these voices as possible to learn from one another and to work together. This ongoing process leads to changes in the church, the church's approach to God's mission, and the practice of missions. The reality is that we simply *must* work with others as we engage the important work of sharing the good news, and that we will never be able to "boil it all down" or "sum it all up" in ways that will be completely universal.

It is not an accident that immediately following Jesus's first announcement of his public ministry (Mark 1:14; Matt. 4:17), he calls a group of disciples to follow him in order that they may participate in learning and doing God's mission on earth. This relationship is marked by Jesus's constant teaching and engagement with the disciples about God's mission for each context in which they find themselves (led there by Jesus himself, of course!). The very disagreements, wrestlings, and various practices of the disciples, both before and after Jesus physically leaves them, model the necessity for engaging in discernment together . . . and the messiness of that process.

Paul's work with the many believers in the variety of places that he traveled also reveals this truth. As the church sought to engage cultures and contexts with the good news of Jesus Christ, there were differences of opinion on methods, strategies, and message. It was often messy, and yet it was also effective.

The process of the community of faith discerning what the gospel is and how it is to be lived out was remarkable in that it brought people together. To be clear, it brought *all* types of people together from all types of differences. This made the first Christian community remarkable, and to the outside world, quite unbelievable. The early church in Acts was imperfect and troubled; it was filled with people from various socioeconomic groups and ethnic backgrounds. In short, it was made up of people who would not normally be found in community together. So too must youth ministries invite all voices into the process of discernment.

---

2.   Bosch himself is quoting and expanding on the work of George Soares-Prabhu's article "Missiology or Missiologies?," *Mission Studies*, no. 6 (1986): 85–87.

Discernment is one of the key roles the church plays in engaging the world in the work of the kingdom. The Gospel in Our Culture Network (GOCN) was formed in 1987 by church leaders and missiologists to provide useful research and encourage local action, realizing the shift in North American culture from modernity to postmodernity. GOCN desired to create a network to help the church engage culture in missiological ways. Their book *Missional Church: A Vision for the Sending of the Church in North America* does an excellent job moving the discussion from the church as a sending congregation to a community being sent.

Missional Church advocates that as the church is a community of the Holy Spirit, it needs to practice discernment:

> Discernment is a process of sorting, distinguishing, evaluating, and sifting among competing stimuli, demands, longings, desires, needs, and influences, in order to determine which are of God and which are not. . . . As the *ekklesia* of God, a people gathered and sent to be about God's business, the church is called to a way of making decisions that articulates and correlates with listening, hearing, testing, planning, and obeying together in the power of the Holy Spirit. (Guder and Barrett 1998, 172–73)

Missional Church advocates for a Christian community that listens to *all* believers, giving time and space for each to share from their experience and giftings, as they sort through Christian tradition, Scripture, and the leading of the Spirit to find God's truth. In this way, each person is involved according to experience and gifts, giving voice to each so that when a decision is reached, the whole community has had their voice heard and now can fully commit to the decision of the community.

In a world with so many different youth cultures and so many competing "stimuli, demands, longings, desires, needs, and influences," discernment is exactly what youth ministry and the church needs. This is a complex task for all people in the church. To ask an individual pastor to do this seems like an impossible task, let alone a teenager with no theological education and little life experience. While a discerning community admittedly takes time to foster, it seems like the alternative—a lone individual "leader" tasked with discerning for the whole community—is so costly that the time and relational commitment are more than worth it.

Most teenagers today have at their fingertips, through their smartphones connected to the internet, access to more information than their grandparents had access to in their entire lives. While this access can be quite helpful, as one can find all kinds of useful information, it can also provide difficult challenges to young people. Which religion should I choose? Which response to racism is best? How should I respond to issues of sexuality? The amount of information that young people have to sift through to discern the truth is staggering. Unfortunately, most young people are left to do this discerning on their own. It is rarely discussed. The church should be modeling and providing a better way of discernment together.

A follow-up book from the GOCN, *Treasure in Clay Jars: Patterns in Missional Faithfulness*, takes the ideas from *Missional Church* and looks for examples lived out in communities of faith. One of the patterns they discover is a "missional vocation" (Barrett 2004), which is described as discovering together God's specific missional call for the entire community and all its members. A missional vocation is a response to listening to God's work in the life of a community as it exists in context. This missional vocation is demonstrated in another pattern they found, "taking risks as a contrast community," where the community is continually asking questions of the church's engagement with culture and suggesting appropriate changes required in this ongoing engagement (Barrett 2004). Some of the changes that the community discerns to be appropriate might very well be new and risky. *Treasure in Clay Jars* demonstrates that discernment can be practiced in community, resulting in a lived-out kingdom commitment.

One of the key takeaways from the missional church literature, the conversation between missiology and ecclesiology, is that the church needs to reinvest in developing and training discernment in its local communities. Youth ministry can learn from this as youth and youth leaders try to engage the cultures around them. Teaching discernment in a community context not only provides an environment that corresponds to developmental needs (identity formation, cognitive formation, faith/moral formation); it also reminds youth that they are not alone in this mission. As missiology has dealt with more communally minded cultures globally, those missionary experiences have much to offer the church and youth ministries.

DISCERNING AS A COMMUNITY

Discernment can be complicated, but it is a part of youth ministry all the time. As most youth are not just interested in their youth cultures but rather embedded in them, it is important that youth leaders learn to help the community to discern truth and good news in the midst of these cultures. As we have discussed previously, if we believe that God is always at work through his Spirit all the time, then part of our role as Christians is to be detectives looking for the fingerprints of God in our everyday lives. But the question is *how*?

W. Jay Moon's book *African Proverbs Reveal Christianity in Culture* is a great resource to help youth ministers see the value and place of what he calls a "hermeneutic community" (2009). "Hermeneutics" is the theory and methodology for interpretation. A "hermeneutic community" is the group of people that turn to each other in order to interpret what is happening in their lives and what they should do about it. It is a place of discernment. Moon uses a narrative example of the proverbs of the Builsa people of Ghana and how those proverbs were utilized in partnership with Scripture to help the church reach the Builsa people in ways that revealed Christ.

These proverbs are used widely across Africa as a way to transmit wisdom. However, most of the church and its missionaries, coming from the outside perspective, had struggled to understand these proverbs and thus had been unable to learn them, reference them, or utilize them. In Moon's narrative, the church was able to begin a conversation about the meaning of some of the African proverbs, which led to connections with Christian Scriptures and thus an engagement with the gospel in ways that were transformational for that community.

As in the case of the Builsa, many youth ministries struggle to help young people connect what they know about Scripture with everyday life. While it is doubtful that many youth ministries in the United States deal with proverbs as utilized by the Builsa, there are other cultural stories and symbols present that can be utilized in a similar manner to contextualize the gospel. Moon's book masterfully points us toward a process of engaging in the conversation about the symbols and stories of our culture in order to find meaning.

STEPS TO A DISCERNING COMMUNITY

Moon starts by noting that most communities do not gather for intentional conversations about discernment naturally. He argues that a leader is needed as a catalyst to initiate and sustain the conversation, doing the work of inviting people to come and handling the logistics around the conversation. In a youth ministry context this often will be the youth leader, who has some relational authority to bring a group of people together. The leader's task at this level is to create the environment where the community can safely gather, share insights, and discern together. For youth ministries with existing small groups, these groups often provide a good place to start practicing discernment together. For ministries without those existing smaller community groups, it might be best to try to start with a group of friends who are walking through a specific difficult issue.

Once invited by the youth leader, a hermeneutic or discerning community gathers together to provide a wider and more informed perspective into which the Holy Spirit can speak. It is helpful if there are both insiders, youth who are embedded within the culture; and outsiders, who are outside of youth culture (probably most adults). This variety of perspectives allows for different viewpoints and experiences to be brought to light by the whole group. In youth ministry, a small group of teens and a few adult youth leaders would be a good example. The group of teens can share from the cultures that they are embedded within. The adults likely are not insiders to cultures represented and so can offer perspective from outside. This gathered community is focused on hearing God's direction on an issue. This shared goal helps the group stay focused on sharing their own perspectives and learning from others.

As the group begins to discuss a particular issue, it is helpful to examine where each person's knowledge about the topic comes from (epistemology). Do they know about the topic from their own experience, from someone they know, or from something they read or watched? This encourages people to engage the larger issue(s) and helps keep people from entrenching along theological or ideological lines. It also opens the door to use Scripture as a conversation partner in the discussion. In youth ministry, when engaging a common cultural genre, say a YouTube video, try to help the group start by making observations about the video. Then ask where those views, ideas, or interpretations come from. This might take some practice to engage, but once the group gets some experience at it, the process will become much easier. This is where the youth leader as catalyst needs to pay attention to his or her role of keeping the conversation safe by helping individuals to listen well and to speak well.

One young man, Zach, had a pretty closed-minded view about the way the government in the United States should treat illegal immigrants. He had been raised around a specific political rhetoric about keeping certain people out and obeying the laws of the authorities. He was quite happy to share with his friends from this particular political lens. One day his small group started a discerning conversation about the issue of how the church should treat illegal immigrants. At first Zach responded as he usually did. His youth leader did not let him stop there, and asked him why he thought that way and where he had heard that particular message. As Zach stopped to think about this, he heard his friend and small group comember José share that his mother was an illegal immigrant and that she could never go and see their family outside the country because she would not be allowed to reenter the United States. Zach, who highly values spending time with his extended family, suddenly had to wrestle with the issue from a different perspective. While Zach was able to share the books and articles where he had learned some of his usual arguments, and this added to the larger conversation, José had shared from his personal experience. Zach's perspective was now only one of many instead of the only right perspective.

A good way to start the conversation with the group is with a local genre. While Moon uses African proverbs in his book, he also recognizes that there are other good places to start. Movies, music, social media posts, and YouTube videos are cultural genres that youth are familiar with and engage the values of different cultures. For example, a youth leader might want to discuss the issue of dealing with racial differences and use a movie clip that illustrates the tension. These local genres are helpful because they are often easily accessible, recognizable, and keep the issue from becoming too personal to one individual.

While analyzing these local genres, the group should look for discoveries about hidden or deeper aspects of culture that are often overlooked. This is where the value of having both insiders and outsiders becomes more obvious. Insiders can see things at a depth outsiders rarely grasp. Outsiders can spot some contrasts and inconsistencies that insiders are often blind to. By making sure it is a safe place, the youth leader invites people to make observations of all kinds. This also allows for people to ask questions of each other. It is good to start with the basic observations. These are important observations that start everyone on a common ground, but it is important to move into deeper observations. The youth leader can ask the more mature in the group to model moving past the superficial to the deeper-level realities.

Moon advocates using a translation of Scripture that is most comfortable for the people engaged in the conversation, since it provides the clearest revelation of God in culture. Using this translation may encourage the discovery of new aspects of Scripture that may have been overlooked in the past. Some examples might be to engage the New Living Translation[3] or *The Message* translation.

Allow time for the Holy Spirit to speak to the discerning or hermeneutical community. Contextualization is not dependent on education level or other

---

3.   For an audio version of the New Living Translation with a hip-hop soundtrack see streetlightsbible.com.

abilities; rather, it is a creation of the Holy Spirit as Scripture is allowed to engage culture via cultural channels prepared by God. The youth leader must trust the Holy Spirit in the midst of the conversation. Allow time for people to make observations and interpretations, and to ask questions. Encourage the group to not just "go along to get along," but to be willing to say what they truly think or feel about an issue. This process cannot be rushed. Some individuals are quicker to speak than others. Some are more thoughtful. The youth leader must be sure to allow time for and give invitation for all to share.

Once the group has had time to discern together, the outcome of the conversation, the contextualization, should be recorded in the heart language of the group. It can be "translated" later to adults or other church leaders if needed. But first allow youth to use their words and language to describe what they are seeing and how it connects with Scripture and theology. The youth leader will have to work hard not to "correct" language. He or she might help the youth to nuance their theology, but the outcome must be stated in ways that the youth best understand and can articulate with confidence themselves. It is also wise to have some means of recording the results of the conversation at the end. This helps the group to come to a consensus and to put into words what they have agreed upon. There are many creative ways to do this recording of conclusions, including simply writing things in a report to share with others, putting it into a social media post or story, or shooting a video summary.

To communicate Christianity in a culture, the relevant and available symbols should be identified and appropriately used. These symbols are constructed and reconstructed by the participants in the culture. For example, movies and YouTube videos function as symbols in North American youth cultures and have been created from within those cultures. As such, they can be used as building blocks to construct a Christian response from within those youth cultures. Youth leaders can ask the youth to help find the best things to engage. Start by going to the media that youth regularly engage. Be okay feeling uncomfortable, like Jonah (Moon 2009, 194–96)!

Teaching a community to share openly, listen well, and discern together can be quite difficult with anyone, but adolescents can prove even more challenging with their various and changing developmental levels. However, when youth leaders choose to engage them in this discernment together, it demonstrates that the church values them as men and women who are significant, who have meaning, and who have capability. This shows young people that the church truly believes that God can and does speak to them and through them.

In addition to helping the community discern what Christ would have them do, it also helps the youth develop as people and as Christians. Research on cognitive and faith/moral adolescent development demonstrates that people who are exposed to higher level of thinking and a higher level or morality are then challenged to move into a higher level themselves. By exposing youth to these types of discussions and discernment, youth leaders invite them to take next steps in thinking and valuing.

As previously stated, this kind of discernment and group process can take time. It also can be difficult. However, comparing the sustainability of this kind of model with a model where youth only follow what their leader states makes the time commitment seem more than worth it. When a youth ministry begins teaching youth to seek out a community of discernment, it teaches them to seek out wise counsel; to commit to a community; to use Scripture and community as filters for discernment; and to be guided, as a community, by God's Spirit. In short, youth ministry is teaching them to be active disciples of Jesus Christ and co-collaborators in building his kingdom on earth as it is in heaven.

THE STORY

Bill could not help but notice how Sophia was beaming as she walked into the coffee shop this week. "I guess it went well."

"It went really well!" Sophia exclaimed. She went on to tell Bill about how she gathered the Bible study group for a special session just to pray with Chloe and help her make some decisions. The group eagerly came together to offer their support. When Chloe explained the situation and the question about the Tupac song, the group was supportive of her emotionally and then they got quiet. "I had to really prompt them to answer her question about the song." To do so, Sophia had printed the lyrics of the song and had it cued up on her phone. She started the conversation by simply asking the group to listen to the song and read the lyrics as it played, asking them to not think about who the song was performed by at first. After the group had heard the song, Sophia started by asking what they noticed in the song.

"Since many in the group have grown up in the church, they had not really listened much to Tupac. They had some preconceived ideas about him and his songs, especially the language he uses. When they read the lyrics and listened to it, they were really positive about the song. They affirmed the overall message that the violence in our culture toward each other has to change," Sophia explained.

"Why do I feel like there is a 'but' coming?" Bill asked.

"Because there is! One of my leaders, who I thought might have a hard time with this, raised a question about whether endorsing this one song was to endorse all of Tupac's songs, which she clearly was *not* comfortable with. I really wanted to jump in and state my opinion, but I just waited for the group to respond."

"Good for you!" affirmed Bill.

"It was so hard, but it was so worth it. A couple of the girls agreed with the adult volunteer that this could be seen as an endorsement of Tupac, especially since it would be played in the church building, but then another girl spoke up and said that she thought the truth of the song was worth sharing because it was not going to be the only thing happening at the funeral. She went on to say that if I were to point out in my funeral sermon that the change Tupac was hoping for is able to be found in Christ, it could be a chance to speak about Jesus to people who do not normally open themselves up to it, *and* she said that it would help them see the Bible and Jesus as relevant. She thought it was important because Chloe and her friends had thought the song was important."

"Wow! That sounds like a really well-articulated point."

"Yes, I was so proud of her. Then it got even better because my other small group leader, Betty, who is a mom and a bit older, spoke up and said that she had not really been interested in playing this song at all when the conversation started, but after seeing the lyrics (and the lack of swear words) and hearing how it could really open the door for a good conversation of hope, she was changing her mind. She went on to point out that some of the Psalms also asked questions without any real answer. She even got out her phone and read Psalm 44 to the girls."

"Then what happened?"

"Well, there was some more dialogue about what I might say to help connect the song to the hope in Christ. I asked them to help me name some things from the song I could build off of and asked them to help me find Scriptures to speak from. This is where the 'church girls' and Chloe really got excited about it and started helping. This gave us a record of what we thought was right and why. Most importantly, to me, was that Chloe left that group time feeling supported and encouraged, and that Christianity matters when life is hardest."

A few days later, Sophia was outside the church doors welcoming people to the funeral service. Many of the people who were there were friends of Isabella, whose funeral it was. Some of the youth group, youth parents, and all of Chloe's small group came, and some were involved in the service by reading Scripture. Very few members of the congregation came, because they did not know Isabella at all. During the service, after some prayers and Scripture readings, the Tupac song "Changes" was played. The lyrics were printed in the service handout. After the song was played, Sophia preached the funeral message, addressing some of the lyrics in the song about the changes that are needed. She said that while it was quite unusual to play a Tupac song in church (everyone laughed) and that the church did not endorse all of Tupac's songs and lyrics, this song was important to Isabella and had a good message. She went on to reference Jesus's message of love for one another and love for neighbor. She connected how true change can only happen from the inside out when we allow Christ to transform us. Chloe got up next and shared what she loved about Isabella, how Jesus was changing her own life, and how she wanted Jesus to change the neighborhood. It was a powerful service, and many people thanked Sophia on their way out for the good message. One woman thanked her for "making a funeral actually make some sense." Sophia was most proud of Chloe's small group and their parents, who showed up in support of Chloe and reached out to love the people at the funeral.

QUESTIONS FOR REFLECTION

1. This chapter references David Bosch's work on the "pluriverse of missiology," which says that we should work to listen to the many different voices that are all trying to pursue God's mission. What are some ways that Scripture demonstrates this? What kinds of people are brought together in this work?

2. What is discernment, according to this chapter?

3. What are the nine steps in developing a discerning community?

4. What do you think are some of the challenges for the church to discern God's direction and will together?

5. What makes discerning with others difficult for you? What are the obstacles in the way?

9

TELLING THE STORY

SOPHIA AND BILL MET AGAIN for coffee at The Daily Grind. They secured their place in The Bunker. It seemed like all the customers knew that it was their space. They had developed a pretty good rhythm for connecting and talking through new issues each time they came together.

Sophia started their conversation this week. "Bill, I have been thinking a lot about the power of story. As we have already discussed, words build worlds. We have been talking about ways to share the good news, and I really like the idea of contextualization. I like the idea of helping people connect to the story. I guess I am now at the place where I am asking '*How?*' We have been doing a lesson in youth group every week, but it feels like the youth are not that engaged. I think that youth really want to hear good news, and I think that Scripture is good news, but I just cannot seem to help youth connect to Scripture in ways that feel relevant to their everyday lives."

Bill added, "I agree with you. Reading *anything* seems to have almost no place in their lives, even Scripture. It feels like social media has captured almost all of their attention."

"I have noticed that it is stories that grab them. Even social media is trying to help people tell a story now," Sophia said.

"Sure, I notice this in small ways and big ways. When I tell a story about my life, especially my failures, people listen more. When we have youth share their stories and what God has been doing in their lives, people listen way more."

Sophia chided Bill, "With all your failures, it seems like you would have a lot to share."

"Thanks a lot!"

Sophia continued, "Back to your point about people listening to stories. We noticed this too and have been trying to incorporate stories more into our regular gatherings. About every other week we have different youth share their stories and how they are doing with God. We have even included some people who are not sure where they are with God yet. We have found that modeling that transparency has been really helpful. But last week was a whole other thing. . . ."

"What happened?" Bill asked, excited to hear the story.

"Last week I asked Joshua to share his 'testimony,' as we used to call it. I called him beforehand and told him the questions I would ask him. We went over his answers, just to give him a chance to practice his responses ahead of time. Joshua is one of our core youth, and a lot of other teens look up to him for his faith and integrity. I was excited for him to share how close he is with God. And then it went a whole different direction.

"During youth group, I brought him up front to share. When I asked him about how he was doing with God, he said, 'Well, to be honest, I am not feeling close to God at all right now. It has been a hard week and a hard semester. I have been praying to God, but it hasn't always worked out like I thought it would. Right now, I have a lot of questions and doubts.' Then he sat down.

"I was very shocked by this because it was a totally different answer than what we had discussed earlier in the week. I did not really know what to say or do, so we just quickly moved on. I shared some looks of concern with my other adult leaders throughout the night, and I knew I would have to follow up with Joshua later.

"But after the service was when the big surprise came. Lots of the youth wanted to talk with Joshua about his faith. They wanted to share their stories and their questions too. There were youth who wanted to support him and pray for him, and youth who just wanted to know that it was okay to have questions."

"How did Joshua do with all of that?" Bill asked.

Sophia replied, "Well, at first he was pretty quiet, but he quickly realized that he was not alone in this. Joshua is a mature teen, and it was cool to see him handle this well. I made my way over and stood by him as he talked to people. It was super-hard not to jump in and try to answer all the questions I heard. But I was able to really listen to the questions and struggles youth have. It just took Joshua's story to unlock it."

Bill said, "Well if stories unlock that kind of reaction and openness, then we need to figure out how to use story more. Back when I was young, in the stone ages," Bill joked, "we learned to teach Scripture with propositions and alliteration. How can we use story more in engaging Scripture? This change of focus reminds me of something. Have you ever read Vincent Donovan's *Rediscovering Christianity*?"

"Yes! I read it for a class in college and really liked it. It has been a long time, though. It was refreshing to see how he used God's story to reach the Masai. I wondered when I read it if that would work for my youth, but never really tried it."

"Me too!" Bill replied.

"Well, let's reread that book, and also look at this other book I picked up called *The Drama of Scripture*. Then we can talk about this more."

Bill and Sophia spent the rest of their time catching up on life before setting a time for their next meeting and leaving.

THE VALUE OF STORY

Stories are everywhere. Every culture has its stories. Social media encourages and even teaches people to tell their stories in a variety of ways. People are binge-watching TV shows hours at a time because the story is so compelling. Movies tell stories and share values. Companies today are working hard to make sure their customers know their origin story. Video games must have a compelling narrative to drive the action and draw participants in.

As the macro culture has shifted from modernity to postmodernity, there has been a big step away from propositions and toward stories. A proposition is a statement that is put forward to be considered true or untrue. Modernity loves propositions because for modernity, reason is king. In modernity people trust things that can be reasoned out. If we all have the same information, then we can all come to the same conclusion using reason and logic, using our minds. Once we looked at the information and determined a truth, then we could articulate that truth in a proposition that was true for everyone, for all time.

But postmodernity has been helping people process the reality that not all truth is true all the time. Propositions, at times, are not that helpful. There can be things that are true sometimes, but not all the time. Context has a lot to do with how something is both said and received. For example, two plus two does not equal four when you are adding drops of water. Two drops of water plus two drops of water can equal one big drop of water.

In the postmodern macro culture, stories and narratives have become much more trusted and favored. They are favored in part because stories allow for context to be explained, and in part because stories allow people to find themselves within the narrative. A story allows for nuance and complexity that propositions often do not.

Story helps people to see the big picture. Story helps people understand how and where things fit. Story invites people into it and allows people to know there is purpose, belonging, and direction. It then challenges one to move ahead, to not stay stuck where they are. Story tells people that conflict is to be expected and that it needs to be overcome.

Stories also invite participation in ways that propositions do not. A proposition is true or untrue all the time. It will be true whether I participate in it or not. But a story invites me into it, to find myself in the details, to have agency to choose, and to help shape the story as it unfolds. Stories have become the ways that young people participate in this postmodern macro culture. Social media, for example, allows young people to both read other people's stories and create their own to be read by others.

Postmodernity has critiqued the idea of metanarratives, those overarching narratives that include everyone. The question is one of power. Whoever gets to write and tell the metanarrative controls the power within the story. It is often said that history is written by the winners. Postmodernity seeks to critique that power and instead allow everyone to write and participate in his or her own story. It emphasizes context.

Scripture is a metanarrative. However, Scripture is different than all the other metanarratives in that it gives voice and agency to all people, especially the disenfranchised. It was written by a wide variety of people from a wide variety of socioeconomic, social, and ethnic backgrounds. It stands out because it highlights the flaws of its heroes and gives value to people who had no value in culture. When handled appropriately, it is a text that everyone can find himself or herself within. But it still is a metanarrative that some people may struggle with just because it is a grand story.

Part of the strength and power of Scripture is that it is a living text. That is, the story of Scripture is true for many contexts; it is true in layers. Scripture is true in a really *big* way.

In the rabbinic tradition, they talk about Scripture having seventy faces. Like a fine gem, the text must be turned so that it can be seen from all sides. Each side contains a beauty that is true and that could not be seen from the other side. When light shines through the gem on one side, the observer might see a green colored light. When the gem is turned and light shines through another side, the observer might see a yellow colored light. There is a beauty to Scripture that cannot be seen from only one side. Part of the task of youth ministry is to help young people turn the gem of Scripture.

One of the ways that youth ministry can turn the gem is focusing on the larger story of Scripture, helping young people to see that something bigger is going on here. This is helpful for youth developmentally as they need to challenge and be challenged in some of their assumptions about the way the world works and their role within it. Story can do this in a way that is less confrontational and more invitational.

Stories can be told many different ways. As macro culture turns to story as a valid way to express values and truths, it is important for youth ministry to learn to tell stories, and in particular the story of Scripture, in a variety of ways.

By telling the story of Scripture and allowing it to stand on its own, youth leaders invite youth into the process of finding truth for themselves. This means opening up to questions, doubts, struggles, and comparison. But in so doing, youth ministry retains a place as a conversation partner, and one who cares, in the lives of young people, while also giving them agency to discover truth for themselves.

Part of the role as a youth leader is to share the story. Storytelling, at least when telling this grand narrative, involves the duel functions of being a prophet and a poet. A prophet is a truth-teller, someone who knows where people are and what God is doing in their midst. This is part of a youth leader's task. Tell the truth and tell it in way that people can understand and hear. Emily Dickinson had a poem entitled "Tell all the truth but tell it slant." The poem describes our need for truth, but our inability to hear it if it comes straight at us.[1] One of the main ways we help youth hear the truth is through the Bible story.

Consider this Yiddish teaching:

---

1.   Emily Dickinson, 1263,
      Tell all the truth but tell it slant—
      Success in Circuit lies
      Too bright for our infirm Delight
      The Truth's superb surprise
      As Lightning to the Children eased
      With explanation kind
      The Truth must dazzle gradually
      Or every man be blind—

Truth, naked and cold, had been turned away from every door in the village. Her nakedness frightened the people. When Parable found her she was huddled in a corner, shivering and hungry. Taking pity on her, Parable gathered her up and took her home. There, she dressed Truth in story, warmed her and sent her out again. Clothed in story, Truth knocked again at the doors and was readily welcomed into the villagers' houses. They invited her to eat at their tables and warm herself by their fires.[2]

By telling the Bible story, we allow truth to enter people's lives. Youth need to be challenged in their assumptions about how the world works and what is right and wrong. They are developmentally hardwired for this. Part of a youth ministry's responsibility is to be that brave space where truth will be encountered, and all will be challenged to change in response.

Another function of a youth leader is be a poet. A poet is someone who puts into words what people are already feeling. This is why when you hear a great song, or watch a scene from a movie, your heart affirms it as true. You recognize it as a deeper truth of something you have experienced or are experiencing. Youth leaders who are striving to share the story of Scripture need to find their poetic voice and put into words what the youth in their community are feeling. This can take a number of different shapes, from verbal to video to viral. The medium is important as a tool to best reach the audience.

One of the best ways to be poetic is to find the best question. Often youth leaders want to give people answers, but answers alone are limited. Answers are limited in their scope because they assume to know the questions people are asking. Answers are limited because they can assume that there is one right answer for every situation and person. In contrast, a good question allows the audience to discover the answer for themselves, out of their own hearts and minds. It puts into words the journey that they are on. A good question is a better place to begin. A good question summarizes what people are feeling and points them toward the truth. The best teachers in history are the best at asking questions. (Jesus was pretty good at this!)

Many churches experience a bulge in attendance after natural and national disasters occur. Oftentimes the groups of people who are stepping back into church looking for meaning are welcomed with a list of answers to questions that the church assumes the people are asking. After the tragic

---

2.   As quoted in Annette Simmons, *The Story Factor: Inspiration, Influence, and Persuasion through the Art of Storytelling* (New York: Basic Books, 2006).

events on September 11, 2001, a church near the nation's capital had many newcomers for several weeks. The pastoral staff, anticipating this increase in visitors, started a new teaching series on "God, the Ultimate Victor." It was an attempt to answer the question they thought the people were asking (in a propositional way). After several weeks, almost all the newcomers stopped coming. In desperation, one of the pastors asked one of the young people who had visited but now had stopped attending, "What is it you were looking for?" The young woman answered, "I am not sure any of us knew, but we sure had a lot of questions." Perhaps the poetic role of the church is to help people ask their questions. This can only be done by helping people put into words the deeper questions they are asking but sometimes do not know how to ask themselves.

Telling good stories oftentimes starts by listening. By using tools like the LASTS model presented earlier, youth leaders can begin to get a sense of the deeper issues involved in the lives of youth. Knowing those deeper issues, youth leaders can then tell stories that help put into words the reality of people's experiences and point them to Christ.

There was a growing youth ministry that had several new young people attending. One of the newly attending young women pulled her small group leader to the side one evening. The young woman shared how she had been sexually abused in the past. Other small group leaders also had members tell them of personal experiences of abuse. These stories came out in several separate situations, with different girls and different group leaders, but all within a couple weeks of each other.

The group leaders individually came and shared this with their youth minister. As she had the fourth small group leader in the last week leave her office sharing a similar story, she knew she needed to do something. They had already begun the process of getting the young women into counseling, talking to parents, arranging mentor relationships, and talking to authorities. The youth minister gathered all the female group leaders together to talk about this issue and to discern what their approach should be to best care for these girls and others like them who might not have shared. After talking about the prevalence of the issue and understanding the core of what was going on, the group of leaders turned to Scripture. They realized that there were several places in Scripture where it addresses sexual abuse, God's heart for the abused, and issues of identity found in Christ. The group of leaders decided that they would begin a Bible study series working through these Scripture stories in the girls' small groups. By starting with the issues that young people were facing, by listening well to the struggles and needs, the youth group then was able to help these young ladies who had suffered abuse find themselves as part of a larger story, with a God much bigger and more loving then they had previously imagined.[3]

In Scripture we see this reality with the Israelites in Exodus. They first experience God as their Redeemer. He literally freed them and redeemed them! But as they began to engage the names of God, they learned that he was not just a Redeemer but also the Creator. They had to start with their own experiences with God before they could really begin to understand the whole of who God is. This is exactly where Vincent Donovan found himself in his missionary work with the Masai.

VINCENT DONOVAN

Vincent Donovan was a Catholic missionary to the Masai people of East Africa. After having been in the mission of Loliondo for a year, having taken the time to understand the context and the scope of the mission, Donovan wrote a report to his bishop. In that letter he gave an overview of the mission with four schools, a small chapel, and a hospital. All of these seemed to be well run, and the schools and the hospital had an enormous impact on the area. The priests had good friendships with the Masai. However, he goes on to report, "The best way to describe realistically the state of this Christian mission is zero. As of this month, in the seventh year of this mission's existence, there are no adult Masai practicing Christians from Loliondo mission" (2003, 13).

Donovan had discovered that despite all the material impact of the mission, the Masai people could not and were not interested in talking about God or Christianity with the missionaries. He also discovered that while the schoolchildren would hear about Jesus, none of them continued practicing Christianity after they graduated from the schools. The priests did almost none of the instruction about Christianity.

> It was the fact that ninety percent of all religious instruction was being given, not by the missionary or the priest, but by the catechist. Even in this directly religious task, preaching the gospel such as it was, the missionary was not immediately

---

3. While this youth group chose to work through the Bible study Scriptures on sexual abuse with only the girls, certainly both guys and girls need the church to address these issues in appropriate biblical ways. Story can be a great way to do so.

involved, was not at the center, but was off somewhere in the periphery. But worse than that, these untrained catechists were ignorant of the true Christian message, and they passed on their ignorance to others. (2003, 6)

Because of these discoveries, and the fact that the schools and hospitals took so much of the time of the missionaries, Donovan decided to cut himself free from those other responsibilities and to go directly to the Masai to talk to them only about God. He later reflects, "As I look back on the whole adventure now, I am certain that if I had known the difficulty involved in the process of meeting a pagan people with a Western version of Christianity, I would never have had the courage to begin. Fortunately, my naivete was boundless" (2003, 20). Donovan went to five different sections of Masai kraals, or villages, and told them he wanted to talk to them about God and not anything about schools, or land, or hospitals, or anything else (as the missionaries had done before). The response of the Masai in all of the sections to his request was the same: "Why have you not come to us before?" All the sections agreed to allow him to come one day a week to talk to the people from their kraals in that section who were interested. He would go to a different section each day early in the morning before their work began.

Donovan quickly realized how unprepared he was to share the gospel with a pagan people who did not have some words or concepts for "person or creation or grace or freedom or spirit or immortality" (2003, 21). He had to do a lot of editing and adapting. "Every single thing I prepared to teach them had to be revised or discarded once I had presented it to them. . . . As a result of this, I know that the original, traditional teaching of Christianity that I presented to them was so revised, adapted, distilled, and filtered in the process that by the end it was hardly recognizable" (2003, 21).

He found himself having to rethink many of the suppositions that he had started with in evangelism. None of the philosophical or theological framework he had been given prior to this was found to be helpful. Liberation theology, which was quite influential in the Catholic Church later and insisted on starting with people's experiences and practice, had not yet come to Donovan or missionary training. He states, "All I knew was that in my work, it would not be a case of going from theory to practice. It would have to be the other way around, a necessity of proceeding from practice to theory. If a theology did emerge from my work, it would have to be a theology growing out of the life and experience of the pagan peoples of the savannahs of East Africa" (2003, 21).

As he began his quest to share with the Masai, he struggled to get to the heart of the message, the actual good news. "At this point I had to make the humiliating admission that I did not know what the gospel was" (2003, 24). This drove Donovan back to Scriptures, to study, and to prayer. He tried to clear his mind of all the preconceived answers and strategies.

Donovan began his attempts at sharing about God with a simple question, "What do you think about God?" and a simple response by one of the younger Masai warriors, "If I ever run into God, I will put a spear through him" (2003, 32). This response was pointing to a larger question about who God really is and why there is evil and suffering in the world.

When working on sharing the story with people, much like Vincent Donovan, youth leaders need to start with the deeper question. In Donovan's case, he started with the young man's claim that if he found God he would put a spear through him. He could have addressed the words of the young man and told him, "God is too big to put a spear through." Or he could have offered something trite like, "God has had a spear put through him before. Let me tell you about Jesus on the cross." Instead, Donovan looked deeper into the question. He found a larger question that the people were asking: "Who is God and how can he allow suffering and pain?" In his poetic role, he was able to put into words the question they were asking in their hearts. In his prophetic role, he tried to tell them the truth from within Scripture.

So Donovan started there: sharing the story of who God is and the character of God. In the midst of his sharing, he came to Christ, sin, and forgiveness. He realized he had to "peel away" a lot of the cultural baggage of his European culture and education. As Donovan did so, he also felt comfortable in adapting some of the stories of Scripture to better fit the Masai's context (see the conversation about translation, adaptation, and contextualization in chapter 6). When after many weeks he had walked through the gospel, finishing with the story of Jesus, he left the different sections to make their decisions about how each group would respond.

After a week or two, Donovan returned and explained that the next step would be to be baptized. Many of the Masai groups chose to take this step together and formed what they called the "age group brotherhood of God," their highest level of community. This community, the church, would be charged with caring for those around them, continuing the faith, sharing the stories, and practicing their belief. Donovan felt called to continue on to other groups, to share with them. Many of the groups chose to be baptized. Over time, Donovan would realize that some groups would not accept the invitation to faith. But this freedom of choice was in fact what gave Christianity great value.

One of the key things that youth ministry can learn from Donovan's experience is that telling the story of Jesus must remain a primary goal. Youth ministry must share this story not because they want to change people's behaviors, but because of love (see the chapter on incarnation). In fact, when the church really tries to share the gospel in a way that reaches its audience, the gospel demands that it be told in a way that is understandable by the audience. The story must be told because it is the ultimate sharing of love, relationship, and the best kind of life. In the midst of all the other good things that youth ministry can be doing, it must not lose sight of this task to share about Jesus out of a loving relationship.

As has been illustrated in chapter 6, contextualizing the message is important. When we seek to tell the story, we must tell it in a way that the audience understands it. Truly communicating the story implies not just that the story has been told, but that it has been received and understood. Telling the story of Scripture well means adapting it to the culture and language of the audience. Paul says it repeatedly in his letters: the most spiritually mature should be the ones who bend the most.[4] The Christians should be the ones to adapt their message so that it is understood by others.

This is done out of love. One of the things that Donovan had to wrestle with in his missionary quest was his motivations and the motivations of the church that sent him. Was it simply to help people physically and materially? That may be easier in some ways to measure. In some contexts, it will also be easier to accomplish. Perhaps in youth ministry the temptation is similar. It is easier to measure the number of people coming, or the number of mission trips or activities planned and accomplished. It is easier even to measure the approval of the existing group. But the motivation of love is not so easily measured, and the results of loving people are not often so quickly apparent in the typically measured ways. Learning to celebrate stories can be a way past the traditional measurements of nickels and noses.

Take for example the youth leader who, along with a teenager from her church, is in an incarnational relationship with a girl named Lisa. Lisa is newly sober and a recovering drug addict. Loving and caring for Lisa in the midst of her addiction may not quickly result in a baptism or Lisa bringing fifty new

---

4.   Paul talks about this need notably in 1 Corinthians 8 and 1 Corinthians 9:20–22; he also models this in Romans and Acts (specifically chapters 16, 17, 21, and 22).

friends to youth group. Loving and caring for Lisa may have to be measured in another day of relationship and sobriety. It may have to be measured in telling Lisa's story.

When we tell the story of God and the good news of Jesus Christ, we must also realize that people have a choice. There is the option for those hearing it to accept it or reject it. The love of Jesus does not relent, and so too must our love also not relent. This does not mean that we continue to try to force something on someone. It does mean that we do not leave relationship even when someone rejects Jesus. If we are not really presenting a choice, then we are just back to trying to change ideology, approaching the relationship with our own agenda, and valuing people only in their potential to behave like the church does.

THE DRAMA OF SCRIPTURE

The great New Testament scholar N. T. Wright says that the "whole point of Christianity is that it offers a story which is the story of the whole world. It is public truth" (2013, 40). He goes on to state that the central task of the church is to "tell this story as clearly as possible, and to allow it to subvert other ways of telling the story of the world" (2013, 41–42). Scripture contains a great story. It is great because it is good news and because it is a grand narrative. It is a drama.

The book *The Drama of Scripture: Finding Our Place in the Biblical Story* is a great resource for mission-of-God–minded churches. It reminds the church of the great story of Scripture and gives some ways to talk about the story. As the authors, Craig G. Bartholomew and Michael W. Goheen, articulate, there are three main emphases or threads that weave through the whole of the drama: God's redemptive work in creation, the believer's own place within the biblical story, and the centrality of mission within the biblical story (2017, 14–15). The first thread helps people see the loving engagement of God with his creation. The second describes the agency given to humanity, each person's invitation to participate in God's work. The third connects to God's mission, as described earlier in this book.

These threads are unveiled throughout the narrative of Scripture. As any good story does, Scripture moves through several acts, revealing characters, conflict, rising tension, climax, and the resolution. Building on the work of N. T. Wright, Bartholomew and Goheen put the drama of Scripture into six acts:

Act 1: God Established his Kingdom: Creation
Act 2: Rebellion in the Kingdom: Fall

Act 3: The King Chooses Israel: Redemption Initiated

Act 4: The Coming of the King: Redemption Accomplished

Act 5: Spreading the News of the King: The Mission of the Church

Act 6: The Return of the King: Redemption Completed (Bartholomew and Goheen 2017, 22–23)

By viewing Scripture as a drama, as a narrative, youth leaders can help young people begin to see those three main threads and locate their own story within the larger story. Youth leaders need to tell the larger story. Sometimes it can be tempting to get trapped in the important details of a passage of Scripture and lose sight of its place as a part of the larger drama of Scripture. There are many examples of the church and popular church culture getting caught up in a small passage and missing the larger story at work (for example, *The Prayer of Jabez* in 1 Chron. 4:9–10; Jer. 29:11; Phil. 4:13; Rev. 3:20). But when youth leaders help youth see the larger story and themselves as part of it, the Scriptures become something that can be integrated into beliefs instead of just "banked." By telling the larger story, youth leaders also move away from the propositions that young people often find arrogant and culturally insensitive.

Lesslie Newbigin believed in the importance of seeing ourselves as part of this grand narrative: "The way we understand human life depends on what conception we have of the human story. What is the real story of which my life story is a part?" (2014, 15). By assisting young people in seeing the Bible as something much bigger than just another religious book, youth leaders can unlock a world of potential as young people find themselves challenged and empowered by a story bigger than all others.

The reality, of course, is that youth in all cultures are struggling with how to live within some of the stories they have been told. There are many narratives competing for the trust of our youth. There are narratives that say that God is distant, that God simply does not exist, that all there is in this world is the material, that our worth comes only from producing, and so on. Scripture is a bigger story than all of these and, we would argue, a story that points to truth. Scripture is the story that should at places contrast with other stories in youth cultures. Scripture should be the story that young people are able to experience as true.

The problem in modern youth ministry and the church has been that people are so sure of the truth of Scripture that instead of telling the story and allowing it to stand for itself, the church has felt the need to stand up for Scripture through propositions. Perhaps Scripture does not need defending.

HOW TO TELL THE STORY

The question, as Sophia had asked at the beginning of the chapter, is "How do we tell God's story?" In particular, "How do we tell God's story in ways that reach youth?"

STARTING WITH CULTURE

One day I (Brian) was talking to my dad about his own story. I had realized that there were parts of my family history that I did not know, including some significant chunks of his life. I wanted to know some of this story, if he would share it, because I wanted to know what shaped him, and in some ways, what shaped me as a person and a father myself. I asked him, "Dad, will you tell me about your life?" He responded with a thoughtful pause followed by this question, "Where do I begin?"

This question of where to begin a story, especially a big story like what is found in Scripture, is one of the most important questions. If my dad had started sharing about how his dad and mom met, a story I had heard many times before, it might have been helpful but it probably would not have been the most interesting. In addition, my children, who were also listening, might not have had a context for a man name Clifford and woman named Margaret (the names of my great-grandparents). My children had never met their great-grandparents and probably did not remember their names. So instead, my dad asked, "What part of my life would you like to hear about?" My kids, who were young at the time, wanted to know about his childhood and how it compared to their own, so he started at his childhood and from there began to tie together how his parents had met, moved with his family to Iowa, and then settled in Indiana.

When youth ministry tells the story of Scripture, it must start with the questions of the culture—the questions that strike where the youth are living today. The church has often started wherever it wants in the story and asked the people to catch up and jump in; but as good missionaries, youth leaders need to start with the experiences of youth themselves. You see Phillip do this with the eunuch in Acts 8:35. The eunuch is reading from Isaiah, curious to learn about God but struggling to understand. "Then Phillip began with that very passage of Scripture and told him the good news about Jesus" (NIV). Starting where people are is a key part of contextualization. It is a valuable way to not start out of arrogance.

We have found that many youth leaders are teaching and sharing the story in the same way they were told the story when they were young. In addition, any changes or modifications that youth leaders make to that way of teaching and sharing the story are based on what the youth leader would have wanted or needed when he or she was a youth. In short, youth leaders are teaching to their teenage selves. This is often not on purpose, but if one does not stop and think about how to share the story, then one will revert to what one knows. One of the main themes of this book is to give youth ministry an intentional approach so that youth leaders do not just keep doing what they have always done, assuming that people have the same needs, hear the same way, process the same way, and experience life the same way as the youth leaders did.

Beginning with people's experiences and questions will help youth see the value of Scripture, see the larger story, find themselves in the story, and understand where in the story they are. So how do you know what young people's questions, struggles, and issues are? As has already been stated, starting with relationship is the best place to begin. When a youth leader is in relationship with a youth, then he or she knows what is happening in that youth's life. The leader knows the struggles, joys, and temptations. Those are great places to begin the story. As you begin to carefully (note the word "care" in there) learn youth culture, questions and issues will also arise. Once you have begun to tell the story, like Donovan found, it will lead you to many of the other big pieces.

FINDING OURSELVES IN THE STORY

On the other hand, there are passages of Scripture, parts of the story, that young people would find foundational. Stories about Jesus, Abraham, Pentecost, creation, fall, the exodus, and Paul's early ministry all are formative pieces to seeing the larger story. Perhaps working those into the teaching in an intentionally planned way every few years would also be valuable.

An important part of seeing Scripture as a grand narrative, a drama, is helping people see themselves as part of the story. This happens in two ways. First, as they allow the story to read into their lives, they begin to find themselves and their issues within the larger narrative of Scripture itself. They begin to sense God at work in their own lives as he has been at work throughout history. Second, as they begin to see the major themes within Scripture, they see themselves as invited to join God in his missional activity.

"What time is it?" the young man asked me while we stood on the train platform. It was not enough to know that trains ran under the city and made stops at various destinations. It was not enough to know that many people used these trains to get around the city in a timely and cheap manner. He wanted to know the time so he could anticipate how long until the next train would arrive. He was going to participate in the journey of the train.

When young people begin to see the larger story of Scripture, they begin to sense that they are invited into the story. Like the young man waiting for the train, they want to know what time it is, so they can know what has come before, what is going to come, and what should be happening now. They want to know where they are in the story. When we begin to tell the story of Scripture as a drama, young people want to know what act they are in.

One of the ways to help young people see where they are in the story is to use a timeline. There are many ways of doing this, but one example is described in the book *Worship-Centered Youth Ministry*. Jon Middendorf explains that to help young people visualize the movement of God in history and in their own lives, a youth group painted a timeline on the wall of the youth room (2014, 67). The timeline starts with creation and then extends all the way to the second coming of Christ. It is a timeline that extended to all four walls. By putting up this timeline, the youth ministry could then begin to place visual symbols representing some of the different Bible stories they are reading on the timeline to help the group understand the location of the story within Scripture and history. Most Bibles that we access today are not put together in the chronological order of the events historically. By helping young people visualize the timeline of the story they are hearing, the group began to see where that specific story fits into the larger story. As youth leaders then worked to help youth make connections to their own lives, the question was asked, "What time is it?" While the events of Scripture happened in the past, the grand story points out that they are part of the story right now—in "Act 5: Spreading the News of the King: The Mission of the Church." By helping youth identify God's activity in history and in the present, youth ministries can help youth view God as active, present, and loving in a world that often portrays him as distant and uncaring. They begin to see the larger threads of God's loving character that weave themselves through the big story.

Youth ministries can also help youth accept the invitation by God for youth to be active participants in the story. By hearing the invitation to join God and his mission in this world, young people cannot help but also ask, "How?" This opens all kinds of opportunities to help young people engage the mission of God, to learn the cultures of their community, to translate and tell the story themselves, and to engage in this work together. There is a natural conversation here about the gifts, dreams, and calling God has placed on each person's and community's life.

SOME METHODS

There are many different methods and mediums to tell story. Youth ministries must use contextually appropriate methods to reach those young people around them. The examples that follow might help you as you begin to think about your context. The methods mentioned below are merely descriptions of what some others have found helpful in telling the biblical story cross-culturally. These are not prescriptions that everyone should follow.

Testimonies. One of the oldest and most effective ways of inviting people into God's story is by sharing the stories of how God has changed other people's lives. Like the testimony times that Sophia mentioned, many youth groups have utilized the stories of the young people in their own group. This of course depends on the youth in your group having had relational encounters with Jesus. It also requires that youth group gatherings are safe places where people can honestly share. But there is great power in hearing someone who has a similar experience share how God has met them and helped them in those times.[5]

One youth ministry in a Middle Eastern country closed to Christianity has found great success in utilizing the stories of other young people. As they have grown, they have utilized an application called "yesHEis," which gathers and collates YouTube videos of young people sharing their faith stories. The app categorizes the testimonies so that users can search for a topic or question that they have and then watch another young person talk about those things. What makes it so helpful is that it is in a medium the young people in this country already use, and the videos are not professional. These are ordinary people who are sharing their encounter with Christ.

Youth for Christ has a whole curriculum called "3 Story" that they utilize to help youth tell their story, listen to the story of the other person, and then invite them into God's story. This story method has been very successful in places as a way to invite people into the story of God's work in the world.

---

5.   Amanda Hontz Drury's book *Saying Is Believing: The Necessity of Testimony in Adolescent Spiritual Development* (Downers Grove, IL: InterVarsity, 2015) does an excellent job of talking about the value of youth sharing and hearing testimonies.

Storying. Another method that has been successful across cultures is called "storying." This is where the leader gathers some people to hear a story. The leader tells one of the stories from Scripture. It may not be memorized word for word, but the leader tries his or her best to tell the story as accurately as possible. Then the leader, instead of telling people what to notice or how to interpret the story, invites the people to begin to make observations about the story. The leader then asks some questions of the group about what they wonder about; it is a time when people might ask questions. There may be some questions that the leader can answer confidently, but there are often things, including some deeper theological issues, that the leader does not have a sure answer to. The value here is in allowing people to ask questions of the story. Then the leader starts asking the group what they are going to do with what they have learned from each other in story.

This gives the audience an opportunity to share their own insights from the story. It is a way of "turning the gem" so that all the people, including the leader, have an opportunity to hear the experiences and insights of each other. It also allows the leader many opportunities to hear what the people in the group are noticing and paying attention to. There is almost immediate feedback about the story and what is found there. The storying method is also effective cross-culturally because it allows the group to make applications that are culturally relevant to them. It does not require the leader to make those applications for them.

This method is particularly helpful for the narrative passages of Scripture like the Gospels, Acts, Exodus, and so on. While it can be done with other parts of Scripture, it is more difficult. Paul's letters, for example, are best told in this way by giving a lot of historical and social background in a story format so that the actual text can be understood within a story.

This method has been around missionary circles for quite some time, but has in recent years been brought to youth ministry by Michael Novelli. His book *Shaped by the Story: Discover the Art of Bible Storying* does an excellent job walking youth leaders through this method and its methodology.[6]

Orality. Missionaries who have been attuned to culture have often found stories to be more helpful when sharing the gospel. Particularly in places where oral tradition is very important, finding ways to share good news in

---

6.   Michael Novelli, *Shaped by the Story: Discover the Art of Bible Storying*, 2nd ed. (Minneapolis: Sparkhouse, 2013).

story form is essential. The missionaries have found it to be more than just a transmission of information but rather a multisensory participatory event.

In the area of Bible translation, there have been some recent critiques from missiology. Translating the Bible only into written form assumes that a culture needs to be literate in order to access Scripture. The critique is that, by forcing literacy in order to access the good news of God's redemptive work in the world, Bible translators can be forcing a written language on a people that the people did not help to write. Taking a spoken language and putting it into written form, and then using that form to translate a text, gives to the translator incredible power over the translations and the narrative and can remove it from the original culture.

There is a new movement within missiology called the "orality movement," which seeks to train missionaries and indigenous peoples to share the story of Scripture in oral form. This values the oral tradition of a culture, as well as gives the people power within the story as they retell it and participate in its narratives. Not only does this movement use the oral traditions of the culture it speaks into, but it also considers the oral origins of Scripture itself. James Maxey, in his book *From Orality to Orality*, says it well: "The activities of Bible Translation have for centuries presupposed literacy rather than orality as the predominant means of communication for the Bible's creation, transmission, and reception. I suggest that this understanding distorts both historical and anthropological evidence. The Bible was for the most part created, transmitted, and received in a predominantly oral context" (2009, 1). Perhaps learning to share story is a faithful way to share good news.

Missionaries in cultures where story is central to their values often have found success is sharing the story of Scripture in a storying way. Many faithful believers in countries that are closed to Christianity might never be able to start a formal church or do a specific Bible study, but they are often invited to share stories.

Something New. The Holy Spirit is doing new things in the world through story. Young people are learning to effectively and authentically tell stories in new and exciting ways. With advances in technology and cameras, youth can make high-quality films with their smartphones. There are youth who are telling compelling stories of Christ and the transformation of their lives through social media. Spoken word, song writing, painting, and other artistic mediums are also being used. Who knows how God might enable youth to tell stories that reach others with good news in your community? The biggest challenge is to listen. As you incarnationally invest in young people, listen for their stories and listen for ways they might already be engaging others through their stories. Find ways to encourage those youth to share those stories more broadly.

SHARING STORIES

The coffee shop was particularly busy when Bill and Sophia met this month. There had been a charity run/walk that morning nearby, and it appeared that many of the runners had gathered at the coffee shop to get some warmth on this cold morning after their event. Sophia arrived a little late and found Bill waiting in the long line and talking to a woman in line ahead of him.

"What's going on?" Sophia asked. Bill briefly summarized the situation and the woman's story of how she was running to raise money for cancer research. Having lost her aunt to breast cancer earlier that year, Sophia was particularly interested in the woman's journey with breast cancer.

After they had waited in line with their new friend for quite some time, Bill and Sophia finally settled into their usual seats in The Bunker.

Bill said, "Well that was a great example of you getting drawn into a story!"

"I guess it was," said Sophia. "It is amazing how stories can connect us to those around us."

"That's the truth!" Bill exclaimed. "I guess I knew that somewhere inside, but I had to move past my cultural baggage that the gospel had to be told in a propositional kind of way. Seeing the power of story has really changed the way I am approaching ministry."

"How so?"

"Last week I had to be a substitute middle school small group leader. One of my volunteer leaders had a last-minute business trip he had to go on, and so I stepped in. Not having had time to prepare using the normal curriculum, I thought about what we had been reading and this time I just told the story. The lesson was supposed to be on Luke 19 and the story of Zacchaeus. So I told that story with a little cultural background stuff thrown into it and then asked the boys what they noticed in the story. It was amazing to see, first of all, how they listened better to a story, and second, how they identified with the social outcast that Zacchaeus probably was. Our discussion was great, and the group was really engaged. Every single one of them shared something. I was really impressed by their insights, and about how much I learned about the world of middle school. Some of it was scary, but it was helpful to hear and understand. We all enjoyed it.

"I know that was only one time, but it really felt like a more natural way to communicate and connect with a group. So this month we are training our youth leaders on storying. We'll see how it goes."

Sophia responded, "I had some great opportunities these past couple weeks to hear more stories from our youth. I have asked a couple of them to put their stories into a spoken word to share this week. I am really excited about it."

"Look at us learning some new things!" Bill said. "I guess we might have some stories to share with some of our other youth leader friends soon."

Sophia nodded in agreement. "And with that I need to go. I have some of my youth today helping me put a timeline on the wall of our youth room! I figure that if we can get our youth to realize that they all are part of the bigger story, it might help them realize not only their place in the story, but the value of the scriptural story for their lives."

"Until next time!" Bill said as they went their separate ways.

QUESTIONS FOR REFLECTION

1. What are some stories that you heard other people tell that have impacted your life?

2. Think about the young people you know best. What are some of the ways they participate in storytelling and listening to stories?

3. Does your youth ministry tell stories in those same mediums? How could you use some of those mediums to tell stories to youth?

4. When was the last time you told your story of faith and encountering God? (Even if you do not believe in God, there is a story you can tell.) Why not make it a goal to tell your faith story to someone you care about this week?

5. What do you think about the way Donovan went about sharing the story of God so directly with the Masai?

6. When you think about the two functions of a youth leader in story-telling mentioned in this chapter, prophet and poet, which one are you most comfortable with and why? What is challenging for you about each of those roles?

10

DEVELOPING LEADERS

THE DAILY GRIND CUSTOMER in line in front of Bill was clearly not having a good day. He was obviously in a hurry and was getting upset that it was taking "so long" for his drink to be made. Even though the coffee shop was even busier than usual, with a long line both inside and in the drive-through, the order was not coming fast enough.

Just get a black coffee like I do and then you will not have to wait, Bill thought to himself as the man got more and more agitated.

When the man's drink was finally set on the counter, Bill was already sitting down next to Sophia in The Bunker with his cup of steaming black coffee in hand. The man said, loud enough for everyone in the shop to hear, "That's the problem with this world! Young people today simply do not know how to work hard." Then he stormed out, shaking his head and muttering to himself.

One of the reasons Bill and Sophia chose this coffee shop as their regular hangout was because so many young people made this a third space and many of the employees were young people. A young woman named Sam, who had made the drink, was the barista, and she was clearly bothered by the man's aggressive demeanor. Bill and Sophia, now seated and watching things unfold, were happy to see the other customers in line offering words of encouragement to Sam.

"I understand that everyone has a bad day," said Sophia, "but that kind of reaction and comment drives me crazy. That's not fair to her. Not only did she do nothing wrong; she does not deserve to be treated that way. Besides, she does not represent every young person."

"I agree," added Bill. "But what bothers me more is the mindset behind some of his comment and attitude. I do not know that guy, but I sense that kind of attitude of looking down on young people throughout our culture. It's not fair or right. We both know some incredible young people who are hard workers, great leaders, and committed to doing things well.

"It reminds me of a book, *Framing Youth*, by Mike Males.[1] It came out about twenty years ago, which shows that this is not a new issue. In the book, Males shows how many news articles and reports implicate youth as the problem or the bad actors in our world. These reports use studies and research to support their claims, but they oftentimes misrepresent or leave out a large chunk of the data. Blaming young people has become an easy way to get a splashy headline, but it often is not correct or fair."

"I will have to check it out sometime," Sophia said. "This brings up one more thing I want to discuss with you. How do we balance believing in teenagers and their capability for leading with the reality that they need some adults to support, encourage, and empower them? I feel like I often go back and forth between extremes of giving youth everything and then taking the leadership back over."

"Well, you have a lot of company in that regard. Not only have I done the same, but that is also the pendulum swing we have seen in the history of youth ministry," said Bill.

"You mean back when you were riding dinosaurs to church?" Sophia teased.

Bill laughed. "Well, I am not quite old enough to remember the beginning of leadership in youth ministry or in missions, but I have read enough to be able to fill you in."

Interestingly, most youth ministry has been done *to* youth and not *with* youth. As we have seen in this book, youth cultures can be their own distinct cultures. In this sense, youth need autonomy to innovate and adapt the good news to reach their peers within their culture. However, it is also true that adolescents are still in the developmental process and need adult influences in their lives. These two realities create a tension within youth ministry. How

---

1.   Mike Males's *Framing Youth: Ten Myths about the Next Generation* (1999) is an excellent example of the ways research and data should be utilized versus how it often is. Males demonstrates well how teenagers are easy targets for misrepresentation and the need for advocates for teenagers in our churches and communities.

much ministry should adults responsibly give to teenagers, and how much ministry needs adult involvement? There are lessons on this issue of leadership from mission history, youth ministry history, and Scripture.

HISTORY OF LEADERSHIP IN CHRISTIAN MISSIONS

The history of Christian missions is, in many ways, a story of discovery. As the Christian church began to discover people who did not know about Jesus, they desired to help those people discover who Jesus is, what Jesus has done, and the transformation his love could bring. The story is also about the Christian church discovering some realities about itself: the ways its theology was enwrapped in its culture, the need to critique its own culture, the importance of words and language, and the need to value all people. There is much youth ministry can learn from these discoveries, not least of which is the openness to discover new things about itself and God's work in the world.

On the one hand, the history of Christian mission has many positives. There was a desire to help others learn about the love of Jesus. There was a willingness to sacrificially go to others so that they could hear this good news. There was a discontent with the Christian church's absence in reaching the world (particularly the Western Christian church), which led to action. There are also arguments to be made that missionaries brought about improvements in parts of the world due to their presence.

On the other hand, the history of Christian mission has many negatives. There was a deep ethnocentrism and cultural elitism that led many missionaries to believe that to be "Christian" was to become like the missionary's home culture. If the missionary was Roman, then the unchristian culture needed to first become Roman (or American or British, etc.) before they could accept Christ. Some of the "improvements" that missionaries brought led to more acculturation and more problems than solutions. For example, where there were cultures that were collectivist (where people thought of themselves as a group rather than as individuals) and the gospel was presented in a very individualistic way, it harmed the very fabric of the culture. The missionary rarely took the time to critique his or her own culture, assuming that it was long before baptized as the best way, while quickly critiquing the other culture for its lack of civilization. In this way, many missionaries confused their Western middle-class ideals with the tenets of Christianity. Their views about morality, responsibility, order, professionalism, individualism, technological progress, and relationships were seen as superior and to be taught to all others for adoption.

Like all movements, Christian mission is an evolving thing. It started in one place and is changing and adapting to become something else. Christian mission very much started out with the goal to import its own cultural version of Christianity to anyone found who did not follow Jesus. As missionaries interacted more and more with other cultures, God's love began to help them discover some things about themselves and their own culture as well. At the end of the eighteenth and beginning of the nineteenth centuries, mission work was recognizing the deep need to help the indigenous church be more reflective of its own culture and values.[2] The "indigenization" principle was developed.

In the middle of the nineteenth century, two separate missionary leaders started articulating a "three-self" principle to establish indigenous churches. Henry Venn, general secretary of the Church Missionary Society, and Rufus Anderson, foreign secretary of the American Board of Commissioners for Foreign Missions, each independently started advocating for similar principles. The three principles were self-governance, self-support, and self-propagation (Anderson and Beaver 1967; Venn 1971). The idea was to move the leadership of church plants on the mission field away from being all foreigners to involve indigenous people. The first principle, self-governance, was a reaction to the structure of most churches that were planted under the direction of a missionary. Before self-governance, churches would usually be organized in ways that were consistent with the home culture of the missionary, not the indigenous people. The second principle, self-support, was an effort to remove the dependence on the foreign missionary's money and resources. The final principle, self-propagation, was to give freedom to the indigenous church to share with others in whatever manner seemed best for their culture.

This three-self principle was a major step forward in mission work. Marking a move away from the paternalism of earlier mission work, it received much praise and was often talked about in the late nineteenth century. In many ways it recognized the problem of the overinvolved missionary, and it also acknowledged the capability of the indigenous people and leadership. Unfortunately, this momentum did not last long in practice. The indigenous churches were often seen as inferior and less-than. Many Western missionaries in the field viewed these indigenous church plants as needing benevolent control and guidance like a young teen not ready for real responsibility

---

2.   There were other examples of a more culturally attuned adaptation of the gospel throughout history, but these did not become widely adopted. Examples include St. Patrick and the Celts and Hudson Taylor in China.

(Bosch 1991, 195). The big step forward of the "indigenous principle" took a small step back in practice.

Fortunately, as time marched on, more and more missionaries and churches moved in the direction of the indigenous movement. In the late twentieth century, Paul Hiebert started suggesting that a fourth self be added to the model: self-theologizing.

> The relationship was that of parent and child, in which the national leaders were expected to learn the missionary's theology by rote. Much was written about the three selves: self propagating, self supporting, and self governing. But little was said about the fourth self: self theologizing. For the most part, national leaders were not encouraged to study the Scripture for themselves and to develop their own theologies. Deviation from the missionary's theology was often branded as heresy. To young nationalistically minded leaders, this was theological colonialism. (Hiebert 1985, 16)

David Bosch agreed, and noted that many truly indigenous churches were already developing their own theology for their context, but doing so out of the view of missionaries (Bosch 1991, 451–52). By the end of the twentieth century, there was a significant movement to have missionaries help indigenous leaders develop their own theology, a theology that would inform the local and global context. By placing more trust and confidence in indigenous leaders, this continued the move away from missionary and other culture dependence.

If many youth are a part of their own culture, it could be argued that adults need to learn to give ministry to young people much like missionaries have learned to give ministry to indigenous people. Youth, much like the indigenous leaders mentioned above, are developing their own theology, but often out of the sight of adults. If they feel that it is unsafe to articulate a different theology than the adults of the church, they will not stop theologizing; instead they will just go "underground" with it. This leads us to examine the separation between adults and youth in the work of ministry.

CLERGY OR LAITY

David Bosch writes, "The movement away from ministry as the monopoly of ordained men to ministry as the responsibility of the whole people of God, ordained as well as non-ordained, is one of the most dramatic shifts taking place in the church today" (1991, 467).

The church, throughout time, has been struggling with the question about leadership. Who will lead us? Who should be doing the work of the ministry? There were, from the early days of the church, leaders who would help coordinate the work and ministry of the church, but were those leaders somehow more sacred than others? In the earliest church, those leaders were not official in position, nor were their positions considered sacred and fixed. Leaders were chosen because of their *charism*, that is, the work or gift of the Holy Spirit in their lives that enabled that individual to accomplish a specific task or role. It was not until around A.D. 80 that the church moved to formalize those positions.

The church, perhaps like Israel of old, has often sought leadership in the flesh. Therefore, it separated clergy from laity, often referring to clergy as "sacred," "special," or "set apart," while others were "normal" or even "secular." This made clergy the givers or communicators of grace and no longer the receivers, thus widening the divide between the two groups of people.

In mission work, there were two different approaches to leadership. In Catholic missions, the elevation of clergy as leadership was passed to the mission field from the West. Catholic missions almost exclusively operated under the leadership of clergy.

Protestant missions in the early days, however, did not use clergy as leadership and was often lay-driven. Clergy were involved, particularly in forming the mission societies, but they always worked closely with lay leadership. The societies themselves were open, democratic, anti-authoritarian, and embracing of all classes. There was a flat leadership model. The layperson was no longer the one who merely accompanied the clergy on mission, but more often it was the other way around. The focus of leadership began to shift to the community, not the clergy, as the primary bearer of mission.

In the history of youth ministry, the leadership of those ministries has also suffered from two major divides: age and office. Usually the leader of ministry to or with youth has been an adult. Sometimes that adult has also been an ordained clergy, but almost always that person has some official title and status given by the lead pastor of that church (e.g., "youth director," "youth leader," "youth coordinator," "youth pastor").

AGE DISTINCTION

There are some definite advantages to having adults involved in the leadership of youth ministries. First, one must acknowledge the differences in developmental levels. Adults can be surer of their identity, more capable of consistency in thought and reason, and more able to make consistent faith and moral decisions. The key word in the above sentence is "can." Age is not the only marker for maturity in identity, cognitive ability, or faith and moral reasoning. But there can be no doubt that having young people exposed to adults who are more mature in those areas helps young people.

Adults often have additional resources to engage in ministry. They also have a larger knowledge of the resources available and how to access those resources than youth with less experience typically do.

Having adults involved and mentoring youth is a great thing. To be clear, we are *for* this. We believe it is vitally important. But we also want to acknowledge the temptations and dangers when adults take too much authority away from young people in ministry.

When adults take all the leadership in a youth ministry, it continues to perpetuate the model that youth need to depend on adults for ministry, theological thought, significance, and meaning. In this way, young people learn to be consumers of what adults produce. Adults become needed for any kind of ministry to happen. When youth are not involved in youth ministry and church leadership, they lose out on all kinds of opportunities to make mistakes, to have success, to fail, and to learn. An unintended consequence of this model of adult-only leadership is that youth miss out on the joys of responsibility, training, and disciple-making. To put it in the terms of the missionary leaders Henry Venn and Rufus Anderson, adult-only leadership creates "dependence."

YOUTH MOVEMENTS

Interestingly, the history of youth ministry holds many of the same movements as mission history, albeit in a slightly different order. A brief look at the history of youth ministry will reveal a ministry that is done *to* youth by adults, then a shift to ministry *with* youth, followed by another shift back toward ministry *to* youth by adults. Now, perhaps, we are seeing a movement back toward empowering youth in leadership.

The first youth ministry as we currently consider it was The Young People's Society of Christian Endeavor. Founded in 1881 by Francis Clark, a pastor in Portland, Maine, Christian Endeavor grew from a ministry at one church with about sixty people to a worldwide movement with societies on every continent and a membership of five million young people.

Before Christian Endeavor, there was very little focus on youth in the church aside from young people patiently observing ministry until they reached "adulthood" or their occasional attendance at sporadic prayer meetings. The Sunday school, which had once been outside the church and focused primarily on young people, had been brought into the church, and its focus transitioned to the younger children of the church. Churches were not willing to allow young people under eighteen years old into church membership and therefore were very hesitant to allow them to serve. When young people were the focus of the church's attention, usually during revival meetings, there were the occasional "bubbling up" of young people's prayer meetings, but almost none of those were sustainable, nor did they move youth to action and serving. Instead, most efforts to involve young people in church included attempts at entertainment and to move the attention away from serving and sacrifice. Those attempts failed in producing disciples and in maintaining attendance.

Francis Clark, a young pastor in Portland, Maine, was trying to find ways to engage the young people of his community. When he recognized the problem that the church offered almost nothing for young people after Sunday school age and before the age of church membership, he adapted, synthesized, and adopted some approaches he had discovered from Theodore Cuyler and Horace Bushnell. Cuyler was a pastor from Brooklyn who advocated for valuing all people no matter age, race, or gender. Horace Bushnell authored *Christian Nurture*, in which he famously argued that children could grow up and remain Christian. On a cold and snowy night in February 1881, Clark invited a group of sixty young people to join a society with high responsibility, involvement, and accountability. The first Young People's Society of Christian Endeavor was born, and it changed the church forever with its focus on training and involving young people in ministry (F. E. Clark 1923).

After Christian Endeavor was born and modeled a successful way of reaching and training young people, churches began to adopt Christian Endeavor or "borrow" the idea. Denominations liked the idea so much that they eventually took the principle of having an age-specific ministry to young people and adapted it to their denominations. In so doing, they created an avenue to propagate denominational literature and curriculum that communicated the importance of denominational values. This started with a few denominations at first, but gradually grew until by the middle of the twentieth century, almost all denominations had their own youth ministry literature and curriculum, as well as denominational leaders, to guide local churches in this ministry to youth (Senter 2010). The early adaptations of Christian Endeavor held to the idea that youth should lead, but quickly the leadership shifted to adults. The emphasis on ministry to youth expanded into the 1940s and 1950s, and specific adult ministers were brought into churches to be youth pastors or youth directors. The main job of these individuals was (and largely is) to coordinate the ministry to youth in this protective way.

Words build worlds. The language of "ministry *to* youth" communicates that the youth are not active leaders in the ministry, but rather are consumers. When youth are seen as consumers of ministry, youth ministry in a church is something the adults do to youth. It is not something that is done with them. This model of youth ministry moves away from Christian Endeavor and the foundational principle that Clark instilled: training. Whereas teaching focuses on giving young people the information, training focuses on allowing young people to experience practicing what they are learning. In short, Clark wanted young people to lead.

This shift from ministry *with* youth to ministry *to* youth reveals a decrease in the value placed on the capability of young people and, therefore, a decrease in the opportunities for youth to *do* ministry. Clark valued young people and saw them as capable of significant ministry. He did not see them as full-fledged adults in terms of development, but he did expect them to be able to practice their faith in meaningful ways.

In both missions history and youth ministry history we see the tension between ministering *to* the people the church is reaching or ministry *with* the people the church is reaching. Both missions and youth ministry have some glimpses of doing this well, but the temptation is great to reclaim the role of "expert."

YOUNG PEOPLE IN SCRIPTURE

There are no age limits on people God chooses to call. Part of the role of the community of faith is to value young people and God's work among them. One of Francis Clark's foundational beliefs was that young people were important to God and to the church. Scripture reveals a God who works through young people.

In Scripture there are almost no stated age limits on serving God and others. In the Old Testament there are only two age restrictions mentioned: twenty years old and twenty-five years old. According to Old Testament law, at twenty years old men are counted in the census, have increased tax rates, can be conscripted for military service, and are required to make offering to God. The other age limit listed is twenty-five, and it is listed only in

Numbers 8:24: "This applies to the Levites; from twenty-five years old and
upward they shall begin to do duty in the service of the tent of the meeting" (NRSV). In the New Testament there are no age restrictions specifically
listed, although some are implied by context. Jesus, as a Jewish rabbi, called
disciples that mostly would have been fifteen or sixteen years old per the
Jewish context of the day. None of these age restrictions have to do with
God's work in their lives.

In addition to few listed age restrictions, Scripture is clear to point out a
number of times and places where God works through young people. From
David being anointed king and killing Goliath to Daniel's stand and leadership to Mary's mothering of Jesus, Scripture is full of examples of God at work
in young people. It is important to also note that the work of God in young
people is not just for the good of other young people but rather for the good of
world![3] Paul states in his instructions to Timothy, "My loyal child in the faith
. . . let no one despise your youth, but set the believers an example in speech
and conduct, in love, in faith, in purity" (1 Tim. 1:2; 4:12 NRSV). God seems
willing to work with all people, no matter their age.

VALUING CAPABILITY IN YOUNG PEOPLE

In addition to recognizing that God is at work in the lives of young people,
the church needs to realize that young people are capable. Capability has to do
with the power, ability, and capacity to do something. Developmental experts
and the largest ever study of youth and religion both are indicating that young
people are capable of significant faith, serving, and leading.

Developmental experts have argued for some time about the physiological realities of adolescence versus the cultural creation of adolescent culture. Using some of the most recent biological and psychological
research, Robert Epstein, former editor-in-chief of *Psychology Today* and
author of the book *Teen 2.0*, argues that young people are capable thinkers, can love, are tough, are creative, and can handle responsibility. Epstein
draws on many studies, from psychological to developmental to physiological, to support his claims. Epstein partnered with Diane Dumas to construct
a list of characteristics that make people adult and then created the *Epstein-
Dumas Test of Adultness* and administered it to a large group (more than

---

3.   Clark utilized these Scriptures often when advocating for the involvement of Christian
      Endeavor in the church. See especially Francis E. Clark, *Training the Church of the Future;
      Auburn Seminary Lectures on Christian Nurture with Special Reference to the Young
      People's Society of Christian Endeavor as a Training-School of the Church.*

thirty-thousand participants). The results revealed that there was not much difference between teens and adults in their "adultness" (Epstein 2010, 147–57). In short, Epstein argues that most young people are as adult as "adults" in terms of capability. Teenagers are lacking adults' experience but are not lacking the capability.

The National Study of Youth and Religion also demonstrates that young people are capable of great faith. According to the study, 8 percent of all young people are considered "highly devoted"; that is, they "believe in God, attend religious services weekly or more often, for whom faith is extremely important in their lives, who regularly participate in religious youth groups and who pray and read the Bible regularly" (Smith and Denton 2005, 110). In addition to noting that there are young people who are highly devoted, the study identified factors significantly associated with this level of faith. Relating to the capability of young people, one thing stands out: none of the factors identified have to do with capacity (Smith and Denton, 2005, 111). That is to say, none of the factors identified would indicate that only certain levels of intelligence are capable of this level of high devotion. Put in another way, it seems that capacity and capability are not the factors keeping young people from this level of devotion.

The problem is not the capability of most young people, but rather the lack of opportunities and encouragement to try out their ideas. If the church can begin to value young people not as some sort of "alien species" but as less-experienced Christians (Dean 2010, 24), then part of the role of the church changes to become a place where youth are given opportunities to experience ministry from a young age. This change in value attributed to youth has to start in the leadership of the youth ministry, extend to the pastoral staff, and then move into the lay leadership. When a church starts seeing young people as valuable and capable, it changes the way the whole organization treats them and the opportunities it presents.

Upon embracing this shift in valuing young people as capable contributors, the first activity that Clark empowered young people to lead was a prayer meeting. Churches today could adopt this as well. Ministries that embrace youth-led prayer meetings give space for young people to lead and to openly proclaim their faith, and demonstrate that they value the capability of young people and the work of God in young people's lives.

From the abandonment issues that Chap Clark mentions to the studies showing that young people are capable, the call for the church moving forward is to value young people as capable contributors to the kingdom.

Francis Clark was adamant in his belief that young people could serve Christ and the church and serve well. Clark's worldwide movement that involved young people in leading core ministry activities should inspire the church today to value and engage youth in similar ways.

SENDING YOUNG PEOPLE

Returning to Jesus's model of discipleship is helpful here. In addition to the apprenticeship that Jesus's young disciples experienced, they were also challenged to "go." In Matthew 10:5–15 (Mark 6:6–13; Luke 9:1–6), Jesus sends out his disciples to go and practice what he has been teaching them. The disciples then return and report on what they had done. This demonstrates that Jesus wanted his disciples to practice what they learned.

Jesus also propelled his disciples onward at the end of his earthly ministry in what is known as the Great Commission (Matt. 28:18–20; Mark 16:15–18; Luke 24:44–49; John 20:19–22; Acts 1:8). In these passages, Jesus is speaking to his young disciples. Jesus expressed full confidence in their abilities to serve the church and the world despite what some might consider their young ages. The call was to "go, make disciples" in the same manner Jesus had made them disciples.

Christian Endeavor adopted this model of empowering young people as well. The genius of Christian Endeavor was that it put youth into places of leadership in the church while still surrounding them with a structure in which they could fail, learn, adapt, and try again. Youth ministry needs to change, just as Clark did, away from things that would only entertain youth, away from ministry *to* youth, and toward expecting youth to be active contributors to the encouragement of believers and the ministry. This is a decidedly active move away from the protective model of youth ministry. This is a movement toward handing youth ministry back over to youth.

Christian Endeavor's compact organizational model allowed for a lot of adult oversight and supervision while empowering the young people to do ministry and to innovate new methods. There is great power in this kind of flexibility. If local churches held to the idea of propelling young people into their communities but allowed young people to be innovative in their ways to do this, then there is no limit to the options. The types of committees of Christian Endeavor were famously adaptable to their local needs. By adopting the principle of propelling young people into their worlds, but not prescribing a method, churches could see young people again sent as missionaries into their schools, social networks, and communities.

OUR DISCOVERIES

Both of the authors of this book have helped to create Youth Theology Institutes that are run through their college campuses and invite high school students into theologically guided leadership. These summer institutes help high school students take the next step in their leadership in the church. Both programs have been running for more than five years and have seen great success. Below are some principles we have learned, adopted, and adapted.

VALUING YOUNG PEOPLE AS CAPABLE

We have articulated earlier in this chapter our belief in the capability of young people. What we have learned through our experiences with Youth Theology Institutes is that young people need to be told that they are capable, and to be given opportunities to step into that capability. We tell the young people in our programs that we believe in them and we believe they are capable, and we do it often. We make sure to prioritize this language and posture.

In our ongoing research with these students, they have articulated the importance of this affirmation. Several mention specifically that the encouragement of their gifts and their capability in utilizing these gifts were both very important to their exploring their personal vocation. In addition, this affirmation allowed young people to start envisioning themselves in leadership starting in the present, not just the future. As one student articulated, "Two or three years ago I felt a call to ministry. I felt like I had to go to college and seminary before I could live out that calling. I got caught up in the preparation, but I can do something where I am at now!" Another shared, "I don't just need to think of calling as something for when I am older."

As we look at the life and message of Jesus, this underlying belief in people seems to permeate his message, spoken and unspoken. Jesus called young men to be his disciples, believing they were capable of following him. Jesus called the Samaritan woman into true worship, believing that, even though no one else thought her valuable, she was valuable and capable. Jesus even articulated a belief in people after they had betrayed him, denied him, and doubted him.

CREATING A CULTURE OF "YES"

Another huge insight for us has been the value of creating a culture of "yes." We seek to be permission *giving* in our time with young people. In a world that seems to be often telling young people "no," we want to echo the words of the good Father and say "yes." Can I ask that really hard question? Yes. Can I express my questions and doubts? Yes. Can I pursue this thing that

God has put on my heart? Yes. Can I put together my passions and dreams even though I have never seen these things combined before? Yes.

By starting with the posture of "yes," we discovered that it unlocked a freedom to dream, to imagine, and to wonder. It also helped young people move past the pressures they feel to perform to certain standards. As we spent time with young people saying "yes," we saw them move away from what often feels like constant comparison to each other and to pursuing what God is calling them into.

By saying "yes" to young people, we also found them more likely and willing to say "yes" to God. By knowing that people believe in them and that God is not a God of scarcity, young people continue to prove their openness to him and to his calling. As one young person said, "I keep seeing that God is on the move. I've been really encouraged to keep saying yes to God. I want to be stretched. I love seeing how present God has been in our relationships here."

We also were amazed at how this posture changed us and our perspective. We became very aware of the many ways that we say "no" to teenagers, often in the form of "well, we'll see." By choosing to make "yes" our default response, it began to open us up to the abundance of God in the midst of a wide variety of contexts, cultures, and socioeconomic situations. It also revealed to us the ongoing revelation of God in young people and their incredible capability.

NEXT STEPS

INVITING AND EXPECTING

Just like Henry Venn and Rufus Anderson articulated long ago and Francis Clark developed, perhaps it's time we allowed young people to take on significant responsibilities for their ministries. In a culture where most responsibility has been removed from the lives of young people, perhaps the church can be a place where they find opportunities to lead, share their faith, and publicly work out their theology. This approach worked for Christian Endeavor, and it grew into a movement that equipped leaders for generations all over the world.

CONNECTING TO THE LOCAL CHURCH AND MENTORS

Before discussing the opportunities the church has to empower young people, it is important that the role of the church in the process is emphasized. Adults still matter. Adults still need to be engaged and involved in mentoring young people. Young people still need adults to encourage, support, resource, and model for them what this life in Christ looks like—a life in Christ that is not perfect but rather full of ups and downs, joys and heartache, sufferings and successes. Young people need to see a real life lived in faith in Christ.

This requires a church, a community of people together putting their faith in the risen Jesus Christ. Young people need to belong to a group that desperately loves Christ and loves them. It is in this context that young people can step into each aspect of the four-self model (more on this below) and learn to lead on their own. We propose that the church thinks of adult involvement in the lives of young people in four ways: prayer, faithful witness, active support, and mentoring.

Every church has people who pray. Let us encourage the prayer warriors of the church to prioritize praying for young people. This feels obvious to say, but the importance of this is almost without parallel. We feel that this emphasis on praying for young people should be placed at every level, in public requests for prayer, in public prayers, in private prayers, and on prayer lists. One church I know set up prayer partners where one adult is praying for every youth their church reaches. Vetted adults get a card with the name of the youth, their school and grade, and their birthday (not year). The youth get a card with the name of the adult who is praying for them. Once a year there is a banquet where the adults and youth come together to celebrate God's faithfulness.

The church also needs to realize the importance of the adults who are faithful witnesses to God's work in their lives. This is not a formal program, but rather a recognition that much of our learning is caught rather than taught. Young people need to be around adults who are worshiping together, responding to Scripture together, sharing their stories, and *being* together. This allows young people to see that God continues to shape and invite us into something bigger. This helps young people realize that God is at work among people of all ages and that God does not stop calling, equipping, and loving. Despite the cultural differences, this faithful witness can be a huge impact on the long-term faith of young people.

Adults from the church can play an important role in a more active way as well. Whatever ministry adults are involved in themselves, they can invite young people to join them. A large part of adolescence is about identity development. This necessarily requires opportunities to try out new things in the context of safe and supportive relationships. Part of the role of the youth leader is to help connect young people and adults in the congregation where there might be some mutual interest. The opportunities are almost as many as the number of ministries you have in the church.

One young adult, Tom, who grew up in the church, cannot help but talk about how Dan changed his life. Dan is not what most people would call a typical youth ministry volunteer. He does not play video games or have the coolest new phone. Dan volunteers his time at the church helping take care of the church vans. Dan is a gifted mechanic who enjoys "getting his hands dirty for Jesus." Tom, who was pretty interested in cars, started hanging around the garage at the back of the church property where the vans received some maintenance. It started one Sunday when one of the vans that shuttles some senior adults to church from their assisted living facility got a flat tire. Tom saw Dan changing the tire and wanted to help. Tom started joining Dan in volunteering. Every other Saturday morning was spent volunteering in this ministry. During their oil changes, turn-signal bulb replacements, and van cleanings, Tom learned about servant leadership (how many people had any idea that this ministry even happened??). Tom also got to hear about Dan's life, his faith in Christ, and his commitment to the kingdom of God using his gifts. Tom cannot tell his own story of faith without referencing the countless conversations with Dan.

There is also a place in the life of the church for adults to mentor teenagers. This is a more intentional relationship where adults and youth meet regularly for conversations, Scripture engagement, and prayer. The church needs adults who are willing to actively disciple young people. This does not mean that adults get to tell young people what to do, or how they would do it, or all the lessons of their own lives. Rather it is a time to build friendship, share in life together, and encourage each other in their faith. It is a place where young people are invited into the real and deep conversations about life. It is where young people are given agency to make decisions but with the counsel of an older and wiser person of faith.

Through our Youth Theology Institutes and our many years of ministry, we have seen the incredible value of these kinds of mentoring relationships. As one young person put it, "My mentor gives me a place to know that someone is going to support me, listen to me, give me advice when I ask, and share her experiences." Mentoring does not have to be complicated, just consistent. One mentor shared, "When I first was asked to be a mentor, I was a little intimidated. I mean, what were we going to talk about? But once we started and got to know each other, we realized that we could count on each other. The questions (the mentee) asks me have been helpful to me remembering what God has done in my life and how I still need him." Each mentoring relationship can look different depending on the needs and interests of each person.

As adults mentor and work alongside young people in the work of the kingdom, there might also be a place for these mentors to help connect young people to the larger mission of the church by creating specific groups. These groups might have a specific purpose, gifting, or calling that would help the mission of the church. These could be led by young people (more on this below) but would be organized by adults.

Now that we have highlighted some of the ways adults can and should be involved in the lives of teenagers, let's look at how young people can lead. The four-self model for mission work seems like it could be quite useful with young people as well: self-governance, self-support, self-propagation, and self-theologizing.

SELF-GOVERNANCE—LEAD AND FAIL

Young people need places where they can lead and serve. Just like on the mission field where the foreign missionaries were making all the choices and guiding the ministry, so too many youth ministries are guided by adults who make all the choices. The result comes to be the same: a dependence on the adults to do the work of the ministry. We believe young people can be great Christlike leaders starting right now. This commitment should lead us to find places for young people to take leadership. Francis Clark, the Christian Endeavor founder, made a rule for the young people's prayer meetings early on: adults can come and pray silently, but they cannot speak. He knew that if the adults were allowed to speak, they would start taking over with proper prayers and long-winded treatises. He wanted young people to be free to pray their way with their words. In our youth ministries, we need to allow the young people to lead.

Francis Clark had one other rule for the young people prayer meetings: every youth who came had to share something. It could have been as simple as a single verse from Scripture they read that week, a line from a song, or something that God had placed on a heart, but every youth was expected to share. Teens praying in a supportive and encouraging environment and adults not speaking—it sounds quite a bit like the move away from missionary dependency.

"But the young people will make mistakes! Shouldn't we protect them from these failures? This is the kingdom of God!" I hear this argument quite often when working with adults and introducing this concept (sometimes from my own lips!). First, it's important to remember that we all fail, adults and teens alike. The reality is that it is in failure that youth learn to innovate and overcome. They learn from the failure, and they learn how to deal with the failure. The role of the youth leader and mentors in this kind of environment is to be supportive and encouraging, helping young people to get back up and try again. It is not to rescue them or keep them from making mistakes. As Venn and Anderson realized, without this kind of authority and agency, the people will keep looking to the outsider.

Adult leaders and mentors should help youth put into words the culture and mission they are trying to embody, and then continue to give the youth the decisions to make that happen. The "how" of the ministry needs to come from young people. Who knows better how to reach teenagers within that culture other than the very teenagers who come to your youth ministry? As mentioned above, sometimes youth might need adults to help them organize and focus their passions and callings in ways that help meet the mission of the local church, but this is not to say that the adults would take over those ministries.

SELF-SUPPORT—GIVE THEM TOOLS TO BE ENTREPRENEURS

As previously mentioned, a lot of young people have had responsibility in their lives removed. Those who do have significant responsibility often are not given any support or direction. What if adults in the church viewed part of their purpose as to help teach young people to not only dream about joining God's work in the world but also discover ways to resource those God-given dreams? Venn and Anderson realized that as long as the mission agencies and missionaries' relationships to indigenous people was tied to money, there would be dependency. We would like to propose that the church help young people to learn to work with the resources they have and to learn to engage more resources in their communities. In this way, youth become less dependent on the adults in their lives and more capable of leadership for the long haul.

Two teenage siblings started to notice all the homeless people they passed on the street and near the stores where they shopped. They started to wonder about how they might help and asked one of the adults from their church who ran an area food bank. He recommended putting together small bags with the essentials that could be given away. The two teens put together a list of needs: socks, toothbrushes, toothpaste, and soap. Knowing that between them they could only buy enough to fill a couple of bags, they went to their pastor to see if they could ask others for help. They made an announcement at church one Sunday to see if others would join them in donating. Not only did they learn how to go to people, cast a vision for a need, and explain how God was calling them to help with the need, they were amazed at the number of donations received.

Another young man saw the passion his sister had for the poor in their town. In an economic recession, this town had been hit particularly hard, with many losing their jobs. His sister, who was a couple of years older, was really good at coordinating with agencies in town and connecting people to those resources. Her organizational skills helped the churches in that town come together and realize that several were serving food to the homeless on the same night of the week. She got them to work together so that all but one night of the week there was somewhere for the homeless to go for food. She wanted her church to start feeding the homeless on the open night. Her brother went to his mentor from the church and shared about how he was frustrated because he could not organize things well and was not very good in working with people. All he was good at, it seemed to him, was mowing the grass. His mentor helped him start a lawn care business over the summer, where most of the proceeds went to funding this feeding of the homeless. The two teens, the church, and the community learned some valuable lessons about working together, using their gifts, and about how to fund the ministries God put on their hearts.

SELF-PROPAGATION—NO TRUST IN AUTHORITY, REACHING PEERS

Another area where teens can take leadership is in evangelizing their peers, sharing with them good news of Jesus Christ. In a lot of current models of evangelism, the teenagers' job is to invite their friends to come to a program put on by adults that will be fun and talk about Jesus. We are all for youth hearing about Jesus and having a good time, but this kind of model might have an expiration date. Youth have more and more distrust in the things that were once considered foundational in our culture. The pillars of our society are crumbling. Youth do not trust the government, large corporations, celebrities, the church, or education. Instead, teens put their trust in each other. There is the sense that other youth are the only trustworthy people.

If most teens do not trust authority, then the model of having youth invite their peers to an adult-led church event will stop working. In many places it already has. Perhaps it is time to focus on training young people to build loving relationships with their peers, including those who do not know the good news of Jesus. Perhaps instead of adults planning the events that will reach the teenagers' friends, adults in the church should start asking young people what they think will work.

Venn and Anderson understood that if the missionaries were the ones doing all the evangelistic work, then the methods would continue to be limited to ones that worked in the missionaries' own culture. They also understood that the ways that a foreign missionary would reach out and attempt to disciple indigenous people would produce Christians who looked a lot like the foreign missionary. In other words, they were just as likely to become disciples of the missionary as they were to become disciples of Jesus.

Youth ministry has long suffered from the same reality. By helping young people realize that they are capable of reaching others and that they know more about reaching their friends than an adult does, the church empowers young people to be responsible for sharing the love of Christ. One youth pastor started asking his youth where there were needs in the community for youth. They told him that there were a lot of youth bands in the area but the only place for them to play were bars. If there was a safe place for youth bands to play, they said, then they could invite their friends. The youth pastor started talking to other churches in the area and discovered that a church down the road had a great facility in place to do this. He shared this with the teens in his church who put together a group of teens from churches in the area to host and run this "battle of the bands" once a month at this facility. The youth asked that the bands be allowed to play all types of music, not just "Christian," but they also developed a small committee that had to approve all the song lyrics to prevent vulgarity and inappropriate content. Adults for the four or five churches involved took turns helping to provide support, but the youth ran everything from setup to running the event to cleanup. The "battle of the bands" became a huge youth event in the county, drawing from all the different schools and bands from all over the area. The youth organizing team started a weekly time of prayer and devotions. Some nights youth would share a testimony. Many young people were connected to local churches, Christian youth, and adults who never would have been reached if that youth pastor had not listened to the youth in his community.

SELF-THEOLOGIZING—WORK IT OUT . . . BUT OUT LOUD IN THE CONTEXT OF MENTORS

The final "self" in the model, "self-theologizing," was added later by the missiologist Paul Hiebert. The goal of this step is to help the indigenous culture begin to talk about their theology, their views of God's work and revelation in the world, in ways that are true to their own culture. It is true that many churches are places where people can and do talk about theology in classes, groups, teaching times, and through the arts. But it is also true that many young people do not feel comfortable or safe in those places to share their own thoughts. This is partly because youth are not sure the church is a place where they can safely ask questions.

A youth pastor, in a parent meeting, was explaining that youth, even non-churched youth, are talking about spiritual things with their peers. A parent spoke up and said, "I think you are wrong. I do not ever hear my daughter talking about these things. I don't think they care." The next week that same parent came up and somewhat sheepishly said, "You were right. I asked my daughter and she said that they talk about God every day on the bus ride to and from school." This is one story of many we could share illustrating that young people are talking about God and the things of God, and that they do not feel like the church is the place to do so.

One of the observations of Bosch about self-theologizing was that truly indigenous churches had been theologizing for a long time but out of the view of missionaries. So too, many of our youth are working out a theology about how God interacts with their everyday lives but are doing so out of sight of the church. Why not create specific and safe spaces and places for youth to do this?

Perhaps the church should prioritize creating these safe spaces so that the church can be a part of these conversations. The goal of being a part is not to "teach them the right way," but to journey alongside them, helping them to engage Scripture and listen to what God is saying. Earlier in the book we discussed creating discerning communities. This is self-theologizing at its best. When a group can learn to come together to talk about their theology, to challenge and interact with each other, to turn to Scripture together, and to develop a theology in their own "language," that is the best of what the church can help young people do. It is trusting young people as capable. It is trusting that God still speaks to young people.

CONNECTING, LEADING, INNOVATING

"I like the four-self idea," commented Sophia, once Bill had finished his summary. "I have always loved that Jesus seemed to invest so much in young people. Christian Endeavor's success in giving young people responsibility seems to follow this model. This has my wheels turning about what kind of opportunities I make available to the teens in my church."

Bill nodded. "It really starts with how we view young people. Youth ministry too often likes to talk about the self-giving love of God to teenagers to encourage them to give of themselves in accordance with what the adults of the church desire to have done. This is born, I believe, out of a desire to help teenagers to learn to sacrifice and to keep teenagers moving toward a 'known' direction. It is usually well intentioned. However, in so doing, youth ministry and the church often wind up creating loyalists to the leaders of the church and youth group, or perhaps to a dogma, instead of helping to create loyalists to Christ, willing to follow his Spirit wherever he might lead them. Young people, seeking to please adults and to find stability of relationship (read: safety), are susceptible to these pleas to take the traveled road.

"But here comes the brilliance of God in adolescence. At some point in this journey of transition from childhood to adulthood, teenagers desire to become their own selves. This journey toward individuation pushes away from the known of the community (family, church, even culture), in order to determine what can be known by the individual. The brilliance of God is to call each of us in this time of adolescent transition, like Abraham, to leave home without any real clear sense of the destination. It is to honor and implore agency. Youth can choose. The temptation for the church is to see this step out as a dangerous move away from the church and to demand compliance with the church's known values and systems as a form of 'safety.' We do this instead of allowing the young to lead us into an uncharted and previously unknown territory where dependence on God is required—a place where faith and culture are questioned, a place where allegiances are revealed, a place of deep discomfort, a place where God meets us."

Sophia listened and paused in thought. After a few seconds of silently finishing their coffees and people-watching from their view in The Bunker, Sophia spoke. "With young people, it is a dance to know when to teach and lead and when to listen and follow. But at the core of what we are saying is a belief that teenagers can lead the church toward an expanding kingdom of God . . .".

". . . if we listen!" finished Bill.

"Just talking about this has me evaluating my own commitment to helping create lots of places for young people to connect and lead," agreed Bill.

"This reminds me of a young girl, Alexandra, that graduated last year who attended my youth group," shared Sophia.

"How so?" asked Bill.

"Alexandra has always had a heart for serving others. She volunteered in our children's ministry and was really good at connecting to all kinds of kids. She would even go with her parents and other adults to visit a housing project just down the road from our church where some of the children from our children's ministry live.

"One summer she went to a Christian leadership program where she was given some help in developing a ministry project. She came back and started something that was pretty amazing!

"Alexandra had noticed in her visits to the housing projects that the families of the children were often less healthy than many of the other families she knew. She started wondering more about this and started paying attention to the food that these families ate. She realized how unhealthy it really was. Her mentor, a woman named Samantha, happened to be a dietician, so when Alexandra started praying about a ministry project, she put the pieces together. She realized that many of these families did not eat healthy meals and that she knew some ways to help them.

"Now Alexandra has three teams of people that work for her ministry at the church. One team prepares healthy dishes that will feed a family. Another team delivers the food to the families in the complex once a month, along with a recipe card so that the families can make the same dish again later. Another team, led by Samantha, goes to the complex once a month and does workshops on how to shop for and cook with healthy food so that people in the complex can learn how to do this themselves."

"That is incredible!" Bill marveled. "How old was Alexandra when this started?"

"Obviously it took some time to get the different teams together and up and running. But she started with just the food-making and delivery once a month when she was fifteen. About a year later they added the other team."

"What else was amazing was how Alexandra was able to talk about *why* she was doing this and how it mattered. Because of her passion, and some organizational skills of some of her adult friends, she was able to plug in a lot of people to this ministry, including some other youth."

"What a great example of a young person catching a vision for something and leading," said Bill. "You have to teach me how to do that!"

"Well, it's not as much about me as it is the whole church. They really rallied behind her," shared Sophia.

"Don't sell yourself short," encouraged Bill. "While I am sure the church had a big part, you had to help her make some of those connections and encourage her."

"There were some obstacles along the way!" recalled Sophia. "But Alexandra really would not be stopped. It was great to see the community help her troubleshoot and to see her desire to serve others lead her to innovate."

QUESTIONS FOR REFLECTION

1. What is the difference between ministry *to* youth and *with* youth? Why do you think it matters?

2. In your experience, how have age differences impacted people's approaches to ministry? Does there seem to be an age limit to who can serve? If so, why do you think that is? How have you seen young people lead?

3. This chapter talks about sending out young people. Why do you think that might be challenging? What are some of the obstacles to doing this? How might you overcome those?

4. What are the four principles of the four-self model? Which of these four do you think would be most challenging to employ for the church or youth ministry you know best? Why?

11

WORLD RELIGIONS . . . IN OUR NEIGHBORHOODS!

INTENTIONAL INVESTIGATION

Bill looked over the list of youth who were planning to attend next weekend's retreat. He paused for a moment when he read Sanjay's name.

Sanjay and his family had recently moved into the community. Sanjay's father was a computer engineer at a local company that produced microchips. Sanjay and his little brother and sister were already making a name for themselves, having helped the local junior high and high school academic teams take high honors in several competitions.

Sanjay started coming to Bill's youth group activities when he was invited by Chris, who knew him from their participation in the academic teams. Sanjay seemed to be a great addition to the youth group community. He was attentive, respectful, and often displayed an infectious, quirky sense of humor. More recently, he had begun to ask some penetrating questions, like, "Why is it necessary to focus so much attention on Jesus?" and "How can one know the right way to God?"

Bill answered the questions with what he considered classic, evangelical responses, but he wondered if his answers were satisfactory. Sanjay's questions and his answers forced Bill to think about Sanjay's motivation for asking the questions. Bill did not really know Sanjay's family very well, but he knew his parents had been born in India, though their children were born in America. He assumed their religious background was Hindu, but he was not sure if they practiced Hinduism as a family.

When Bill started out in youth ministry, the question of other religions was just an academic exercise. All the people he knew in his community were churched or at least church-influenced, even those who never attended. Sanjay's active presence in his youth group, though, was representative of a new reality: the religions of the world had come to the neighborhood! What was once an academic exercise was now real, personal, and intimate.

With these thoughts, Bill looked over to the shelf of missiological litera- ture he had been collecting over the year. He remembered that several of the books mentioned encountering other religions.

"It's time for me to do some intentional investigation on the relationship between Christianity and other religions," Bill said out loud.

APPROACHES TO OTHER RELIGIONS

In walking through the issue of the relationship between non-Christian religions and Christianity, Timothy Tennent (2010) presents a valuable discussion on the main approaches to a theology of other religions and then sketches an outline of an evangelical theology of religions. Tennent works within the classic threefold paradigm, to which many writers from a wide spectrum adhere, and suggests a fourth category.

EXCLUSIVISM

On the conservative side of the spectrum is exclusivism, also called particu- larism or replacement model. This position operates with three nonnegotiables: (1) the unique revelation, thus, authority of Jesus Christ; (2) the historicity of Jesus's crucifixion and resurrection; and (3) the necessity of explicit repentance and faith in Jesus Christ for salvation (Tennent 2010). For many who hold this position, there is a "'radical discontinuity' between the Christian faith and the beliefs of all other religions" (Tennent 2010, 197). For others, they hold on to the three nonnegotiables but make room for the accessibility of general revela- tion in non-Christian religions. Even so, what these other religions offer falls short in providing salvation and reconciliation to God. There are some in the exclusivist camp who talk of fulfillment, who see "God working through philos- ophy and non-Christian religions to prepare people to hear and respond to the gospel" (Tennent 2010, 199). The tendency, though, in the exclusivist view is to see the supremacy of Christianity in stark contrast to other religious systems.

Tennent clearly affirms an exclusivist position, even as he notes problems with the traditional nomenclature and structure of the positions. He sees exclusivists' strength in the clear assertions of scriptural authority, the ultimate revelation in Jesus Christ, and the clarion call for salvation in Jesus. He also notes how these tenets historically have been encapsulated in the early creeds of the church and handed down through the generations. Tennent, however, identifies some cautions with the exclusivist position. These include a defensive posture and lack of honest engagement when faced with challenging questions from other religions, and a failure to acknowledge God's activity in the lives of non-Christians. God's revelation is not limited to Jesus Christ, even though that revelation is unique and salvific, for "God is not passive or stingy in His self-revelation" (Tennent 2010, 212).

INCLUSIVISM

The inclusivist position, also called the new fulfillment model, calls into question the third nonnegotiable, the necessity of explicit repentance and faith in Jesus Christ for salvation. Based on passages like John 3:16 and 2 Peter 3:9, inclusivists suggest that everyone must have access to God's saving grace regardless of personal knowledge or decision. Tennent summarizes the position this way: "In short, salvific grace is mediated through general revelation, not just through special revelation" (2010, 202). The result is "universal access to the gospel."

Tennent appreciates that inclusivists hold to Christian tradition by affirming the centrality of Jesus Christ for salvation. Additionally, he upholds the inclusivist's recognition of God's activity beyond the specific revelation in Jesus Christ. However, he offers a sharp rebuke for their "selective" biblical hermeneutic, which divides the requirement of Christ's work and humanity's conscious response to it. The unfortunate result is that it removes Christ as the crucial object of faith.

PLURALISM

Pluralism, also known as the mutuality model, is the all-roads-lead-to-the-top-of-the-same-mountain view of religions. In the pluralist's scheme, the exclusivist nonnegotiables, centered as they are in the special revelation of God in Christ, are seen as problematic. Rather, all religious systems are viable paths to God and salvation. Christianity, then, holds no uniqueness among the world's religions, so biblical support for pluralism is unneeded. As this logic is extended to other religions, there is no appeal to any sacred texts. For pluralists, the controlling principle resides in human experience as expressed in "a kind of general revelation through universal religious consciousness" (Tennent 2010, 204).

Unsurprisingly, an evangelical like Tennent finds little or nothing of positive value in pluralism and offers a fairly sharp critique. The pluralist position downplays all religions' truth claims, while holding their own relativism as somehow fundamentally true. This leads to an ambiguous conception of God, making any definitive statement about God virtually impossible. Topping it off, basing the reliability of the pluralist position in human experience as "final arbiter of all truth" makes religion little more than "filling a market niche" and meeting "consumer preferences" (Tennent 2010, 209).

POSTMODERNISM

Following recent developments in the field of theology of religions, Tennent identifies a fourth position: the postmodern, or acceptance, model. The postmodern view suggests that religions really are different and that there is no universal truth. In contrast to the pluralist position, it is an all-roads-lead-to-the-top-of-different-mountains view. Religions "have multiple goals, multiple salvations, and multiple deities," with nothing common that they share (Tennent 2010, 205). The goal, then, is "swapping stories" rather than forging some type of metanarrative.

Tennent appreciates that the postmodern position recognizes the real differences between religions, making discussion of religious similarity a moot point. However, Tennent has little fondness for the postmodern claim that truth is a "socially constructed narrative" that "float[s] autonomously in the sea of religious discourse" (Tennent 2010, 206). With truth conceived this way and partnered with a weak view of history, Tennent declares that the postmodern view dissolves into a sea of rampant relativism populated with bobbing individual perceptions.

CONTOURS OF AN EVANGELICAL
THEOLOGY OF RELIGIONS

Tennent notes shortcomings in the classic framework presented above and presents the following guidelines to help evangelicals move forward in developing a theology of religions. First, labels matter. The labels attached to the various positions should be able to be embraced by the people who hold each position. Furthermore, it would enhance discussions across various views if the labels indicate the "performative practice" of each position.

For example, Tennent suggests renaming exclusivism to revelatory particularism.[1] This phrase appropriately emphasizes God's revelation in both Scripture and in Jesus Christ. Additionally, the particular primacy of Jesus Christ is held up as the historically true Christian proclamation.

Second, the Trinity matters. A revelatory particularistic view, then, should keep focus on a Trinitarian view of God, seeing God the Father, God the Son, and God the Holy Spirit as "the hub around which all the doctrinal spokes of the Christian proclamation are held together" (Tennent 2010, 223). This keeps the incarnation of God in Jesus Christ as the center and summit of his revelation.

Third, the Word matters. As an evangelical position, revelatory particularism emphasizes God's revelation in the Bible. Tennent asserts that the Christian Scriptures should be held as the language of truth. It is this biblical truth that is the final arbiter of competing revelations and conceptions of reality. This truth should be thoughtfully, respectfully, yet boldly, proclaimed.

Fourth, theology matters. To avoid mere proof texting and overindividualized applications, an evangelical theology of religions should be articulated in light of God's grand narrative of redemption revealed in Scripture. The guideline captures the thrust of God's missional intention in creating, redeeming, and restoring his creation.

Fifth, the global church matters. Tennent calls for "recognizing the global dimension of religious pluralism and world Christianity" (2010, 209). This means that revelatory particularism needs to be evangelical, holding to the primacy of Jesus Christ; and global, recognizing the breadth of legitimate Christian expressions around the world. In short, we need to learn from Christians in other contexts, ones that are not as influenced by the Western Enlightenment. Doing so will tap into the knowledge of Christians experienced in "living side by side with actual practitioners of non-Christian religions" (Tennent 2010, 220).

A MISSIONARY ENCOUNTER

Tennent's appraisal of the classic approaches to a theology of religions is much needed, particularly as he addresses issues from an evangelical viewpoint. His modifications, especially the updates on nomenclature, are an improvement and should aid in interreligious dialogue. Finally, he sets out the guidelines well in his five-part standards for an evangelical theology of religions.

---

1.   Tennent also suggests the following changes: inclusivism to universal inclusivism, pluralism to dialogic pluralism, and postmodernism to narrative postmodernism (221–22).

We turn now to Michael Goheen (2014), who moves the conversation forward by speaking to the posture and practices of Christians desiring to engage sincerely with their family, friends, and colleagues who are practitioners of other religions. Goheen calls for a "missionary encounter" in the context of pluralism (2014, 334). He explains:

> A "missionary encounter" is an encounter between ultimate and comprehensive religious commitments that shapes different ways of life. The word "encounter" advocates an unflinching commitment to ultimate and all-embracing claims and precludes the accommodation of any religious vision into another more ultimate and comprehensive one. . . . The word "missionary" advocates an invitational and appealing approach and precludes a violent and coercive meeting. (2014, 334–35)

Two key comprehensive components sustain a faithful missionary encounter. First, a missionary encounter should embrace and proclaim the universality of the Christian gospel. The gospel of Jesus Christ encounters, penetrates, and transforms all areas of life. The impact is not only deep for an individual's life; it is broad, for it is meant for every person in every place and time.

The second key is the recognition that a comprehensive scope of religion counters the prevailing Western, Enlightenment notion that religion can be compartmentalized to a small, often neglected aspect of life. In contrast, a missionary encounter sees religion as "an all-embracing vision of life" (Goheen 2014, 336). Therefore, it is a stance against the dualism, individualism, and secularism that marks much of Western thought about religion. Because a missionary encounter employs this robust view of religion, clashes between religious truth claims and perceptions of reality are expected. Goheen, though, offers an important reminder that these clashes should be "noncoercive, nonviolent and gentle" (338). He goes on, "It will be an uncompromising call to conversion but will offer the gospel in life, word and deed as an attractive and credible alternative in an invitational and appealing way" (2014, 338).

PUBLIC TRUTH OF THE GOSPEL

With inspiration from Tennent and others, Goheen presents a sketch of the missionary encounter model that overcomes the theological neglect and the "rampant radical relativism" that often stymies effective engagement with other religions (2014, 344). Drawing on the first comprehensive component stated above, he indicates that the starting point is the "public truth of the gospel" that "humbly—yet boldly—confesses that salvation is found in Christ alone" (2014, 344–45). Jesus Christ is the center of a missional reading of Scripture (see chap. 3). From the apex of God's revelation in Jesus, the story looks back to creation, fall, and the initiation of redemption in the calling of Abraham and the formation of the people of Israel for the sake of the nations. From the culminating work of Jesus's birth, life, death, and resurrection, the story looks forward to the Spirit-filled witness of the church through history, coming to fruition in the restoration of God's people from every tribe. Hence, God's ultimate word is Jesus, meant for everyone (Heb. 1:1–3). In this sense, Goheen embraces the exclusivist position of the classic paradigm. Tennent's modification is valuable here, for Goheen is speaking of revelatory particularism. Jesus is the particular, primary, and authoritative revelation of God to be proclaimed to all nations.

REVELATION OUTSIDE THE GOSPEL

Goheen notes that exclusivism or revelatory particularism raises questions for some who do not want to affirm the third nonnegotiable as described by Tennent: the necessity of explicit repentance and faith in Jesus Christ for salvation (Goheen 2014, 346; Tennent 2010, 197). As mentioned above, those who hold to a more inclusivist position doubt the need for a definitive faith response on the part of people for salvation. Some even suggest that God's salvific grace flows through non-Christian religious systems. All of this points to the issue of the role and efficacy of revelation beyond the specific vehicles of the Bible and the incarnation.

Goheen tackles this issue effectively. First, he indicates that Scripture itself is open in acknowledging a broader revelation. This is seen in places in the Old Testament, such as the introduction of Melchizedek as king and priest of the Most High God (Genesis 13). It appears in the New Testament in Paul's proclamation of God's general revelation in Acts 14:17 and in Romans 1–2. God's general revelation negatively affirms guilt in human consciousness, but it also positively pushes humanity to recognition of God through the benefits of community, compassion, and beauty. However, Goheen maintains, "revelation in creation does not bring salvation" (2014, 350).

It does, however, generate "in humankind a religious consciousness that in turn gives rise to historical religions" (2014, 350). This is Goheen's second point. There is a foundational religious nature to human beings, stemming from the creational hand of God. This religious nature seeks out God's revelation in this world, but human perceptions and insights are always marred by sin. The result is idolatry, reverence for items, concepts, and values apart from the one, true God. "As religious creatures, human beings give answer to God's revelation, but as sinful creatures, their answer is always idolatrous—truth distorted" (Goheen 2014, 352). The distorted attention that humans give and have given to these crafted counterfeit idols result in the various religions of the world. "The empirical religions are the historical answers that certain communities collectively give to God's creational revelation" (Goheen 2014, 353). In a concise formula, Goheen puts it like this: "God's revelation + a corrupted response + various historical circumstances = particular religion" (2014, 354).

Origin of Religions. At this point, it is beneficial to bring in another voice to the conversation. Winfried Corduan, in *Neighboring Faiths: A Christian Introduction to World Religions* (2012), offers an important discussion on the origin of religions. Corduan categorizes one set of religious origin theories as subjective approaches. He describes six theorists, who range from the liberal theologian Friedrich Schleiermacher to analytical psychologists Sigmund Freud and C. G. Jung. The concern of these varied theorists is not in the historicity of religions. Whether locating religious origins in human feeling (Schleiermacher), in the search/need of a perfect father (Freud), or in symbolic archetypes (Jung), the common feature of subjective approaches is that they assume the source of religion lies in the human impulse. It rises out of the subconscious, nonrational human experience in thoughts, feelings, and symbols, attaining a kind of subjective reality in conscious human activity. Corduan finds limited value in these subjective approaches. They are an incomplete explanation, essentially disregarding any discussion of the historicity of religions (Corduan 2012, 29–32).

Another theory of religious origins that comes under Corduan's critique is the evolutionary approach. This approach emerged during the early development of the field of anthropology in the 1800s. Influenced by the work of Charles Darwin and inspired by the hope and commitment of human progress, a model of evolutionary cultural development arose that assumed societies moved from primitive to complex (see chap. 6). For religion, the evolutionary approach proposed a unilinear movement from fetishism and animism through polytheism up to monotheism in continual progress. It is a supposed sequence from a world of magic and localized spirits to the formation of many gods, finally arriving at a belief in one God. The major problem, Corduan explains, is that this unilinear development has never been observed. Another thing that clearly undermines the evolutionary approach is the documented belief in a high God that exists in many primitive, animistic cultures. While the evolutionary theory for cultural and religious development essentially has been debunked, its influence continues to linger in academic and everyday thought (Corduan 2012, 32–40).

Original Monotheism. In contrast to the subjective and evolutionary approaches to the origin of religions, which are human centered, Corduan offers an alternative in original monotheism. He explains,

> This approach finds a home within the religious context itself. Someone who believes in the Bible or the Qur'an, for example, would hold that the reality of God preceded human awareness of God. People responded to God's self-disclosure, and religion came into existence. Any changes in religion consist of either a closer approach to or a deviation from the divine disclosure. (2012, 40)

In short, religion begins in humanity's response to God's revelation.

In his discussion of original monotheism, Corduan provides a huge favor by reviving the work of culture ethnographer Wilhelm Schmidt.[2] Using a culture-history research method, Schmidt provides the documented research for original monotheism. In brief, he found in almost all traditional cultural contexts a belief in a high God. This God is described similarly across cultures. He (masculine terms are typically used to describe this God) is creator; he sets standards of good and evil, and humans are expected to follow them. Interestingly, "it was the most ancient . . . cultures that featured exclusive worship of God and almost no magic" (Corduan 2012, 44).

Three basic inferences describe the move away from original monotheism. First, there is "one decisive" turn away from God. People look to other objects or spirits to help with the anxieties of life, such as sickness,

---

2. Here are some excerpts of Corduan's description of Schmidt's work: "It is customary in scholarly circles to credit the anthropologist (or better ethnologist) Wilhelm Schmidt with the theory of original monotheism. . . . Wilhelm Schmidt's contribution lay in the scholarly documentation he provided concerning original monotheism. . . . He refined a method called culture-history, which had already been used by other scholars. . . . The purpose of culture-history was to identify a chronological sequence among prehistorical cultures" (Corduan, 2012, 41, 42). Because Schmidt was a Roman Catholic priest, many of his conclusions were questioned by secular scholars. Schmidt maintained, however, "that his conclusions not only paralleled the biblical narrative but verified it from a scientific standpoint as well" (Corduan 2012, 44).

crop failure, and infertility. Second, while there is "no clear pattern" to the move away from God, it does give rise to a turn toward ritual and magic as a replacement or an overshadowing of the worship of God. Third, after the initial move away from monotheism, there are additional changes. Sometimes there is a return to the worship of God, but it usually comes with a tension between an elite and a folk version of the religion (Corduan 2012, 45–46).

Some Answers. With the insight of the discussion on original monotheism, Corduan offers some answers to typical questions about truth, salvation, and religion. First, in answer to whether Christianity is true, Corduan posits that, yes, "it is exclusively true," which negates the possibility that it can be one of many ways to God (Corduan 2012, 57). Second, regarding the truth of other religions, since Corduan affirms the truthfulness of Christianity, "simple logic" indicates other religions are not true (2012, 57). He calls them "fictions, speculations, and counterfeits" in contrast to worshiping God. However, he notes, third, other religions do "contain truths" (2012, 57). Containing simple factual truths and assorted wisdom, though, "does not mean that the entire set of beliefs is true" (Corduan 2012, 58).

Fourth, Corduan moves to the question of salvation. In responding to whether Christianity saves, he responds, "Of course not. No religion saves a person" (2012, 58). He indicates that salvation is an act of God, accomplished in the person and work of Jesus Christ, who is the object of personal faith. So, fifth, what about the possibility of salvation in other religions? The same answer applies to other religions—there is no salvation without Jesus. Moreover, the understanding of redemption in other religions varies from the Christian view. Finally, sixth, do other religions provide any benefit in moving people to salvation? Corduan says there is "indirect contribution" (2012, 58). Here he indicates that other religions function in the same way Paul describes the Old Testament functioning in its identification of human sinfulness. "We can say that other religions (just as Christianity without personal faith) demonstrate the futility of attempting to live life without the true God" (Corduan 2012, 58).

SUBVERSIVE FULFILLMENT

Corduan's presentation affirms Goheen's contention: it is the corrupted response to God's revelation by humans in their historical context that results in particular religions. Goheen navigates the issue of God's revelation and the possible presence of truth/grace in other religions by embracing two, seemingly contrasting, approaches.[3]

One is a "sympathetic, insider approach" (Goheen 2014, 356–57). As fellow human sojourners seeking out God, Christians legitimately can commiserate with the heart cries of practitioners of other religions. Indeed, to really understand and hear the unanswered questions in the lives of Muslims or Hindus, effective cross-cultural communicators of the gospel must enter their world. This point of contact is necessary, lest our missionary encounters and apologetics always be combative and confrontational. Christians can offer compassionate friendship to those who share a desire for God, holiness, and salvation. Goheen remarks, "God's common grace opposes the destructive power of sin in human life. Thus, we can see much that is good, right, just, beautiful and true in people who do not confess Christ and in their empirical religions" (2014, 357).

Simultaneously, Goheen encourages a "critical, outsider approach" (2014, 357–58). The recognition of human sin and of an ongoing spiritual battle that twists and blinds people to the true reality of God calls us to "bring the light of the gospel to bear on all religious life outside the gospel" (Goheen 2014, 357). There is a real suppression of God's revelation in other religions, and it is expressed in idolatry and false notions. These things need critique. They need to be called out and exposed, if people's deepest longings to really connect with God are going to be satisfied.

In order to employ a missionary encounter with other religions that is both confirming and confronting, it is helpful to see both the continuity and discontinuity other religions have with Christianity. For example, Islam and Christianity share a reverence for the one God of the universe, who is the majestic creator. However, the Qur'an's description of Allah is an incomplete and inaccurate view of the God of the Bible. The continuity, remnants of God's general revelation, is impaired by "the vinegar of idolatry that has transformed the wine of God's revelation" (Goheen 2014, 360). The result, according to Goheen, is that the gospel subversively fulfills other religions. "The gospel challenges and subverts each of these notions as it offers Christ as the true answer to the religious longing. . . . The gospel both fulfills religious longing and subverts its twisted expression" (Goheen 2014, 360).

---

3.   There is a similarity between Goheen's two approaches and Andrew Walls's pilgrim and indigenizing principles discussed in the chapter "The Translatability of the Gospel." Both describe operating in the creative tension of two somewhat opposite, yet biblically inspired, methods.

Seeing how the Christian gospel is subversive fulfillment to the religious search of people who follow other religions, Goheen recommends two aspects to employ in the communication of the gospel for a true missionary encounter. First is to "attend to the point of contact" (Goheen 2014, 362). There is an amazing phrase that describes very well what should happen when cultivating a point of contact. When someone of particular charm, wit, or pleasant disposition is in attendance, it is often said that the person has "graced us with his or her presence." Disregarding the sometimes sarcastic use of the phrase, that is what Goheen is suggesting. Christlike attributes, such as love, forbearance, and gentleness should mark communication that seeks to be attractive. Also, achieving a mutual point of contact encourages gospel communication to be understandable, which means a witness embracing both relevance and challenge. It's a witness that identifies and relates to the orienting core of a religion as it grasps for God, while at the same time faithfully pointing to Christ for the solution to life's dilemmas. As the Christian gospel brings both light and correction, it should always be remembered that the person in front of us is not just a representative of another religion and a potential convert. He or she is also a potential friend and fellow sojourner who we are inviting to walk with us.

Second, Goheen highlights dialogue in the context of missionary encounters with other religions. When it comes to interfaith connections, dialogue often gets a bad rap, particularly from evangelicals, and perhaps rightly so. When tied to a pluralist agenda, interfaith dialogue requires a stripping away of truth claims, undermining evangelism. However, is there a legitimate way to participate in dialogue that does not demand a dilution of Christian doctrine and beliefs?

Two evangelical missiologists offer a way forward. Terry Muck (2011), a professor and former editor of both *Christianity Today* and *Missiology: An International Review*, presents several characteristics of faithful and effective interfaith dialogue. He locates his missional theology of dialogue in the "orthodox recognition of God's revelation to all" (2011, 191). Dialogue, then, is a two-way participation in the lives of others, seeking out and sharing the confirmations of God's glory. Within this two-way conversation is a commitment to the existence of the absolute. But the commitment comes with Christian humility and an acknowledgement that absolute truth is known imperfectly in our cultural contexts. When communicated with sincere love of neighbor, sincere Christian witness can, and should, occur in interfaith dialogue. Matthias Zahniser (1994), missiologist and Christian evangelical expert on the Qur'an, indicates that this kind of dialogue requires vulnerability. There is power in allowing ourselves to be vulnerable to the diversity of cultures while at the same time calling ourselves and others to transformation in Jesus. Zahniser declares that these "close encounters of the vulnerable kind" require "dialogical proclamation" in the context of intimate relationships. When we become vulnerable in relationships, then God's Spirit has opportunity to engage us and our partners "in dialogue in the painful but liberating process of conviction" (1994, 77).

Goheen concurs with Muck and Zahniser by stating that dialogue is an act of extending love for our neighbors. It is an intentional missionary encounter, an emptying of oneself for the benefit of the other. As such, it should be foundationally Trinitarian. It flows from the work of the Father in creation and throughout history, always unequivocally witnessing to the incarnational identity and work of Jesus Christ and relying on the convicting and reconciling work of the Holy Spirit. For our missionary encounters are a participation in the missional work of God.

"WHAT ARE YOU GOING TO DO ABOUT IT?"

"So that's what I've been reading and studying lately," said Bill, as he leaned back in The Bunker.

Sophia looked across the table at Bill, a little slack-jawed. "You look like you're catching flies with your mouth half-opened," chided Bill.

Sophia smiled and said, "I guess I was thinking about how you really grappled with this subject of other religions. It can be difficult to be firm in one's faith on one hand, and still be open and respectful to other religions on the other."

"You're right, but I really think that the kind of dialogical proclamation that Zahniser talks about is a more characteristically Christian position and that it actually takes a firmer faith to enact," replied Bill.

"I think you may be on to something there," added Sophia. "Here's my question, though: How do you communicate these ideas in a way that's understandable to a normal member, youth, or adult? I have a feeling their eyes will glaze over once you mention revelatory particularism or original monotheism."

"I have thought about that," Bill said, "and I have come up with a four-part statement as a summary. First, there is some truth in all religions of the world. Second, as Christians, we should seek to discover the truth of other religions, remembering that the only source of truth is God. That truth exists in other religions need not cause us to doubt the veracity of our Christian faith. Neither should it compel us to embrace every other religion as a viable way to establish a saving relationship with God. It simply is recognition that God is active in the world, searching for the lost. He is the good father of the parable who sees his lost son returning even 'while he was still a long way off.' That's from Luke 15:20.

"Slow down, Bill," said Sophia, "because I'm trying to write this down."

"Okay," said Bill. "The third part is, the fact that truth exists in other religions does not negate the ultimate uniqueness of Christianity. This distinctiveness centers on the person of Jesus Christ. The historical nature of Jesus's life, death, and resurrection provides the essential foundations of Christianity. Jesus is the incarnation of God, fully human and fully divine, the one and only manifestation of God, all holy and all loving. Through Jesus's reconciling work on the cross and through the resurrection, Jesus has conquered sin and death, making a saving relationship with God a possibility for all people. No other religion makes such audacious claims."

"I like this so far," commented Sophia.

Bill continued, "Finally, any person, no matter what religious heritage, including Christian, lives an unfulfilled life apart from Jesus. Our attitude and response to people, no matter their religious background, then, should be one of respect and an appropriate encouragement to find ultimate fulfillment in life through Jesus.

"I appreciate the summary," said Sophia, "and I can tell you've been doing a lot of thinking."

"And praying," Bill added.

"So, getting back to what started all this studying, what's going on with Sanjay?" Sophia asked.

"That's really interesting. As I was doing all this reading and thinking, I would share my thoughts and findings with Stan," began Bill. "Then, one time Stan asked, 'So, what are you going to do about it?' Well, that pretty much hit me between the eyes because I knew he was talking about Sanjay." Bill paused.

"So . . . don't leave me hanging!" cried Sophia.

Bill continued, "So, I knew he was right. All my studying needed to lead to some application. So . . .". Bill took a slow drink of coffee.

"Oh, just get on with it, will you?" Sophia practically yelled.

"Okay, okay. So, I decided to visit Sanjay's parents. I did this, obviously, because I wanted to get to know them since their son was part of our youth group. But I also wanted to demonstrate that I respected them as Sanjay's parents and that I respected their family's values and heritage."

"How did it go?" asked Sophia.

"Really well!" replied Bill. "I went on a Saturday afternoon. When I walked into their home, I was amazed at the display of tea and food. They really laid out a spread. I came hoping to show my respect, and here they were treating the visit like I was some kind of bigwig. Their hospitality was almost overwhelming. Anyway, we settled in and chatted awhile about our backgrounds. Their story is fascinating. They are so well-educated, and they came to America after they were married to give their future children more opportunities. That allowed us to begin talking about Sanjay. I mentioned that we really enjoy Sanjay's presence in our youth group and that he had begun to ask some penetrating questions."

"What did they say about that?" asked Sophia.

"Mostly, they politely listened," answered Bill. "I explained the answers that I was giving to Sanjay. Essentially, I walked through the narrative of the Bible. I told them I believed in one God, who is the creator, and how humanity made a decisive move away from God. I said that while God was not pleased with this rebellion, he still reached out to humanity in love. This reaching out culminated in God coming to us in the person of Jesus Christ, and that in Jesus we can be fully restored into relationship with God. It was a bit more detailed than that, but you get the idea."

Sophia asked, "How did they receive it?"

"Pretty well, I think," Bill said. "As I said, they were polite and mostly quiet once we got to the religious part of the conversation. At that point, I told them that I really respected them as Sanjay's parents. I told them how I appreciated Sanjay's inquisitiveness, good manners, and humor. I said it was obvious that Sanjay had really good parents. They were pleased, as any parents would be. I told them that, as good parents, I knew they would want to know what I was teaching Sanjay. I told them that I hope Sanjay would continue to be part of our youth group."

"So where did you leave it?" wondered Sophia.

Bill explained, "I invited them over to supper with my wife and me. They immediately accepted the invitation, and they said they would think about the things we discussed. They will be coming over next week. I am hoping it's the beginning of a long friendship. I'll listen to their religious journey, and I'll speak about mine. You know, this whole process of looking into this issue of other religions has given me a freedom to speak firmly about my faith, and it's given me a freedom to be kind and respectful to others. It's given me a way to be clearly invitational and to point unequivocally to Jesus."

Sophia remarked, "Well put, Bill, well put!"

QUESTIONS FOR REFLECTION

1. In presenting an evangelical theology of religions, Tennent offers five guidelines. Which of these guidelines are most formative in your approach to other religions? Why?

2. How does a truly missionary encounter with other religions confront the dualism, individualism, and secularism of Western society?

3. In what ways does acknowledging revelation beyond Christianity bring about a fuller, more holistic witness of the Christian gospel?

4. How do the concepts of original monotheism and subversive fulfillment provide helpful launching pads for answering youth's questions about Christianity and other religions?

5. Think about a family member, friend, or youth in your ministry who is seriously considering other religions. How might you adapt your approach to them based on the ideas in this chapter?

12

SOCIAL JUSTICE

BACK AT THE DAILY GRIND with large caffeinated drinks in hand, Sophia and Bill spent some time catching up on life. It had been a while since they last met. Bill shared greetings from Stan, who had been traveling recently. They both commented that they would be glad when Stan returned. Finally, Bill got down to business.

"Three books!" said Bill. "That's a lot of reading."

"Well, at least it was light reading," joked Sophia.

"What's easier and more relaxing than reading about the marginalized people of our world and how the church should be engaging them . . . and realizing how we are *not*?" added Bill.

"Issues of injustice and justice, poverty, marginalization, and social justice are not new and certainly are not going away. I cannot count how many times people have asked me to represent all black pastors or black churches just because of the color of my skin. After the killing of another young black man by the police hit the news, someone stopped me and said, 'That may have happened there, but it would never happen here. You have nothing to worry about.'"

"I am so sorry. I was on a Zoom conversation with some other youth pastors last week. One of them started to share about what he thought minorities needed from the church right now. He happened to be white and so I simply asked if we should be hearing from one of the youth pastors who is from a minority. He responded that he thought he could accurately represent the issues of the people in his community. I cringed and the conversation quickly changed."

"This has happened often to me, which is why I want to unpack our readings. I have tons of notes and thoughts. Let's get started," stated Sophia.

"Okay, where do we begin?" asked Bill.

"Let's do Gustavo Gutiérrez's *Theology of Liberation* first, then we can talk about *Marginality* by Jung Young Lee, and then finish with Miroslav Volf's *Exclusion and Embrace*."

"Sounds like a plan! *Theology of Liberation* is a classic. I like starting with that one," said Bill, as they dove into their coffees and their notes.[1]

A THEOLOGY OF LIBERATION

Gustavo Gutiérrez's book *A Theology of Liberation*, originally printed in Spanish in 1971, continues to be one of the most influential books in missions and justice conversations. A Roman Catholic priest writing out of the incredibly difficult living situations in Latin America in the late 1960s and 1970s, marked by oppression, poverty, and marginalization, Gutiérrez sought to move theology from thought and theory into everyday practiced life. He was seeking to address the question of how faith should interact with the injustices of the world—injustices the people there were facing every day. He states:

> Theology as critical reflection on historical praxis is a liberating theology, a theology of the liberating transformation of the history of humankind and also therefore that part of humankind—gathered into *ecclesia*—which openly confesses Christ. This is a theology that does not stop with reflecting on the world, but rather tries to be part of the process through which the world is transformed. It is a theology which is open—in the protest against trampled human dignity, in the struggle against the plunder of the vast majority of humankind, in liberating love, and in the building of a new, just, and comradely society—to the gift of the Kingdom of God. (12)

For Gutiérrez, theology must be active, locally practicing, and liberating. Theology must be lived out by the church.

---

1.   There are many great books on justice issues; here we kept the interaction with formative texts in missiology. This is not to devalue any other texts, and we would recommend reading widely on this issue.

In *A Theology of Liberation*, Gutiérrez first tackles theology and uses the term *liberation*—to liberate is to give life—to indicate the holistic meaning of salvation, including justice across relationships with others and with the Lord. Second, he argues that traditional approaches are not adequate in helping the Latin American context, and therefore new approaches are needed, approaches developed by the oppressed group. Third, he examines the presence of the church and its practices in the midst of the oppression.

THEOLOGY FROM THE PERSPECTIVE OF THE POOR

Popularizing the phrase "liberation theology," Gutiérrez argues for a theology that is done from the perspective of the poor and oppressed. Gutiérrez finds support for this approach in the life and teaching of Jesus Christ. Jesus came to give life, to liberate, to set free those who are oppressed. Liberation theology seeks to level the playing field of classes, stratification, and hierarchy, instead hoping to see everyone on equal ground.

In the case of Latin America, Gutiérrez saw two extremes that did not seem to fit together. On the one hand were the few people in power who were using systems of economics, politics, and military might to oppress others in order to keep and grow their wealth. These people were also associated with the church. On the other hand, the vast majority of people were living in poverty, many in abject poverty, oppressed by the very people who belonged to the same church. For those in power, the theology that stated that the rich had a right to what they earned and the wisdom to set forward laws and rules was working great. For those impoverished and oppressed, it was not a theology that made any sense.

A theology done from the perspective of the poor asserted that all people are created in God's image and have worth. It said that the church should be a place to call out injustice and to work against those who would oppress others for their own gain. It said that the church should be active in correcting relationships of power, especially where the government or political parties were dominating certain people groups for their own gain or when the church was complicit in those activities.

SIN AND TRUTH

Gutiérrez rejects the idea that sin is exclusively individualistic. He argues for a threefold nature of sin. The first is the social, economic, and political oppression that exploits the oppressed, particularly the poor. Second is the historical determinism that discourages the oppressed from determining their own destiny in history. Third is the breach of communion with God and neighbor. For Gutiérrez the current systems are broken, unjust, and sinful. The church needs to rise up and stand with those who are oppressed, working to liberate them from these sins of injustice.

To this end, the work of liberation theology is to practice the truth. The first step to practice the truth is to analyze the social situation. Gutiérrez calls for the church to recognize the injustice done to people and the role larger systems play in creating these injustices. The second step is a theological critique, which for Gutiérrez includes pointing out how the church has been complicit in the injustices done to the people by participating in the systems that lead to the injustices. The third step is practice. Liberation theology calls for the church to confess its role and to change.

The purpose of liberation theology for Gutiérrez is to "create a new humanity." He sees that this purpose can be reached by understanding that humanity is the temple of God (106–11). It means that God dwells everywhere and will be present in the very heart of every human being (108). Additionally, this particular purpose can be reached by rethinking our attitudes toward our neighbor. One can find in Scripture a call to a close relationship with God and neighbor (110). To build a new society is to know God, but knowing God can be expressed only in the attempt to do justice for one's neighbor. To love one's neighbor is to love Christ, because Christ is within the neighbor (112–16). He concludes that building a more just society is to know that real spirituality is "participation in the struggle for liberation of those oppressed by others" (116). In the Latin American context, Gutiérrez argues, this is to participate in the revolutionary process.

To join the revolution is to work to change everything, including the economics of Latin America. Gutiérrez critiques capitalism as the source of the materialism that is leading to the oppression in Latin America. In his critique of his current situation, he turns away from capitalism as a conversation partner and to Marxism. He turns to Marxism because of its call for an equality of all classes. He sees it as a better way to love one's neighbor.

BIG PICTURE

Ultimately what Gutiérrez is arguing for, as well as others expanding on a theology of liberation, is that those who have been oppressed can move out of oppression into equal footings with all. He writes,

> The theology of liberation attempts to reflect on the experience and meaning of the faith based on the commitment to abolish injustice and to build a new

society; this theology must be verified by the practice of that commitment, by active, effective participation in the struggle which the exploited social classes have undertaken against their oppressors. Liberation from every form of exploitation, the possibility of a more human and dignified life, the creation of a new humankind—all pass through this struggle. (174)

He advocates for the church to help actively participate in this liberation of people. He continues:

We will have an authentic theology of liberation only when the oppressed themselves can freely raise their voice and express themselves directly and creatively in society and in the heart of the People of God, when they themselves "account for the hope," which they bear, when they are the protagonists of their own liberation. (174)

This is to give life to everyone, especially those who are oppressed.

Liberation theology is helpful because it tries to shift the vantage point of the church and theology from a position of power to the margins in solidarity with the poor. One of the reasons that liberation theology continues to have a strong voice is this vantage point. Those who are in the midst of oppression resonate with a theology from their own point of view. In addition, Jesus Christ's own words and life resonate with this approach.

However, liberation theology is not free from critique. Many point out that it is impossible to adopt Marxist principles about economics without also adopting Marxist views on humanity and God (which are humanistic and atheistic). In Marxism, the response to materialism is to focus on the class struggle, whereas traditionally in Christianity the response is to focus on sin and repentance. When adopting Marxist principles and the ideologies behind them, the call comes to step forward with revolutionary violence. Jesus seems to be more interested in non-violent social action in his life and teaching.

Perhaps the biggest critique of liberation theology is in its historic practice. In joining in the revolutionary violence to remove oppressors and free the oppressed, the church also sacrifices its own call to repentance and to the view that all of humanity is equal. When practiced, the oppressed, after removing the oppressors, often become the oppressors themselves. This is seen in Scripture with the Israelites again and again. The cycle of oppression continues.

"There is a lot in this book to process and a lot I agree with," said Bill. "The ties to Marxism make me uneasy, but the desire to see God and faith through the eyes of those who are oppressed rather than those in power seems pretty valuable and scriptural."

"I can definitely see how this kind of theology would resonate with those who are oppressed," says Sophia. "One of the things that young people I know who are marginalized often are saying to the established church about Christianity is 'Of course your religion is good in your eyes, it has worked well for you. But it is not working for me.' This always breaks my heart because I have seen Jesus to be *with* them in the midst of their struggle. But they do not feel like our Christian faith is for them. They do not feel like our theology has ever been done from their point of view. They see it as just one more thing supporting the systems that have helped to keep them down."

"And other young people I know who may not be marginalized themselves see how their friends and peers who are marginalized are treated, even by the church, and they know it's not right. They want change too," added Bill.

"I find myself wanting to take action and *do something*. Talking about it is a start, I suppose, but it sure doesn't feel like change," Sophia shared.

Bill nodded and said, "I think this is what Jesus wants: a church that will move to the margins and be with people. That's what this next book was all about, *Marginality*."

MARGINALITY

Gutiérrez does an excellent job helping the church theologize from the perspective of the poor and oppressed, and liberation theology pushes an agenda to empower those who are oppressed. Empowerment is good in terms of putting everyone on an equal playing field, but it falters when it leads to the once oppressed becoming oppressors themselves. Jung Young Lee's *Marginality: The Key to Multicultural Theology* adopts a similar viewpoint (the lens of doing theology through the eyes of the marginalized) while also moving the church to reconciliation.

Lee begins by recognizing that there is a center and that there are margins to society (see figure 12.1). The center contains the power, influence, resources, and decision making. The margins are where people do not have power, influence, resources, or control. Those at the margins in this dichotomy desire to be at the center. Lee states,

This inclination to be at the center seems to be an intrinsic human drive. In the history of civilization, the center attracted humanity more than any other thing in the world, for the center has been understood as the locus of power, wealth, and honor. This inclination has been and is a powerful drive in building civilizations, while it remains a destructive power in creating justice. (31)

Lee's work helps the church to define marginality and see it not as a negative thing to be avoided, but rather, the way of transformation.

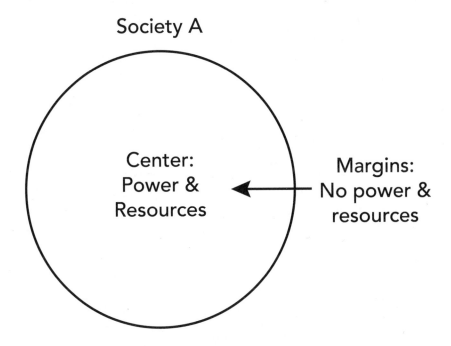

Figure 12.1. Desiring the Center

MARGINALITY DEFINED

Marginality can have many definitions, so Lee tries to give it a new definition. Marginality "describe[s] the individual who lives in two societies or two cultures and is a member of neither" (43). Those living in both cultures are often frustrated with the center because they see where the power needs to be changed. Living on the margins is to be fully "in-both" these worlds, as different and even antagonistic as they may be. However, to be on the margins also means to be "in-between" both worlds, living out the tension of not being fully in either world (see figure 12.2). This divide between two worlds leads to a sense of nothingness and dehumanization. W. E. B. Du Bois called this a "double consciousness," where you always look at yourself through the eyes of another (1897).

For example, my friend who is Asian American says that she lives "in-both" Asian and American worlds. There is identity with being Asian; it is clear by appearance. There is also identity with being American, for it is where she geographically lives. However, the Asian American is also "in-between" both worlds because Asians would say that the Asian American is not fully Asian. The Asian American is also told that she is not fully American by being asked where she is from or when she arrived in the United States.

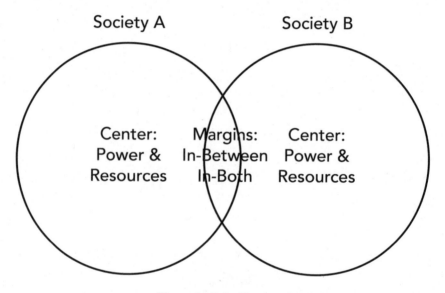

Figure 12.2: In-Between

We all understand what it is like to live on the margins. Even if we find ourselves as part of the center at times, we are never fully center. For example, I (Brian) am a Caucasian male in the United States, part of the center. I also live in Kentucky, but I am not *from* Kentucky. As a Caucasian male I am part of the center of society with more opportunities for privilege and resources than others. However, I grew up in Michigan and have lived in four other states before moving to Kentucky. Therefore, in the eyes of most Kentuckians, I am not from here, despite my more than ten years of residence. Because I am in-between, my opportunities in the community to have voice are limited.

When my children were younger, I volunteered to coach one of my son's basketball teams in a noncompetitive church league. When I volunteered to help out, because I was a white man, I was immediately put into the pool of head coaches, even though I had not asked for that. Once it was discovered that I was not from Kentucky, I was told that I "did not really understand Kentucky basketball" and was given a team of young men who mostly had never played basketball before. I later realized that most of the other teams had young men who had been playing for many years at a competitive level. While this is a simple story and the marginalization felt was minor, it illustrates that marginality can be felt by everyone.

CHOOSING THE MARGINS

One cannot ignore the reality that some people and people groups have a history of being more in the center and others more on the margins. This history often makes navigating the center and the margins complex and difficult. Even more difficult is purposefully choosing to move away from the center after years of being in or near the center.

The question then is, How do we live in the margins, and not desire to live in the center where we would only work to marginalize others ourselves? Living on the margins can feel lonely and isolated. Often there is a tension between feeling anger and longing. Lee states, "The condition of in-between and in-both must be harmonized for one to become *a new marginal person who overcomes marginality without ceasing to be a marginal person*" (emphasis in original, 62). Lee terms this harmonizing "in-beyond." "*To transcend or to live in-beyond does not mean to be free of the two different worlds in which persons exist, but to live in both of them without being bound by either of them*" (emphasis in original, 63). What does this look like? Lee points to Jesus Christ as the ultimate in living "in-beyond."

Jesus Christ is the lens through which all Christians should view the world. Jesus "was truly the new marginal person who was not only in-between but also in-both worlds. He was the man who lived in-beyond racial, cultural, gender, and class divisions, but was also the man of the whole world. He was, therefore, the new marginal person *par excellence*" (72). For Lee, looking at Jesus Christ through the lens of marginality changes everything. Marginality uses reception rather than dominance to change the world. "The way of Jesus Christ is to love one another as he loved us. This love denies all and accepts all. Love denies our selfishness in order to accept others; love accepts others in order to deny our selfishness" (72). This way of love in the midst of our marginality is the way to true transformation.

Lee challenges the church's sometimes exclusive focus on the lordship of Jesus. He chooses instead to focus on the marginality that Jesus continually chooses. "Although they are inseparable, Christ's marginality precedes his lordship. If Christ is present in the world, the self-emptying process continues. It is a mistake to stress the lordship of Christ alone, and neglect his servant-hood, as if it were only a historical phase of who he is" (83). Jesus chooses marginality. He does not choose to be in the center of society. Lee explains,

> A theology of marginality is different from most liberation theologies, which seek only to liberate the poor and the oppressed through reaction. . . . The goal of marginal people, however, is more than liberation from central-group people, rather it is a harmonious coexistence of all people in a genuinely pluralistic society. In this respect, a theology of marginality is holistic, the whole is inseparable from the parts. (73)

Jesus's desire for harmonious coexistence and choice of marginality is seen throughout Scripture.

There is not time here to go through the whole of Scripture to see Jesus's choice of marginality exemplified, but it would be useful to highlight three examples: Jesus's incarnation, his temptation in the wilderness, and his death. In Jesus's loving choice to "empty himself, taking the form of a slave, being born in human likeness" (Phil. 2:5 NRSV), Jesus chooses to come to the very world that was created through him, "yet the world did not know him . . . and his own people did not accept him" (John 1:10–11 NRSV). He knowingly chooses to be fully human and fully divine, living "in-beyond" both worlds. Jesus is born in a manger in Bethlehem but is proclaimed the same night to be the Messiah by an angel from heaven (to shepherds—culturally some of the lowest people on earth!).

In the temptation of Jesus, we can recognize a theme in the temptations presented to Jesus by Satan. All three of those temptations would move Jesus from the margins to the center of society. The power that Jesus would display and the attention that he would receive would move Jesus into the center. But Jesus chooses instead to stay in the margins.

In Jesus's death and resurrection, we see the choice of marginality. Jesus experiences a loneliness that is incomprehensible in his suffering, humiliation, and rejection (even by the Father!). But in so doing, he is conquering sin and death for all. Jesus chooses this path of marginality. Jesus's resurrection again would give him opportunity to move to the center, but instead Jesus chooses to appear first to marginalized women and never to the centers of power.

By choosing marginality, Jesus models the reception and love that is the only truly transformative force. By choosing marginality, Jesus models for us the embrace of the "in-beyond" so that something different from center seeking can be experienced. "*God is not central to those who seek the center, but God is center to those who seek marginality, because the real center is the creative core, the margin of marginality*" (emphasis in original, 97). When people get caught up in seeking the center of society, they accept an attitude of competition, comparison, and uniformity. When people seek marginality, they seek to identify with Jesus Christ, who fully embraced the different worlds he belonged to. By embracing the "in-both" and "in-between," Jesus Christ leads us to a place where we can find a true identity that is also receptive of others.

To be clear, this is not an acceptance or an approval of systems that oppress or lead to injustice. Rather, it is a way to transform those systems. This new marginality allows us to accept who we are and to accept others where they are. The center as created by society seeks to force others into the mold of the dominant culture. By choosing the marginality of Jesus Christ, we choose to reject the "mold" of society that fights for power and marginalizes people who do not fit that mold.

MARGINALITY AS TRANSFORMATIVE

Marginality then leads to unity, whereas centrality leads to uniformity. By rejecting the center and its comparison and competition, we are able to receive others. "The unity of difference is possible through harmony, and harmony is possible because of individual plurality. So, we can affirm our global inclusiveness and claim our right to be different without losing our identity. Thus, the harmonious coexistence of all kinds of people is possible," writes Lee (105). Differences are part of God's design for humanity, and "if racial and gender difference is the base of creative order, the denial of such difference is the most serious sin of humanity" (107). When differences are not taken seriously, order disappears, and harmony is broken. But when we see *and accept* others' differences as part of God's plan, then we no longer seek to make others into the mold of the dominant society.

The church, the community of marginality, is not to seek a central place in society, but to stay at the margins. In this way the church becomes creative, transforming, and authentic. Scripture is full of warnings against seeking out centrality and power because it leads to a singularity.[2] "All those called to discipleship were marginal people. . . . Thus, we cannot become disciples unless we give up our power. . . . Because marginality is a condition of discipleship, God chose the foolish, the weak and humble (1 Cor. 1:27–28), or he chose the poor who were rich in faith (Jas. 2:5)" (118). Lee calls the church to move away from the temptations to move to the center and to instead embrace its marginality: "As Jesus Christ was a marginal person, the norm of the church should be marginality. A church based on the norm of centrality contradicts the church of Jesus Christ" (123). By choosing the margins, the church becomes a "movement of marginal people."

The church that is marginalized transforms centralist culture. The marginal approach finds its creativity in living in the margins. By being outsiders to the dominant culture, the church can be acute and able critics of the dominant ideologies. By being insiders of their own culture, they can bring insights and knowledge. The creativity is found in the in-between. Lee writes, "Love is the dynamic catalyst that transforms the power of centrality. The love of new marginality is inclusive, while the power of centrality is exclusive; the former serves, while the latter dominates; the former cooperates, while the latter controls; the former derives from spirit, while the latter drives from matter" (153). Love and service are the catalysts for change: "the love that Jesus-Christ exemplified contrasts with the power of centralists. Love cooperates for the benefit of the whole. New marginality's love is communitarian and, therefore, relational and pluralistic. It acts and thinks inclusively in terms of the community as a whole" (155). The invitation in following Jesus Christ is to love and serve others, even and especially when the church finds itself on the margins. Lee explains, "To be at the margin means to be a servant of world, even of the world at the center. This idea is a paradox of the Christian faith. Jesus-Christ, who came into the world in the form of servant, leads the church to be marginal and to become servant. Because servanthood is the function of marginality, those who are marginal must be servants" (146). This service and love are what lead to transformation of society: "when all become servants to others, everyone acts as a marginal person, but no one is marginalized; so, marginality has been overcome by marginality" (154). This

---

2.   Some examples include the tower of Babel, Isaiah's describing the marginalized remnant of Israel as the model of the Messiah, Hosea describing God as the marginalized husband, Ezekiel calling out Israel for taking advantage of the marginalized, Jesus's teaching in the Beatitudes, and Jesus's interaction with the rich young ruler.

movement to the margins then leads to true liberation, liberation that does not then oppress others, but levels the playing field.

What does this move to marginality look like? Lee provides this description:

> When heights descend to the valley, the valley is filled and lifted, the mountain is lowered. Everything becomes even. Just so, dominant ideology is abolished, and everyone becomes a servant. From the marginal perspective, every person is marginal to each other, and each becomes a servant to another, for new marginality is depicted in the symbol of the suffering servant, the margin of marginality. When everyone becomes marginal, there is not centrality that can marginalize anyone. Thus, marginality is overcome through marginality. (151)

This love of Jesus Christ invites Christ followers to participate in the cultural and ethnic activities of the marginalized. In so doing, Christians can experience marginality. This participation in love causes them to realize the injustices toward the marginal and creates a desire to free themselves from the centralist ideology. It looks like trying to find places to serve and love others, seeing and receiving them. It is embracing the call of the kingdom of God as described by the prophets and young Mary in her Magnificat (Luke 1:46–55).

Lee takes the approach of Gutiérrez, theology from the view of the marginalized, and adds to it a desire to stay on the margins, to not desire to move to the center. By shifting this emphasis, Lee attempts to focus the church more on the love and service of Jesus Christ and less on the temptation for power.

In young people's critique of the authority of the church, they often point to failures in authenticity. Many studies on adolescent spirituality have discovered that young people desire for the church to live out the service, care for the poor, compassion for the marginalized, and solidarity they find in Scripture.[3] The church can feel attacked by this critique, but the reality is that the church has often chosen the steadiness and security of the center over the insecurity of the margins (e.g., evangelicals' desire for political power in the religious right, the counter-movement for political power of the Christian left, pastors being more like CEOs than servants, etc.). Young people's desire to help the church see and serve those on the margins, to move the church to the margins, to be creative and to implement change, and to truly trust Christ in courage can be transformative . . . if we let it. When we give up security

---

3.   See the National Study of Youth and Religion and Fuller Youth Institute's *Sticky Faith* and *Growing Young* for some strong examples.

and rely on God, we find ourselves trusting while we are insecure, living at marginality's edge, exactly where Jesus is found and courage is given.

This journey into the margins is difficult because it does require loving and serving, a reception of all others. Much in the way the incarnation models a movement toward the other out of love and a desire for relationship as the end goal, not a means to an end, a move to the margins helps us receive others as they are without an agenda to change them into the previously developed mold of our own image. Young people already feel the pressure of "fitting in" to the molds of culture. Lee's *Marginality* invites the church to embrace and seek out the margins, and it seems many young people are there as well.

Marginality can be critiqued as well. There are questions as to the boundaries of the margins. Lee is writing about multicultural theology, referencing the ways dominant culture often marginalizes different cultures. However, one could ask the question of the extremes of this approach. For example, murderers and pedophiles are marginalized in most every culture. If they claimed they were "created this way," should Christians then identify with their marginalization too? Lee allows Christ's love of all to be his hermeneutic, so we do not believe he is stating this, but without more clarity, the extremes of the margins are tested.

After Bill wrapped up his summary of *Marginality*, Sophia thoughtfully added, "This resonates so well with my experiences. It seems that all of us who are trying to follow Christ can get upset with the church and its leadership when we see them as pandering to the center. But the reality is, we all do it. We seek the center. There is such a tension here because youth want to be in the center because that is where they perceive love and acceptance to be. They also see the disparity for those on the margins."

Bill added, "There is a game I play in some of our short-term mission trip training sessions called Star Power. Each person gets an envelope with some beads in it. Different colored beads have different values and certain combinations of beads have bonus values. The participants trade beads for a round, trying to improve the value of their collection of beads. After each round, the scores of each person are tabulated and individuals are placed into one of three groups: the group that has the highest scores, the group that has the lowest scores, and the middle group. The group with the highest score gets to make one new rule after each round. Can you guess what kinds of rules they make?"

"I would make rules that would help me win!" laughed Sophia.

"Exactly!" Bill affirmed. "That is exactly what they do every single time. The first group, who already have the most points, start to make rules where those in that group can get further ahead. Then they make rules to protect what they have. You can imagine how those in the lower groups start to feel."

"If I was in the lower group, I would be pretty mad. I am super-competitive, so I would try to get in that top group."

"And if you realized that almost no matter what you did, because of the rules the top group put in place, you could never move up?"

"Ooooooohhh, Bill. I am afraid that is where the not-so-nice side of my competitiveness might show up!" laughed Sophia.

"This is what usually happens. And when the game is progressing, I sort of poke the lower group by saying things like, 'You guys need to try harder! You just aren't really trying. Don't give up. The people in the top group got there by hard work, you can too!'"

"That is mean! When does this chaos end?"

"The game ends when the lower group starts to get mad at the top group and quits playing or threatens to boycott or worse. When it is over, we debrief the experience and talk about how this pretty much represents our economic system in the West. We talk about how counterintuitive it is to move to the margins, to help those in need, to not make rules that help only ourselves.

"I know this is just a game, but in my many years . . ."

"Many, many years!" joked Sophia.

". . . in my many, many, many years," Bill laughingly continued, "I have done this game with people of all ages and all walks of life. The outcome is pretty much the same. The top group pretty quickly makes choices to help themselves no matter the cost to others."

"I can see the value of the game and the insights it provides. And I already can see that this is where our next book can help give us a model for moving forward."

Bill nodded, "Yep. *Exclusion and Embrace* by Miroslav Volf really does help us with that."

EXCLUSION AND EMBRACE

Equality. Black Lives Matter. "Say their names." These phrases and many more have become commonplace. They represent a complex ongoing journey of experiences, decisions, privilege, oppression, intersectionality, stories, and research. Perhaps partly due to the powerful images on social media, these words have struck a chord with young people. These words are pointing to a multitude of issues, values, and yearnings. At the core of these, we believe, is a deep desire to experience love as a value for us as individuals and as a society.

Love that is lived. Love that is received and given. Love that is embodied in practice and words. Love that is every day.

This kind of love is yearned for but not often seen. For young people it might be even less frequent because of the agendas that adults bring to their relationships. God brings no such agenda. As was mentioned in the chapter on the incarnation, God starts with love. Precisely because of this longing for self-giving love, young people have much to teach the church and the world regarding social issues. They will take us to places of challenge, revelation, journey, and trust if we let them.

Miroslav Volf, a native Croatian who writes out of his own firsthand experience of teaching in Croatia during the war in former Yugoslavia, will help us bring some of these ideas together. Volf writes out of incredible pain at seeing firsthand the cycles of violence and oppression. Where Gutiérrez helps us see a theology of liberation that is done from the perspective of the oppressed and marginalized, and where Lee helps us see Jesus's modeling of continually choosing the margins, Volf helps the reader approach justice from a relational perspective, recognizing the differences between others and the boundedness to others. He does this through the metaphor of God's embrace.

In his book *Exclusion and Embrace*, he writes, "A genuinely Christian reflection on social issues must be rooted in the self-giving love of the divine Trinity as manifested on the cross of Christ; all the central themes of such reflection will have to be thought through from the perspective of the self-giving love of God" (25). It is this love that is yearned for, that can guide the church and youth ministry into a more just and loving response to a world divided and broken.

SEPARATION OR DIFFERENTIATION

The Christian story is a story of relationship. Relationship requires others. Others are different. Differences are real. After a short amount of time with children, you become aware that they know they are different from others. "Why is John's skin white and mine is brown?" a young child might ask. After a short amount of time with middle schoolers, you become aware that those differences are important to their identity. I overheard a middle school girl asking one night, "Why does Jill's brown skin have to be so beautiful compared to my pale white skin?" Recognizing these differences is not wrong; in fact separation is a vital part of the creation account. In Genesis 1 God creates and then he separates: light from darkness, land from sea, humanity from the rest of creation. Being different is important to the process of knowing one's identity.

But in the creation narrative, things are not just created to be separated. Rather, things are separated in order that they can be in relationship to each other. They are immediately separated *and* bound together. Humanity is different from the rest of creation but is bound to it with the relational charge of caring for it (Gen. 2:15). This separation and binding is what Volf calls "differentiation" (65). It is because we are differentiated that we can be in right loving relationship.

> The human self is formed not through a simple rejection of the other—through a binary logic of opposition and negation—but through a complex process of "taking in" *and* "keeping out." We are who we are not because we are separate from the others who are next to us, but because we are *both* separate *and* connected, *both* distinct *and* related; the boundaries that mark our identities are both barriers and bridges. (emphasis in original, 66)

Barriers and bridges: both are necessary to love the other. Too often the church has failed by only teaching one or the other.

Trinitarian theology models this differentiation. The Father is separate from the Son and the Spirit. The Son is separate from the Father and the Spirit. The Spirit is separate from the Father and Son. Yet the Father, Son, and Spirit are bound together in perfect loving relationship, constantly serving and pouring out love for one another. This differentiation allows for a perfect community of right relationship. As noted earlier in the book, humanity is invited into this perfect relationship, one of differentiation. Rightly seen, all of humanity should be differentiated from God and from all others—separate and bound.

But of course, things are not perfect. Things are broken. Our young people are often the best at seeing this brokenness and calling it out. A high school student named Brooke started attending a large youth group at a church situated in a multicultural neighborhood. Brooke visited for a couple of weeks and was clearly getting comfortable. The youth pastor was asking her one night how things were going and if she had any questions. She responded, "Just one: why are there no black teens here? Are they not welcome? There are Asians and whites, but no one who is black." Brooke could see the exclusion of others.

In the twofold nature of differentiation, separation and binding, we also find two temptations for humanity. One is to completely separate ourselves from others without seeing the need for right relationship, what Volf refers to as "exclusion." The other temptation is to see ourselves as only bound up with all others and thus see no separation, what Volf calls "radical inclusion."

Neither of these temptations is truly relational, for in separation the other is seen as only different and unable to relate to us outside of our own self-pleasing categories. The other becomes an object. Binding ourselves to the other with no separation leads to a loss of self, where the self is absorbed into the other and therefore incapable of true relationship.

RADICAL INCLUSION

Radical inclusion is where all people, ideas, and values are included. While this may seem a productive correction to exclusion (and it has potential to be), it often leads to more exclusion. There are two major dangers in radical inclusion that lead to more exclusion. "The first is that of generating new forms of exclusion by the very opposition of exclusionary practices" (64). Historically, radical inclusion has meant a defining of who is "right" and who is "wrong." Those who are "wrong" stand in the way of inclusion the "right" way and therefore are excluded. Those who are "right" then must oppose all those who are not in agreement with their "good" conclusions. Jesus was crucified, not by those who would have been thought to be the bad guys or those in the wrong, but rather by those who were "good and right." It was not that Jesus stood in radical opposition to them, but rather that Jesus challenged their definitions of who should be included, of what was wrong or right. He did not fit within their category of "right" and therefore was ultimately excluded.

"The second danger arises from the attempt to escape the first" (64). It is an absence of all boundaries. Attempting to include everyone and losing our boundaries leads to a loss of the other (and ultimately a loss of self). One example of radical inclusion is when people say they are "color-blind" when it comes to race. To proclaim that we are all the same and that there are no differences between us (or that no differences are seen) is incorrect and devalues the uniqueness and beauty that diversity brings. This radical inclusion seeks not to truly see the other, but rather to normalize all people into an image of "normal." It refuses to acknowledge the "abnormal," seeking to either assimilate or exclude them. So instead of losing all of ourselves, losing the differences, radical inclusion leads to making others into our own image. When the narrative of radical inclusion has been invoked, it has necessarily meant excluding some. Slavery, apartheid, and ethnic cleansing are part of the story of modernity's radical inclusion as they refused to see the uniqueness and differences of others and sought instead to assimilate or exclude them. "Those who are conveniently left out of the modern narrative of inclusion because they disturb the integrity of its 'happy ending' plot demand a long and gruesome counter-narrative of exclusion" (59). Neither the complete loss of boundaries nor the exclusion of the "wrong" lead to the embrace necessary in the kingdom of God.

EXCLUSION

Exclusion is the process of reconfiguring the interdependence that God has created, changing what is bound and what is separated. Volf writes, "Exclusion takes place when the violence of expulsion, assimilation, or subjugation and the indifference of abandonment replace the dynamics of taking in and keeping out as well as the mutuality of giving and receiving" (67). It is only separation from the other. There is no taking in, but only keeping out.

Volf identifies three forms of exclusion: false purity, elimination/assimilation, and abandonment. False purity insists that evil lies outside the person in impure things. Someone is "unclean" or does not belong because of their actions, culture, or looks. When pursuing false purity, "sin is here the kind of purity that wants the world cleansed of the other rather than the heart cleansed of the evil that drives people out by calling those who are clean 'unclean' and refusing to help make clean those who are unclean" (74). Jesus insisted that impurity was not outside of a person but rather within each person's heart.

Elimination seeks to remove those who are different completely. In its extreme form, it has resulted in genocide and ethnic cleansing. The more common and "nice" form of elimination is assimilation into the dominant culture. Assimilation occurs when the other is invited to survive and even thrive alongside the dominant culture—as long as the other abandons all of their identity and joins with the dominant culture. Jesus clearly was against such exclusion and sought to make space for the other as a fully valued person, no matter their cultural differences (e.g., the woman at the well in John 4).

Abandonment is where the dominant culture fully moves itself away from the other. The dominant culture moves to the other side of the road or to the suburbs, or returns to their safe enclaves. If others do not have anything the dominant culture desires, then others are kept at a safe, closed-off distance.

Exclusion can be easy to condemn because it seems fairly simple to understand. However, it is much more complex. Volf reminds us, "Exclusion is barbarity *within* civilization, evil *among* the good, crime against the other *right within the walls of the self*" (60). There are many examples in Scripture of how boundaries (healthy ones even) can become exclusion. The Pharisees were religiously pious, trying to remain holy and in right relationship with God. They were trying to remain separate from the things that would lead to broken relationships with God and others. But Jesus clearly feels that by the time he shows up in the flesh, those boundaries have become exclusions, excuses for separateness without relationship.

One must wonder if the "markers" of Christianity today have become more about exclusion than holiness, more about separation than piety. Choosing law over love may be easier, but it is not very Christlike. The young man who walks into the Sunday morning service with a hat on and is told to take it off or go home is reminded of the law, not of love. The teenage girl who comes to youth group, and everyone stops and stares because she has a different color of skin, is told that there is no place for her.

Volf is careful to stand against the frequent response by the oppressed to exclusion: retributive justice. Retributive justice occurs when the oppressed are somehow liberated and then begin to oppress those who were once their oppressors in the same way. It is the view that one who was hurt or excluded now has the right to do the same to the one who wronged them. Children on the playground often live by this standard—you push me down, I push you down. Teens, with their newfound ability to think abstractly, can be more complex in their practice, but the principle is the same. You said something bad about me on social media, so I will post this unflattering picture of you on social media. Historically, the violence of this model bears itself out over and again. Ironically, though humanity continues to repeat this model, retributive justice does not work to bring restoration or reconciliation. Rather, it continues to exclude the other, making them only separate.

Volf encourages his readers to see that when we simply accept the categories typically applied, such as "oppressed" and "oppressor," we fail to recognize the complexity and the messiness of most confrontations. Often there is no blameless innocent; instead, there are people who both instigate and harm each other.[4] We also fail to frame the relationships in ways that lead to love and reconciliation. There is a pressing question of what would or does happen when the oppressed overcome the oppressors. History tells us that often the roles then become reversed. Surely this is not the desired outcome! The goal of the gospel must be that of right relationship and love. This is what Volf terms as "embrace."

---

4.   This statement is not denying that sometimes the dominant culture does horrible things to others. Indeed, this has happened and is the case. This should not be condoned or "swept under the rug." Volf argues that these atrocities *need* to be named, but also that we cannot allow ourselves to fall into these false binary arguments.

For most young people today, overt exclusion is clearly wrong. Further, they often are able to feel the subtlety of exclusion within culture. This is why so many young people are resonating with the social justice issues facing the world. However, they also often lack a framework for a response to that exclusion.

EMBRACE

If exclusion (and radical inclusion which often leads to exclusion) is the usual way of responding to the other, is there an alternative? Volf offers up embrace as a way forward. Embrace is found in the self-giving Christ. He writes,

> Central to the Christian faith is the belief that the Spirit of the crucified Messiah is capable of creating the promised land out of the very territory the Pharaoh has beleaguered. The spirit enters the citadel of the self, de-centers the self by fashioning it in the image of the self-giving Christ and frees its will so it can resist the power of exclusion in the power of the Spirit of embrace. It is in the citadel of the fragile self that the new world of embrace is first created (2 Corinthians 5:17). It is by this seemingly powerless power of the Spirit—the Spirit who blows even outside the walls of the church—that selves are freed from powerlessness in order to fight the system of exclusion everywhere—in the structures, in the culture, and in the self. (92)

Embrace, for Volf, is centered in Christ and his love. It is a way forward, out of the cycle of violence, victim, and revenge. Volf articulates four elements of embrace: opening the arms, waiting, closing the arms, and opening them again.

Embrace is something all have experienced. Physically, it is a hug. Heather Flies is a long-time youth worker and frequent speaker at youth events. Heather has also been a powerlifter. Heather is very strong. One of my favorite things to do is to tell anyone I know who is going to meet Heather to ask for a hug. Little do they know that when Heather hugs, she fully embraces you, wraps you up, picks you off the ground, and squeezes the breath out of you, before gently placing you back down and releasing you to resume breathing. A hug from Heather is unforgettable!

Relationally, we first find embrace modeled by God himself. Somewhat like Heather's hugs, God's embrace is experienced even if it is not fully understood. Accepting God's embrace only leads us to the same gesture toward others. It is to experience a radical love that knows us, accepts us, makes space for us, and desires to be in our presence no matter what we have done. "Having been embraced by God," Volf says, "we must make space for others in ourselves and invite them in—even our enemies. This is what we enact as we celebrate the Eucharist. In receiving Christ's broken body and spilled blood, we, in a sense, receive all those whom Christ received by suffering" (129). Earlier it was mentioned that radical inclusion has the potential for being good. Embrace is radically inclusive in the right sense. It invites and welcomes all, in their own uniqueness and differences, to experience community and love. God shows us this kind of inclusion in his embrace, an embrace we seek for ourselves and seek to show others.

The first movement of embrace is that of opening the arms. "Open arms are a gesture of the body reaching for the other. They are a sign of discontent with my own self-enclosed identity, a code of *desire* for the other" (emphasis in original, 141). When we realize that we need others, that we are created for community, then we open our arms willingly to the other. "More than just a code for desire, open arms are a sign that I have *created space* in myself for the other to come in and that I have made a movement out of myself so as to enter the space created by the other" (emphasis in original, 141). Opening the arms is more than just discontent with the self. It is recognition that the other is needed. It is the work of opening one's self to the other and clearing out room for the other in their uniqueness, in their difference, in their own will to join. Finally, open arms are a gesture of *invitation*—"a *soft knock* on the other's door" (emphasis in original, 142). Open arms are not demanding but inviting.

The second step in the act of embrace is waiting. "Waiting is a sign that, although embrace may have a one-sidedness in its origin (the self makes the initial movement toward the other), it can never reach its goal without reciprocity (the other makes a movement toward the self)" (143). Space is made, the invitation is extended, and now the self must wait for response. It is a vulnerability that is difficult to extend. There is a risk of rejection.

A youth worker was recently picking up a teen, Tim, to attend youth group. Arriving at Tim's house, the youth worker got out of his car and greeted Tim with an extended fist for a "fist bump." The teen did not respond, instead walking around the outstretched fist of the youth worker and opening the door of the car to get in. Tim's father, watching this unfold from his porch, loudly called out, "Tim, what are you doing?" Tim, embarrassed at this call out, mumbled some excuse about not feeling well. The youth worker, undoubtedly hurt by this avoidance, responded, "It's okay! I love Tim no matter what. He can fist-bump me if he wants, but he doesn't have to." The youth worker understood what Tim's dad perhaps did not. The open arms of an embrace are an invitation, a "soft knock," not a demand or a barging in. Just because space is made, one must not insist that someone enters in; this would be to deny the vulnerability of the waiting and the true hospitality of the gesture.

If the invitation is accepted, the soft knock answered, then comes the third step, the closing of the arms. As Volf notes, "This is the goal of the embrace, the embrace proper, which is unthinkable without *reciprocity*" (emphasis in original, 143). The closing of the arms is a sharing of presence. Two come together. The differences and the boundedness are acknowledged. It is worth noting that the two coming together are rarely offering the same things. One may be giving more than the other. This is part of what makes each different, and the differences are usually known by both parties. But the vulnerability and the presence of each is the same. "Though one self may receive or give more than the other, each must enter the space of the other, feel the presence of the other in the self, and make its own presence felt" (143). Closing the arms is invitation accepted, space shared, and presence connected.

The final act of embrace is the opening of the arms again. "What holds the bodies together in an embrace is not their welded boundary, but the arms placed around the other. And if the embrace is not to cancel itself, the arms must open again" (144). This is what allows for embrace to be a gift. Each individual must release the other to be different but in relationship to each other. Without the opening of arms, embrace becomes an inclusion where the identities, uniqueness, and gifts of each are lost. Embrace releases the other to keep being the other and allows the self to keep being the self.

Embrace is risk. When I open my arms, I open myself to misunderstanding or abuse, as well as to appreciation, support, or validation. "Embrace is grace, and grace is a gamble, always," writes Volf (147). Embrace challenges our sense of control and power and invites us to see, to be with. He states,

> The will to give ourselves to others and "welcome" them, to readjust our identities to make space for them, is prior to any judgment about others, except that of identifying them in their humanity. The *will to embrace* precedes any "truth" about others and any construction of their "justice." This will is absolutely indiscriminate and strictly immutable; it transcends the moral mapping of the social world into "good" and "evil." (emphasis in original, 29)

May God's Spirit inhabit us and recenter us in the Christ who transforms us to see and welcome our neighbors.

Critique of Volf's work lies in the practice of his theology of grace and love. Is it really possible to open our arms to those who have chosen to abuse and would choose to do so again? One wonders whether there might be a call to establish boundaries for those living within abusive domestic and national situations. However, Volf's credibility in his own experience helps us see that perhaps there is a way to do both, have boundaries and open arms.

EMBRACE PRACTICED

"Wow! This is a lot to sort through!" exclaimed Sophia. "I like the concepts here, but how do we start to apply all of this?"

"Very carefully," said Bill.

"I feel like these approaches from the missionary world are helpful to give me new lenses with which to see the world. It also helps expand my hospitality toward everyone."

"That's great!" said Bill. "How do we proceed?"

"Let's take Volf's model of embrace—open arms, wait, close arms, and open arms again—as our model to help us adapt," replied Sophia.

"I like that," said Bill. "It is easy to remember and in some ways easy to teach."

"And I think it is big enough to enwrap the other two authors' ideas as well," said Sophia.

OPEN ARMS

The first step of embrace is to open our arms. As Volf says, it is invitation and it indicates a "discontent with my own self-enclosed identity." It begins with listening. It is a posture of reception and not dominance.

In order to be discontent with our own closedness, we must first help young people encounter their identity. Developmental theory helps us to describe the cognitive ability in most early to mid-adolescents as moving into the formal operational thought stage. This means that many adolescents are now capable of abstract thought. This impacts the identity development of young people because they are now able to see the world from viewpoints that are not their own.[5] This means that adolescence is the perfect time to begin to help people expand their view of the world and to see how self-enclosed it may be.

One way to help young people begin to open their arms is to identify their own story. Simply inviting young people to articulate the story of their

---

5.   Of course, "ability to" and "practice of" are not the same. It would also be worth mentioning that developmental theory is helpful as a descriptive tool, not as a goal- or benchmark-setting tool. In other words, it helps us see and name where a young person is developmentally but should not be used as an evaluative measure.

lives, or portions of it, can be very helpful. Ask them about their family back-ground, ethnicity, and origins. By giving space and opportunity for young people to share their own story and listen to others, we help them begin to see and articulate the differences.

For youth who are in the dominant culture, sometimes they do not even see their own ethnicity as part of their identity, because it has become norma-tive. A youth leader was helping to prepare his group for a short-term mission experience. In one of the trainings several months before the trip, he asked the group to write out the story of their family. As the youth were sharing those stories, he noticed that the white youth did not even mention their ethnicity as part of their story, while the students of all other ethnicities did. As more of the group shared, the pattern remained the same. Finally, he asked one of the white students, "What ethnicity is your family?" The student replied, "We are Ameri-can." The youth pastor was then able to follow up on this encounter with the group, helping them to discover their ethnic heritage, the role it has played in their own lives, and the role it plays in how they approach others. The students went back and asked their parents where their ancestors were from, and then the youth leader helped some of them research the cultures of those places.

Cross-cultural experiences can also help us see the larger cultural differ-ences. Short-term mission trips can be helpful for immersing youth who are of the dominant culture into a context where they are no longer cultur-ally dominant. These experiences can be quite disorienting and need careful attention. Culture shock can be difficult. But once the heart and the head can see the role our cultural differences play in the ways we live and treat others, then those new lenses can be applied when we return home as well. It is worth noting that this can create a reverse culture shock that also needs support. (This will be addressed more fully in the chapter on short-term missions.) This kind of cross-cultural experience often leads to a discontent with our closedness and a desire to open our arms.

Another way to help youth understand their identity is to help them begin to name and describe the people around them. When starting this process, youth will begin naming their family and friends. But challenge them to move past those closest to them and to identify all the people they interact with in a week, including the people that serve them in the store, the school cafeteria, and so on, even if the teens do not know their names. Using concentric circles as a guide, this practice can be quite helpful (see questions and exercise at the end of the chapter). The center circle represents those closest to you—who you spend the most time with who you know best and who know you best.

Have youth name the people in that circle. Keep expanding the circles and asking youth to identify and describe the people in those circles. When you reach the outermost rings, you often find people there that we might be able to recognize, even though we don't know their names or their stories.

Sometimes there are people around us who are "invisible" to us. Invite youth to look at the census data for their town, city, or county. Help the group identify the ethnicities or other demographic groups that are listed as present in your community that may not be seen or known. Help youth know who the key leaders in their community are and encourage youth to think through equity issues. By helping youth name some of our blind spots, we begin to help them see how self-enclosed our world and identity can be.

Many communities offer different cultural events that are open to the public. Whether it be a specific celebration of a holiday from another culture, a cultural heritage event, or an artistic event from another culture like an art exhibit or a musical concert, these are great events to participate in with youth. First, it can be a lot of fun to try new things! Second, it begins to help us see and appreciate other cultures that are around us. It also invites relationship and dialogue with others. Reading through the Gospels reveals that Jesus went to a lot of parties and events thrown by others, but it does not seem like Jesus threw many himself. If we attend events from another culture with open hearts, seeking to learn and to appreciate, then we can start to dialogue *with people*, not ideologies.

But seeing that others are there is not enough. Once we recognize that there are others around us with whom we do not interact, we can begin to ask about their stories and experiences. As youth hear these stories, we can invite them to see the world from that person's point of view. As Gutiérrez invites, we can begin to join in theology from their perspective. We seek to see and receive them as they are.

As we invite young people to know their own story and then discover and empathetically interact with another's story, we begin to move past our closedness. In my experience, young people are more willing than adults to truly wrestle with the realities of the differences in experiences and the ramifications of doing theology from the viewpoint of another. Often this leads to repentance. It also leads to a deep disappointment that they had not seen this before. By seeing another's story, we begin to see how we have taken part in not seeing the other and recognizing our boundedness to them. When we do not know someone else's story, we cannot see how we are connected.

When we begin to see other people, particularly those who are different, we also begin to see a different Jesus. We begin to see a Jesus that is moving to the margins, seeking and saving the lost. Opening our arms also means letting go of our inadequate pictures of Jesus to make room for a Jesus who is present in the lives of everyone. This can be difficult. Questions like "How did I miss this?" and "How did my faith not help me see this?" can arise. Part of opening our arms is to wrestle with these questions and let go of our previous closedness.

Opening our arms can also be an act of repentance. If repentance is turning our gaze in the right direction, then opening our arms is to acknowledge that the church has often been silent and at times complicit in the marginalization of others. Opening arms is naming that, asking for forgiveness, and purposefully turning our gaze.

Opening the arms can take a lot of time. It can involve a lot of emotion. It is more of a process than an instance. Be patient with yourself, the youth you love, and the adult volunteers you are working with. New views of the world can be disconcerting.

We begin to open our arms by seeing others and becoming curious to know about them. This is a way we move to the margins, as Lee invites us to do. By helping youth develop new vision and the tools to continually look to the margins, we begin to help them see the larger world. When we see and interact with the larger world, especially on the margins, we begin to see our connectedness to it. Youth are ready, willing, and able to engage in these practices if given the chance. Open arms.

WAIT

The next step in the embrace after the arms are open is to wait. Waiting requires vulnerability. It is an opening of self to the other. It is an invitation sent, with no response determined. It is an invitation that allows the other the choice to accept or decline.

When we wait with arms open, we have invited the other to share with us, but there can be no demand of a positive response. Jesus models this in his move to the margins. Jesus comes to us out of love. There is no demand that we respond. There is not a condition in place where he will stop being there for us. It is reception and not dominance.

For young people, it is important that we model the posture of open arms and waiting. This begins with our posture as youth leaders toward young people. In a time when most adults in young people's lives have an agenda, are looking for something, or are wanting something, to just open our arms and invite relationship is significantly different. The willingness to wait signifies a desire for relationship that does not demand it.

Steven and Ben were brothers, a couple years apart in age, who started attending youth group with some friends. Ben, the younger of the two, quickly jumped into everything he could. He came to faith in Christ and started attending a small group focused on discipleship. He was growing by leaps and bounds in his faith, and it showed in his life. Steven was also enjoying his time at youth group. He was a part of the community, and he really enjoyed the people there. But he was more skeptical and less interested in discipleship than his younger brother. Some of the youth were pressuring Steven to "be like his brother" and come to the small group. Jack, the small group leader, overheard one of these conversations one day and quickly interceded. He pulled the young men to the side and told them that Steven did not have to follow any specific formula for growing in his faith and that his journey would be different from his brother's and anyone else's. While Jack appreciated the young men's attempts to invite Steven to join them, this pressure was demanding and not loving. Jack did not know it at the time of the conversation, but Steven was listening in. When Steven realized that Jack was willing to wait, to extend the invitation and not demand any specific outcome for the relationship to continue, it meant the world to Steven, and he and Jack became great friends.

Waiting does not demand response. A way this can be modeled is in our efforts as a youth group to serve others. Seeing a need in the community and offering to help is invitation. Demanding to be allowed to "serve" is not loving or honoring. As a long-time youth pastor, I have called many community organizations to inquire about potential needs for volunteers. Often my calls are met with excitement and optimism, but not always. Once I had called a ministry in the area that fed the homeless twice every week. When I asked if they would like some help from our youth group, the phone grew silent. Then I asked, "It is more than okay if you do not need any help. But are there any jobs or tasks that no one else wants to do that we could help with?" That question was met with a list of jobs that could use our help. It became apparent during our time serving with that ministry over several years that other youth groups were interested in serving in the ways the youth group wanted or thought was best. One day the volunteer coordinator for the ministry accidentally arranged for too many groups to come in and help. I overheard the leader of one of the groups demanding that the volunteer coordinator find a place for his group to serve. This is not waiting.

Waiting for people to respond can be difficult at times because it can remind us of our role in excluding others. While we wait, we are confronted with the reality that we may have previously walked by this person many times and they were invisible to us. Or perhaps we even saw them as less than we were. For young people who want to resolve the disequilibrium of this brokenness as quickly as possible, it is important that we help them put this discontent into words. By giving them opportunities to talk about how they feel about their role in exclusion, we help them move past paralyzing shame and into repentance and love.

The biblical concept of lament includes naming the grief or sorrow we feel. It is more than just complaining about something. It is a conversation with God where we are willing to reflect on our role in the brokenness we are experiencing. Sometimes we have a role in that brokenness. We can teach young people to lament well, giving them freedom and space to name the emotions they are feeling and the sources of their grief, and to repent of the places where we have participated in the brokenness.

One predominantly white youth group went on a short-term mission trip to a Spanish-speaking country and had a great experience. Their "eyes were opened" to see some of the Latino people in their own community—including the Spanish-speaking congregation that met in their own church building. Realizing that the Spanish-speaking congregation and their youth had been invisible, the youth group upon returning began to seek relationship with the Spanish-speaking church and youth (open arms). But rather than getting a quick affirmative response to their invitations to join together for an event, they were met with silence. And so, they waited. Recognizing that some of the youth were confused by this silence, they began to evaluate their previous interactions with the Spanish-speaking congregation. This led to some uncomfortable realizations. At this point, the youth leaders led the group through a time of reflection, teaching through some of the Psalms and Lamentations. The group did an exercise where they each wrote their own lament or prayer about the situation and their role in it. This became a powerful moment for the group as they began to put into words their emotions, their repentance, and their hope for a better future. And they waited. Arms still open, but perhaps more equipped for a potential positive response to their invitation. They maybe noticed that the Spanish-speaking youth group's arms had been open to them the whole time.

God also uses waiting to help us fight the allure of the center. As Lee mentions when explaining marginality, there is a huge pull toward the center because it is there that we find power and influence. Young people see this pressure all the time as they interact in the social structure of their schools, clubs, or jobs. Waiting releases control and our need to be needed and to have influence. It refines our love for the other.

CLOSE ARMS

The third step in Volf's embrace is to close the arms. It is the moment when Heather Flies wraps her arms around you that you know for sure you have been hugged. Closing the arms brings the two together, both parties engaging in the embrace. The invitation given is received and reciprocated. This is the goal when the arms are opened. God desires unity with us and so he sends his Son. The arms were opened. God waits for us to respond. But the desire of God is the response! We move into God and experience the closed arms and shared presence of God.

The same is true in youth ministry. We open our arms, extend the invitation, and wait. When the response comes, the arms are closed and the hug is on! Just as the invitation should be given to all, so too must the closing of the arms be available to all—especially those on the margins. This is one of the ways we move to the margins and away from the center. If we are seeking only control, power, influence, and resources, then we close our arms only around those who can help us get those things.

In a former occupation, I (Brian) planned large events with up to ten thousand people in attendance. One time I was invited to visit at another conference so that I could meet a potential speaker. We were introduced, the speaker greeted me, and we began talking. We were having what I thought was a good and meaningful conversation until someone else entered the room who was very well known and influential. The speaker immediately walked away from our conversation and introduced himself to this person of influence. It was like I was never even there! In this moment when I thought that I had been welcomed into presence, I realized I was not in the center enough to matter at that moment. We've all felt the sting of those moments.

Jesus of course closed his arms around all types, especially those on the margins. From Zacchaeus to the lepers to the woman caught in adultery to a Samaritan woman, Jesus embraced. So too must we make our youth groups and our own presence safe places where the invitation is given to all; and to all who respond, the arms are closed in shared presence.

As I was talking to my friend Mark, a youth pastor, at a community event, a woman came up and interrupted our conversation. She disdainfully looked at Mark and said that she had heard that a teenager named Doug was attending his youth group. Then she said with much indignation, "You and your youth group will take anyone." With that declaration, she stormed off. Mark and I looked at one another. I was embarrassed for the woman and slightly concerned how Mark would take it. He beamed and said, "That's the nicest compliment I have ever received in ministry!"

When the arms are closed is when presence is shared. In these moments, both parties are fully committed to each other—acknowledging differences, but coming together in love. It is a deep caring for the other. It is awareness and attention to the other. It is being fully present.

As youth leaders, we often are not the center of society or culture. We often do not have money. Other adults rarely listen to us. People do not understand us. People do not often know what we do ("A youth worker, huh? Is that, like, a job?"). However, there can be a great temptation in working with young people to develop a fondness for being at the center. Where adults do not listen to us, sometimes youth do. Where we rarely have influence, in our youth group we do. It is important in this rare place of being in the center that we model being fully present, especially to those on the margins of our groups and of our communities.

It does not take long in youth ministry to have an event when not very many people show up. Inevitably one of the youth will ask, "Where is everyone?" Because you care, you too are wondering in your head where some of the people are, but you also have this incredible opportunity in this moment to close your arms around those who are actually in your presence, who have answered the soft knock of invitation. It is here that we get to say with our actions (and occasionally our words), "*You* matter! *You* belong here!" and be fully present to those who are there.

For Gutiérrez, the church in Latin America was consistently choosing to ignore the realities of the marginalized and oppressed. The church would experience those in need and mourn with them, but it failed to acknowledge that there was a significant problem with the systems of culture. In so doing, it failed to truly see those on the margins and therefore could not close its arms around them. The church could not be fully present because it was interested in keeping its position of authority in that society. So, too, have many churches in North America struggled to actually embrace African Americans because they claimed to be "color-blind." By claiming they could not see color, the church was claiming to not really see the differences or the plight of the other. When we fail to see the differences, we perceive others in our own image. You cannot embrace yourself. We must get to the place where we are willing to be fully present to each other in the midst of those differences.

Sharing presence also means that we are willing to accept the presence and embrace of the other. It is *both* parties closing arms. As Volf mentions, a true embrace does not often come among equals. We are not equal with God, yet we can join the embrace. Only giving and never receiving from others is one of the temptations of ministry. Closing the arms gives agency to the other to choose to be present with us as well, to choose to extend a love that is beyond ourselves. And as youth leaders in ministry, we must be willing to receive the embrace from others. Too often we who are called to serve forget how important it is to accept being served.

When we in the church and youth ministry make relationship—the sharing of presence—the end goal, then we most resemble Christ. When we see our differences but come together anyway, we most resemble the kingdom of God. When we allow others to embrace us, we model shared life.

OPEN ARMS AGAIN

The final step in Volf's embrace is to open the arms again. By opening the arms, we release the other to be him- or herself and to be different. By opening the arms, we acknowledge agency. Opening arms relinquishes control. Open arms validate the embrace as gift.

Once someone has been in the closed arms of embrace, it can be quite difficult to let go. I can think of several young people in my years of youth ministry that I did not want to let go. Sometimes it was because I was unsure of the future decisions they would make. Sometimes I was unsure of the situations that they would return to. Sometimes, if I am honest, I wanted to reshape that young person to be more like me. But we must let go. An embrace is not forcing others to meld into us. An embrace trusts God's work in a person's life.

There was a young man, Jon, who had been active in his youth group. He first attended church and youth group through a friend. He quickly came to faith in Jesus and invited his older brother to do the same. One of the first people to meet Jon when he started attending was Ralph. Ralph was a volunteer in the youth ministry and became a close friend to Jon. As Jon grew in his faith, he would often turn to Ralph for advice and prayer. Jon and Ralph developed an almost weekly rhythm of meeting for smoothies and talking about life.

After a couple years, Jon's friends began to change, and Jon had less and less time for church or youth group and less and less of a relationship with Jesus. Jon also started moving away from Ralph. Jon stopped answering Ralph's texts and calls. Jon stopped meeting with Ralph for smoothies. But Ralph kept his arms open. Ralph had embraced Jon but had also truly released him. He would still call or text Jon once a week and just let Jon know that he cared about him and missed him. Ralph did not guilt or shame Jon for not being at youth group or church, nor did he try to make Jon feel bad for "ghosting" him. Ralph just kept his arms open so that Jon would know that if he ever wanted to reengage the relationship, Ralph cared and desired that. Ralph did not chase Jon down and confront him. He loved him with open arms.

After about a year, Jon returned to church, to youth group, and to Christ. He said it was because of Ralph. At first it was just a returned text. Then it was a phone call for advice. Then it was a smoothie meeting. Several years later, Ralph was moving out of state for his work. The youth group threw a sending party for Ralph and Jon shared, "In the midst of my move away from Jesus and the church, I wanted to believe that there was no place for me. I wanted to believe that God did not love me. I wanted to believe that no one loved me. But then, about once a week, I would get this text from Ralph saying he was praying for me and cared about me. Occasionally he went old school and left a voicemail. I did not return these texts or phone calls. But I knew that somehow Ralph loved me and cared for me. And because Ralph loved me and cared for me, I knew that God still loved me and cared for me. Thank you, Ralph, for not giving up."

The response is not always going to be like Jon's. We cannot guarantee that kind of response. But that's the point of the full embrace. We desire true relationship. Just like God does with us.

The Eucharist is a great way to teach, model, and embody this rhythm of embrace. It tells the story in its enactment of God's invitation to us all. It invites us in with open arms. It waits for us to respond. When we take the bread and drink from the cup, we experience the arms of Christ's love and Christ's community closing around us. We come together in shared presence. Then we are released to continue in freedom of self and choice. We love, and we are loved.

Emily attended youth group with a friend. She loved the community that she found there but struggled with faith. She was very intellectual and wanted there to be clear answers to all of her questions. Despite her frustration with not getting all the answers (and getting more questions!), she continued to attend because of the relationships. One day, the youth group was sharing Communion together. As they moved through their liturgy the youth pastor, Madison, noticed that Emily was deeply moved. When the invitation was given, Emily slipped into line with some of the other youth and received the elements. Madison noticed Emily's big step and asked her about it later. Emily told Madison that despite her lingering questions, she knew she wanted to partake in the Eucharist because she felt so much love in the invitation. She wanted to be a part of this community that loved and invited everyone in, even those with "so many annoying questions" like her. Now that she had accepted this invitation, she knew something was different, that she belonged to this loving community and, while she would continue to pursue her questions, she had this certainty that this love was real.

CONCLUSION

After sharing their insights from the readings, Bill said, "This reminds me of something that happened in my own life about five years ago."

"Oh, yeah?" replied Sophia, sipping her drink. "Do tell."

"You know how church life and ministry can just take over your schedule?" Bill asked Sophia.

Sophia nodded in response and said, "It feels like every day and every night. Sundays are full of church stuff. Monday is staff meeting all morning and administration all afternoon. Tuesday is preparation for Wednesday service, followed by time with teens after school. Tuesday nights usually have some sort of church meeting. Wednesdays is youth group, so that day is full. Thursday is a lot like Tuesday. Friday, I try to take off. Friday night is going to youth events. Saturday often has a youth event . . . and preparation for Sunday."

"Right!" said Bill, taking a drink of his coffee and gathering himself to tell the story. "As you just pointed out, it can be easy to let this take over your life. If we are not careful and intentional, we lose sight of anything outside of the church."

"I can see that and feel that already."

"I had been at this church for a few years, and that is exactly what was happening to me. And its not just the time, its also the relationships. The only people I ever spent time with were church people. Now, don't get me wrong—I love these people and I have great friends here, but most of the adults at this church look and think like me.

"About that time, I was in a pretty close discipleship relationship with a young man named Devin who was on the high school soccer team. He was all about soccer. 'Futbol life,' he called it. He is a good guy, but I had noticed that he was only spending time with other soccer people or, if he was with anyone else, all he ever talked about was soccer."

"Sounds like an evangelist!"

"That would be a good way to describe him: a futbol evangelist. Anyway, I said to him one day, 'You know, Devin, every time I see you it is all soccer all the time.' 'You mean futbol,' he corrected me. I said, 'The point is I want to challenge you to talk to some people who do not know or like soccer . . . er, futbol . . . at all. I want to challenge you to expand your circle of friends.'"

Sophia replied, "That sounds like a fair challenge."

"I thought so!" said Bill, "Until he replied."

"He said, 'Okay, I will do it. But what about you?'"

"I asked him what he meant, and he continued, 'All you do is spend time with church people who look like you and have the same skin color as you. Why don't you expand your circle too?'"

"It was like getting hit by a bus! I had not even realized how true that was. In my mind, I started to try and think of all the things he did not know about my life and about how he was wrong, but . . . he was right. The more I thought about it, the more right I realized he was.

"I muttered an 'Okay, I will try too.' Then I changed the subject."

"'Out of the mouths of babes,' said Sophia quoting Scripture. "That sounds like you took that realization hard. What did you do?"

"Well, first, I took some time and tried to take stock of my life. I wanted to evaluate what was important to me and the relationships I had. God brought to mind Psalm 139:23–24 (NLT), 'Search me, O God, and know my heart; test me and know my anxious thoughts. Point out anything in me that offends you, and lead me along the path of everlasting life.' As I prayed these verses, I realized how much the bubble that was created by my job and ministry kept me more and more isolated from people who were different from me. I also recognized that this was my fault. I had not been intentional about relationships, so the only ones that were happening were the ones that were right in front of me. I started to pray that God would help me reprioritize my life and that he would bring people into my life that were different from me."

"Okay, after this conversation we have been having, I can see where you are going. This was creating a discontent in you with your current life and thoughts, and so you knew you needed to open yourself up, to 'open your arms' as we have been saying," said Sophia.

"That's right. And I was not proud at all of the realization that I was living in such an isolated bubble. Again, this was my fault. I started to pray and ask God to open my heart and to bring some people into my life that were different from me."

"What happened?"

"Well, my prayers began to open me up to God and I believe open my eyes to people who were around me the whole time. I began to see some people who were in my life but were not the center of my focus. It was like when you get so focused on something that you miss all kinds of other things happening right under your nose," Bill said.

"Like when my dad used to watch football when I was a little girl. I could get away with almost anything when he was watching the game. One time I even rearranged some of the furniture in the room without him realizing it until the game was over." Sophia added.

"Wow! That's funny!" Bill said. "And that's pretty focused. I realized that is exactly what had been happening to me. So, God started to show me some things about myself and started to open my eyes. That's when I met Harvey, who was a counselor at a local high school. He also happens to be black. One day I was at the school picking up a teen from my group after his practice. Harvey saw me standing there in the lobby of the school waiting and asked me who I was. He thought I was a parent."

"Wait a minute! He thought you were a parent?" Sophia laughed. "Are you sure it wasn't a grandparent?"

"Very funny," Bill deadpanned but smiled. "I introduced myself to Harvey and he said, 'Glad you are investing in young people. We probably have some things in common.'

"I replied that I thought we did, and so he shared his number and told me to call him. Then he said, 'You won't call, but you should.' I promised him I would call in the next two weeks.

"I called about a week later and left a message. I waited another week and then called and left another message. After another week, I thought that I would probably see him at the school again but that would be it. Which is fine. We all have busy lives."

"You were waiting. With arms open," Sophia said.

"I did not have those words for it at the time, but yes, that's right. So I thought at this point it has been three weeks and nothing. I ran into Harvey at school again when I stopped by to drop off a gift basket from the church for teacher's appreciation week. Harvey saw me and laughingly said, 'I wish there was a counselor appreciation week!' I laughed and said, 'Well, I appreciate all you do.'

"He looked at me and said, 'I know I owe you a phone call, but I have been busy.'

"'Yeah, I am sure. Busy not getting appreciated,' I joked. He laughed and said, 'How about coffee right now?'

"We walked back to the break room there in the school offices and shared a cup of really bad school coffee. We talked for about twenty minutes before he had to go. I got to hear a little of his story and some of the things he deals with as a counselor."

Sophia was connecting to the story. "So now you were closing your arms like in the model. You were trying to embrace him as a person. You probably had other things to do that day at that time, but you prioritized that relationship."

"Yes, I did," said Bill. "God was really clear to me in that moment when Harvey invited me for coffee that this was an opportunity. Where I normally would have said, 'Not today, I have to go to . . . ,' this time God made it clear that I could choose to be present to Harvey and embrace that relationship."

"You also opened your arms again!" added Sophia. "You did not demand to meet again or hold it against him that he had not called you back."

"Again, I did not have language for it at the time, but that is exactly what God led me to do," replied Bill. "And that began a great friendship. Harvey and I are good friends to this day. He called me a few days later and we met for a good cup of coffee one evening. We discovered we were very different in a lot of ways, from favorite sports teams to experiences growing up to how we see the world. But we somehow realized that we both cared a lot about teens and we were able to be honest with each other. I am not sure what clicked so well with us, but something did, and I am so grateful. Harvey has been a good friend and has helped me expand my world."

"Did you ever tell Devin?" asked Sophia. "Tell him what his question had done for you?"

"Yes, I did," said Bill. "As I was wrestling with my closedness, I asked Devin to help hold me accountable to being more open. That became a great conversation for both of us. But my reflections went well beyond just that relationship with Devin and Harvey. It expanded to the church too."

"What do you mean?" asked Sophia.

"I had to start thinking more about the ways we programmed ministry and the willingness to enter long-term relationships with others. Were we as a church willing to hold open our arms to all others?" Bill responded.

"I have to get going, but this leads to what I want to talk about next time!" Sophia said.

"See you in a few weeks. What do we need to talk about then?"

"Mission trips!" said Sophia. "I have been wrestling with our approaches to mission trips for a while, and this reading has really got me digging deep into the why and how of youth mission trips. Plus, I am in the midst of planning one!"

"I look forward to talking about all my mistakes," said Bill. "Send me the name of a book to read and I will be ready!"

QUESTIONS FOR REFLECTION

1. What is the main goal of liberation theology, as expressed by Gutiérrez?

2. What does Lee mean by "marginality"?

3. What are the four steps in Volf's model of embrace?

4. Self-evaluation exercise: There are different kinds of community. It can get complex, but on a basic level, there are three layers of community we surround ourselves with. There's an inner circle of those closest to us, a middle circle of those we engage with regularly but have some level of separation from, and an outer circle of those we interact with on occasion but have the least in common with (see figure 12.3 below).

    a. Take a minute to think about all the people who make up your inner circle of community. Imagine their faces and think of the stories that explain why they're a part of your inner circle.

    b. Take a step out from your inner circle and think about those who make up your middle circle of community. Imagine their faces, their personal journeys, and how they're different from those in your inner circle.

    c. Take a moment to think about your outer circle of community. Imagine the people who are in those furthest corners of friendship. What do they look like? How are they different from you? Why are they at such a distance from your inner circle?

    d. Are there ways you've tried to draw the outsiders into your middle or inner circles? How much effort have you put into drawing them in, and what did it feel like when you tried?

    e. Now think about those who aren't in any part of your community. Why are they so distant from you? Is it because of who they are, where they live, what they believe, or how they look?

    f. Think about the people you see on a daily basis and focus in on one person. What is one simple thing you could do to connect with this person? How might you create room for this person in a part of your community circles? Ask God to help you see and value this person out of love with just an agenda for relationship.

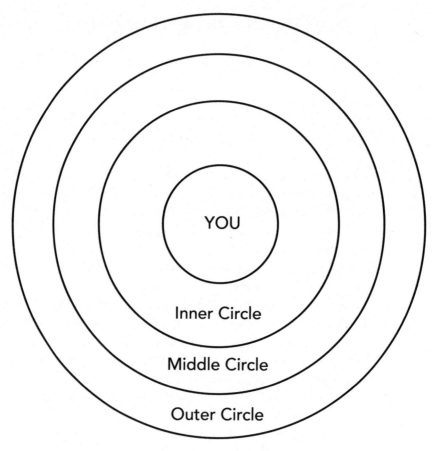

YOU

Inner Circle

Middle Circle

Outer Circle

Outside of your community

Figure 12.3 Circles of Relationship

5. What is your next step personally in this process of embrace of others? What is one practical thing you can work on in the next couple of weeks?

6. How does this chapter impact your own personal philosophy of youth ministry?

13

SHORT-TERM MISSIONS

EVERYBODY'S DOING IT

Sophia felt the tension rising in her as she sat in her office. She thought, "I need some advice." She reached for her phone and texted Bill and Stan.

Sophia: I need to call an immediate meeting at The Bunker. Can you be there in an hour?

Bill: Sure! What's it about?

Sophia: I'll tell you all about it when we get there.

Stan: I can make it. See you in a bit.

The three arrived within a few minutes of each other, ordered and received their drinks, and sat in The Bunker.

"What's going on?" asked Bill.

Stan looked on expectantly. He was glad to join his friends after being away on his travels.

Sophia replied, "I've been asked by my church board to do a mission trip with my youth this summer. And the whole prospect worries me a bit."

"Why the worries?" asked Stan.

Sophia explained, "Part of it is the church board's motivation for wanting a mission trip for the youth. It seems to be coming from a desire to be like other churches' youth groups. Several of the board members mentioned the mission trips that other churches in town have sponsored, and they think we should be doing something similar. The reasoning didn't seem to flow out of any sense of understanding missional theology or any real indication that such efforts are an extension of being sent by God. I guess all that we've been reading about missiology this past year has started to soak in, and I don't really want to lead something that seems so half-baked, especially if it has the word 'mission' attached to it."

"Well, I appreciate where you are coming from," said Stan, "because you want whatever you do to be on a solid foundation."

"Yes, I do," said Sophia. "Now, for the sake of full disclosure, I have been on a number of short-term mission trips. They were fun and meaningful at the time, but I have to wonder about the long-term effects on me and the other participants. And I can't help but wonder if we really helped the people we served. With all the money, time, and effort we poured into the projects, I can't tell you if it made one bit of difference. That's problematic."

Bill finished Sophia's thought, "And now your church wants you to launch something you are really unsure about."

"That's about it," said Sophia. She looked at Bill and Stan, her eyes pleading for some guidance.

Bill offered, "I think I can help. A few years before we met, I had some similar misgivings about short-term mission trips. I had led numerous trips, but I had begun to question the value of them. With Stan's help, I have begun to reimagine our youth mission trips as a coherent piece of an intentional discipleship process for the youth and as a vital piece of our church's missional outreach."

Sophia said with relief, "I need to hear about this!"

"Sure, let's talk about it," Bill said. "My thinking was initially challenged by our old friend Kenda Dean, and since then I have drawn some ideas from a couple of missiological sources. Let me gather everything together, and we can meet again next week to talk about it."

MORE THAN A TRIP

Kendra Creasy Dean (2010) addresses the frustration Sophia expressed to Bill and Stan. Dean notes that many youth ministries operate from a truncated view of mission that has reduced missional activity to a one- or two-week summer trip. While it is notable that many youth ministries promote these summer trips, and there are some good outcomes, typically the agenda of the trips and the theology that compels them gets submerged in the larger church's limited view of mission. As Dean says, these efforts "unwittingly perpetuate anemic understandings of mission and witness" (2010, 96).

How, then, can youth ministries conceive, plan, and enact short-term mission trips that are not malnourished? One answer, perhaps, is to cease doing them. However, estimates indicate that between one and two million US church members annually participate in short-term mission trips (Priest and Priest 2008). The numbers for youth are not as clear, but anecdotal information indicates that large numbers of youth have joined the short-term mission enterprise. Calling for an abrupt halt seems unrealistic. Maybe, though, youth ministers can take a cue from Timothy Tennent, who suggests a *"selah"* moment in the world of mission, in order to pause and reflect for adjustments, to find fresh ways of approaching missions in a changing context (2010, 50–51). Applying Tennent's suggestion to the world of short-term missions is a good idea. Perhaps the COVID pandemic of 2020–2021, with the limitations of travel, has provided a kind of *selah* moment. Can short-term missions be more than just a trip?

Short-term mission research has began to emerge in the mid-1990s. Much of it has been focused on the participants' experiences, and there has tended to be a lack of in-depth missiological research interest. Often there has been hostility. Priest comments, "When students more and more brought up the subject of short-term missions, I reacted negatively—with every anthropological bone in my body" (2008, 53). Over the years, however, there has been more insightful studies. Simone Mulieri Twibell (2020) offers a valuable literature review on short-term mission research that highlights both sides of the short-term mission effort, from that of the participant and the host community, and points to the future possibilities of congregational partnerships. Her review provides some needed evaluative parameters.

LET'S GO! THE PARTICIPANT VIEW

Twibell (2020) points to a number of studies that indicate positive outcomes in short-term mission participants. She describes several studies that speak to participants' developmental formation in areas of spiritualist and personal identity. Other studies try to get at the impact on behavior, with several showing a higher tendency toward social trust and a lower tendency toward racial stereotyping. There also seems to be an indication among youth that their faith is strengthened and their beliefs solidified through short-term mission participation.

One caution, though, is that positive changes from short-term mission trips often seem to be like the experience itself, short lived. This, along with the cultural insensitivity that participants can display on these trips, indicates the ineffectiveness of or lack of trip preparation. These challenges invite criticism of short-term mission practice.

It raises the question: Can short-term missions be done well, or at least better? Looking at the participant side of the short-term mission experience, Dean points out the significant role these kinds of trips can play in Christian formation. She describes them as "'decentering' encounters with 'otherness,'" in which youth can begin to see and participate in how God works both through themselves and through others (2010, 159).

In a real sense, short-term mission participants experience the trips as a kind of spiritual pilgrimage. It is an event in which one detaches from the regular activity of life, invites new insights through some kind of intentional episode, and reenters "normal" life as a renewed person. As pilgrimages, they serve as a kind of rite of passage.

Drawing from the work of anthropologists Arnold van Gennup (1960) and Victor Turner (1977), Matthias Zahniser (1997) describes the importance of a ceremonial rite of passage for disciple-making. The function of a rite of passage is to move an individual from one status in society to another. The individual is not only changed in the sense that one performs within a new role, but the individual's new role within the society is also culturally recognized.

Three phases comprise a rite of passage: (1) separation, (2) liminality, and (3) reintegration. Separation symbolically and actively removes the participant from one's old status in society. Liminality is a transitional state in which a person possesses none of the clearly defined rights or privileges of one's former or future condition. Reintegration returns the participant back to society with a new status.

Turner (1977) observes that people in the liminal state operate within a "statuslessness" that allows them to "develop an intense comradeship and egalitarianism" (1977, 95). Turner calls this *communitas*, a generic human connection and equality (96). This creative community elicited by a liminal state, Zahniser notes, is "ripe for bonding" (1997, 95). Participants bond to the community, and "they also bond to the beliefs and values of that community. This *discipling function* of the rite of passage—*bonding to meaning*—makes rites of passage a powerful tool for discipling" (Zahniser 1997, 96).

This discussion on rite of passage reveals that seeing youth participation in short-term mission trips as a type of pilgrimage or rite of passage makes it, to borrow a word from Zahniser, ripe with disciple-making possibilities. For example, Dean asserts,

> Spiritual detachment enacts the liminal principle of the gospel. . . . In youth ministry, liminal practices leverage dissonance for the sake of divine transformation. Thrust into spaces where none of our usual cultural tools work, we are forced to step back and scan for new ones. In so doing, we observe ourselves and our situations anew, rethinking our former understandings of God, self, and others. Such reflexivity indicates a maturing consciousness. (2010, 160)

When does a youth become an adult? Is it the onset of puberty, which typically occurs around the age of twelve? Is it when a student gets a driver's license at sixteen and experiences some sense of geographical independence? Those ages seem a bit young. What about high school graduation at eighteen? No? Then surely college graduation at twenty-two is the start of adulthood, or maybe the average age for marriage, about twenty-five.

The reality is that American society offers no clear marker for when a youth crosses into adulthood. The physiological reality of puberty at twelve is disconnected and distanced from the cultural reality of marriage in the mid-twenties. The result is a long, murky limbo of adolescence that stretches for at least a decade.

Participating in a short-term mission trip could be one of the several events that gets lost in the seemingly never-ending process of moving from adolescence to adulthood. Or, more fruitfully, it could be intentionally leveraged as part of a holistic discipleship program for youth to help them embrace a more mature Christian faith. When pursued with this kind of forethought, and coupled with appropriate missiological training, short-term mission trips could double down on the positive outcomes that Twibell (2020) highlights and mediate the cautions that she raises.

HERE WE ARE! THE HOST VIEW

Twibell's (2020) review of short-term mission research from the host's view reveals a mixed bag at best. On the positive side, even critics of short-term missions indicate the potential for the experience to be a joint exercise that exhorts the local community. For example, studies describe growth among the hosts in areas like evangelism, relationships, and cultural acuity. Cultural sensitivity on the part of the participants, though, is a key to lasting positive effects.

The challenges and cautions are real. Lack of cultural sensitivity often leads to miscommunication of expectations and outcomes. The result, all too often, is broken relationships, bitterness, and a poor depiction of the gospel. The participants swoop in, create havoc, and leave the hosts to pick up the pieces.

Twibell presents several ways that could mitigate the common negative outcomes of short-term missions and make these efforts more positive for both participants and hosts. First, as already mentioned, participants need to be culturally sensitive. This points to the need for missiological preparation for the participants. Missiological preparation would include teaching on missional theology, basic cultural anthropology, mission practice, and the history and culture of the destination. Participants do not need to know everything about each of these topics, but they should arrive at their destination with enough self-aware and others-aware knowledge that they avoid blundering miscues. In concert with the missiological training, there needs to be concentrated spiritual formation for the participants. Cultural awareness is an outgrowth of spiritual maturity.

Second, an effort should be made to establish healthy, mutual relationships between participants and hosts. The history of missions is littered with examples of paternalism, typically on the part of Western missionaries. Too many short-term mission enterprises lean into that unfortunate historical narrative. Well-resourced and privileged short-termers arrive at their destination providing "solutions" to problems they know little about. There can be a tendency to overwhelm the hosts' contribution and knowledge. A better approach is to establish clear roles. Recalling the lessons from Donald Larson (1978, see chap. 2), short-termers, especially youthful ones, need to adopt the role of learner. A learner's posture of "dependence and vulnerability" is a better communicator of the gospel than dominance (Larson 1978, 314). For youth, then, the short-term mission experience becomes part of one's ongoing training to spiritual maturity. In addition, it reveals that the hosts are not only receivers. They have gifts and knowledge to share with their guests. Mission can, and should, go both ways.

This leads to a third point. Twibell (2020) calls for collaboration between participants and hosts through relationships based on partnership. When short-term mission efforts are seen in the context of long-term, sibling-like, mutual relationships, then several opportunities open up. One is instilling a pattern of missional living in congregants of both churches. Twibell explains,

By emphasizing relationships over projects, focusing on long-term goals and sustainable development, honoring the agency of locals, and replacing philanthropy with solidarity, proponents of partnerships that deploy STM [short-term mission] groups believe that these types of relationships mitigate some of the pitfalls of STM and tend to be more effective in their impact both for those who go and for those who host. (2020, 352)

This kind of mutuality highlights another opportunity: "reverse short-term missions," according to Twibell (2020, 353–54). She cites Dan Mueller's example of several Mexican students coming to Rochester, Minnesota, to participate in an evangelistic outreach (2020, 353). Creative use of monetary resources and sharing of ministry expertise serves to revitalize both communities. "These types of exchanges have the potential to help the American church reinterpret familiar experiences and see the mission of the church in a new way" (Twibell 2020, 354). Finally, partnerships draw attention to globalization, which is "the intersection of the global with the local" (Moreau 2015, 16). For missions, this is the realization that every geographic location potentially is both a sending and receiving venue. In today's world, mission is two-way everywhere. As Dean has said, "Mission is not a trip" (2010, 96). It's the heartbeat of the church—and short-term missions, when employed intentionally and intelligently, can be a catalyst for missional invigoration.

BILL'S PLAN

"As I looked at the literature on short-term missions," said Bill, "three things began to emerge. First, it's pretty much assumed that short-term missions are here to stay, at least for the conceivable future. The COVID pandemic has pushed a big pause button on it, but it's likely to return as strong as ever."

Sophia and Stan sat next to each other on one side of The Bunker, Stan listened intently and Sophia scribbled down her usual copious notes. Each of their cups were nearly empty, The Daily Grind providing the caffeine nutrition.

Bill continued, "Since most people think short-term missions will continue, even with its critics pointing out the cautions and challenges, there is a body of literature that attempts to make the most out of short-term missions. They tend to emphasize two approaches. One looks primarily at participants' experiences. There is plenty of anecdotal evidence and even more formal research that shows participants benefit from short-term missions. Those focusing on the participant view propose viable ways for the positive outcomes to be more effective and long lasting. Clearly, the call for more missiological training is needed. I also appreciate leveraging the short-term experience as a model of pilgrimage. The insights of rites of passage is especially fruitful for those of us in youth ministry."

"Yeah, that's my favorite part," said Sophia. "My youth seem to be floating through life, and society gives them unclear or even contradictory indicators about how to move on to adulthood."

"Right!" said Bill. "The other approach draws in the hosts' view, which ironically has often been neglected. However, when the hosts are considered, then it pushes us to consider short-term missions in light of a fuller missiological understanding. It begs the question: Is there a solid, missiological way to do short-term missions?"

"Well, that is a good question," commented Stan. He took the last swallow from his cup, peered over the rim, and asked, "So, are you going to talk about your plan now? Sophia is waiting for some help."

"Yeah! Let me hear about your big plan!" said Sophia.

"Well, let's call it a modest plan for now, and Stan gave a lot of input to it," replied Bill. "Okay, here we go! The first aspect I want to address is discipleship. I have always wanted the youth in my ministry to grow in their faith so that, when they move on in life, they will have a mature, vital, integrated faith that launches them into adulthood. Admittedly, it's been a bit of a hit-or-miss process. In recent years, I have noticed my juniors and seniors detaching from the youth ministry. Too many are becoming spiritually apathetic. I've begun to consider what I could do that would capture their attention."

Bill took a breath and continued, "I think the issue is that, quite frankly, what I'm regularly offering in my youth ministry is too immature for the juniors and seniors. They need to be pushed and guided forward. So, I am developing a discipleship program specifically for students to do in their junior or senior years. It's a one-year program that culminates in a short-term mission trip. Here are some of the key components."

Bill handed Stan and Sophia each a one-page summary.[1] He spoke as they followed along. "First of all, each youth is placed with a mentor from the church. I'll help with the recruitment and placement of the mentors. The mentors commit to meet with their youth one-on-one each month and to

---

1.   Bill's plan is inspired by the high school theology programs administered by LeTourneau University (Passage Institute for Youth and Theology) and Asbury University (Youth Becoming Leaders).

attend a monthly seminar with all the youth and mentors, which I will lead. This will run from August to June. Also, both the youth and the mentors commit to going on a short-term mission trip in July."

"That's a lot to ask," Sophia said.

"You're right, it is," agreed Bill, "but I'm intentionally setting the bar high to indicate the importance of the venture." He continued, "At the one-on-one mentor meetings, mentors will read and discuss one book in the fall, *The Drama of Scripture*,[2] and one in the spring, *Delighting in the Trinity*.[3] I'll provide some study questions to help them process what they read. The idea is to help youth and their mentors understand their role in God's missional story and grasp more deeply this God who calls us into his story."

"Are there other resources that could be used?" asked Sophia.

"Sure," answered Bill. "These are just two that I have found most helpful."

"Cool, so what about the group meetings?" Sophia inquired.

Bill responded, "In the fall I plan to walk through a biblical theology of mission, which will somewhat mirror their reading in *Drama of Scripture*. By the end of the fall, I want both the youth and the mentors to work toward writing out personal mission statements that reflect their understanding of God's mission and their calling into it. In the spring I'll turn to missiological training in the understanding of culture and cross-cultural communication, and then I'll focus more specifically on the culture they will be encountering on their mission trip."

"I think I'm beginning to see what you're doing," expounded Sophia. "You're really playing into the rites of passage model. Placing youth with an adult mentor begins the process of separation and moves the youth into a liminal phase, where they are not just a youth any more but not quite an adult either. And then the mission trip becomes an affirmation of their new status as fellow workers in ministry, which they use to reintegrate into the life of the church."

"Yes, well, that's the ideal!" exclaimed Bill. "What's interesting is that the mission trip serves as a small rite of passage within the larger one you describe. The trip itself is a separation from normal routine. The trip is a liminal phase in which both youth and adult participants in effect become equal and bond as they become learners in a new culture. Returning from the trip is a literal

2. Craig G. Bartholomew and Michael Goheen. *The Drama of Scripture: Finding Our Place in the Biblical Story* (Grand Rapids: Baker Academic, 2014).

3. Michael Reeves. *Delighting in the Trinity: An Introduction to the Christian Faith* (Downers Grove, IL: IVP Academic, 2012).

reintegration into the life of church. For the youth, the return is a time to fully take on a more adult role in leadership and ministry. I'm still working out the details for how this happens, but I want the youth to see their return as an opportunity to use their gifts and graces for ministry in our church and community."

Sophia nodded and pondered for a moment, then said, "You mentioned that you wanted your short-term mission trip to demonstrate solid missiology. So, I guess you're addressing that with your spring seminar teaching."

"Yes," Bill said, "but there's more. This is where Stan helped me think strategically about our short-term mission trip."

"I do my best," Stan declared as he dramatically bowed his head.

Ignoring Stan's affectations, Bill plowed on. "I have a friend from seminary, Martin Gonzalez, who has been ministering at the church in his hometown, San Luis Potosi, Mexico. Over the years, I have taken a few short-term mission trips with my youth to his church. Anyway, I have proposed to my church's missions committee that we form a mission partnership with Martin's church. His church will be the site of the youth/mentor mission trip every year. Beginning next, our church will host an annual short-term mission trip from his church. In fact, he's going to start a missional discipleship program with his youth that is similar to the one I just described. After these trips get established, then the next phase will be longer-term exchanges where we'll be sending youth and young adults to intern at each other's churches. Finally, we are hoping this leads to our two churches sending a joint team to minister in India, where we both have contacts."

Stan added, "We really hope that this partnership with Martin's church gets our church to grasp a more complete vision of mission. We want to participate in God's mission in Mexico, and India, and also among the cultures represented in our local community. For example, we have several Spanish-speaking immigrants relocating around our church, and we keep fumbling around trying to reach out to them. We're looking forward to the people from Martin's church helping us figure out how to holistically and effectively communicate the gospel to them."

"Wow! I think I'm impressed," Sophia said as she flashed her brightest smile. Then she dropped her head into her hands and moaned, "But I've got to get a plan to my church board pretty soon, and I think they would be overwhelmed with what you just described. They're not ready for all that, and I'm not sure I am either."

"Hey! I've been there, Sophia. I think I understand a little about your dilemma," comforted Bill. "To quote from my favorite movie, *What about Bob?*, 'the way forward is baby steps.'"

"Oh, good grief!" Sophia said, rolling her eyes. Stan just shook his head.

Undeterred, Bill continued, "Baby steps are, indeed, the way. Plan a small mission trip, but be sure to include some solid missiological preparation. Stan and I will be happy to help you with the training, and I'll help you put the proposal together for your church. If you need a destination, Martin's church may be a possibility. Who knows? Maybe down the road your church can join in the partnership."

Sophia beamed at Bill and Stan. "You guys are the best. You really are God's gifts to me."

"That's about the best compliment anyone's ever given me," Stan said, almost blushing. His face slowly shifts into a mischievous smile as he asked, "You're still paying for the coffee, right?"

QUESTIONS FOR REFLECTION

1. Recall the short-term mission trips you have participated in or led. What were the highlights? What were some things that needed improvement? How would Bill's plan make them better?

2. Using the rite of passage model, analyze various aspects of your youth ministry. Use the model to review your youth ministry as a whole.

3. Make a list of churches, parachurch ministries, and other organizations that could become mission partners for your youth ministry. Note the possible strengths and weaknesses of each potential partnership.

14

EPILOGUE: KEEPING THE CONVERSATION GOING

AS HE ENTERED THE DAILY GRIND, Bill was greeted by the familiar sounds and smells. He ordered his coffee—sticking with his basic brew—got his cup from the barista and headed to The Bunker. His colleagues were sitting and chatting across the table, Stan with his dark espresso and Sophia with some kind of latte made with special syrup or milk or whatever. Bill smiled to himself and thought, "I guess coffee will never be just coffee anymore."

Sophia looked up and called out, "Look! Bill's here. Hey, old man!"

"Watch out, Punky Brewster!" Bill retorted.

"What's a Punky Brewster?" Sophia said really slowly, as if she had trouble pronouncing it.

"Never mind, you'll never understand," Bill responded with exaggerated exasperation and a dramatic eye roll.

Stan butted into the repartee and said, "Hey! If you two can finish up there, then we can find out why Sophia called us all here."

"Yeah, why the sudden call for a meeting, Sophia?" Bills asked, as he slid into the booth. "Your text sounded a bit urgent. Is it something good or bad?"

"It's good, it's good. Sorry about the mystery. I just wanted to talk to you two at the same time."

"All right, we're both here and all ears," Stan said.

Sophia interlocked her hands in front of her, sat up straight, beamed a smile at Bill and Stan, and commenced, "First of all, I want to say that the last eighteen months of meeting with you two and discussing youth ministry and missiology have been some of the most meaningful moments of my life. Not only has my ministry grown richer and deeper, but my own personal spiritual growth has blossomed. These conversations have really been life-giving, and I want to sincerely thank you both."

"You are very welcome," Bill replied. "When I met you at that meeting, I could tell that you had a special spark. You are so earnest and sincere. Actually, I think it is me who should be thanking you. You have pushed our discussions forward by your inquisitiveness and persistence. We started out with me kind of the leader or teacher. But I have grown so much because of your insights." Bill nodded toward Stan. "And neither of us could have figured it out without this guy!"

Stan held his hands out in a kind of air embrace. "Listen, I am so inspired by the passion you two put into your youth ministry. Being around you makes me feel decades younger."

Sophia explained, "It's because of this kind camaraderie that I have called us here today. We've all benefitted from our conversations. We're better youth ministers and, hopefully, even better disciples." Bill and Stan nodded in agreement.

"So, I want to keep the conversation going. But there is one thing that's started to bother me."

"What's that?" asked Bill.

Sophia hesitated a little, then said, "The name of our booth here, The Bunker."

"What's wrong with the name—too militaristic?"

"No, it's not that. It's the meaning that's implied, especially in light of our conversations about mission. A bunker is a reinforced shelter that you hide away in to keep safe from outside hostile forces. I get why we started calling this place The Bunker. It became our little hideaway, our retreat, to have these important discussions. But then, something started to click in my heart and head. Everything we have talked about in The Bunker is about getting out and engaging our culture with the gospel, and here we sit safe and secure in The Bunker right in the middle of a mission field." Sophia swept her hand around to indicate the people in The Daily Grind.

The three looked around the coffee shop for a few seconds, pondering Sophia's words. She continued, "Now, that's not really a criticism about what we've been doing. But I do feel we are at a crossroads with our discussion group. Where do we go from here? And what do we do about this space, this holy space, that I really think God has called us to?"

"I'm starting to get the feeling that you have a plan," encouraged Bill.

"I do!" Sophia smiled sheepishly. "I've been thinking that we need to enlarge our conversation. God has brought us together and brought us to this coffee shop. I think we should put into practice all the missional principles we've been talking about right here. I've been talking with the manager of The Daily Grind, and she has agreed to let us host a theology night once a month. I've read about this kind of thing at different pubs and coffee shops. You have a panel of 'theology experts,' usually local pastors, that make a short presentation on a theme and then take questions from the audience. There are established ground rules about using respectful speech, but it's no holds barred regarding being able to express your views."

"Okay, well I've got to get my mind around this," said Bill.

"Well, you better hurry, because I've already told the manager that you, Stan, and I would be the expert panel for the first three months. The first event is next Thursday."

"Who is this missionary firecracker that we've created?" wondered Stan.

"I guess the only thing I can say is . . . yes," Bill stammered a bit helplessly.

"Get this!" Sophia blurted out excitedly, "I've thought of a great name. No longer will this be The Bunker. These theology nights will be called The Forum!"

She reached in her backpack and pulled out a stack of fliers. "I've already had these printed up. Look at the subtitle: 'a conversation about theology and culture.' What do you think?"

Bill and Stan looked over the flier that Sophia handed them. Slowly, but inevitably, they both began to smile.

Stan finally said, "We used to do this kind of thing with university students in Prague, only we'd use various popular movies as theology discussion starters. I look forward to entering this kind of theological fray again. I'm in!"

"I guess you're really kicking us out of The Bunker and into The Forum," said Bill.

"I'm planning to invite my youth to show up at The Forum. You should, too. It will be great for them to see how we engage this mission field. I'm hoping it will inspire them."

Bill looked up from the flier and stated, "It is inspiring. This is a great way to keep the conversation going!"

QUESTIONS FOR REFLECTION

1. What are the three or four key concepts from the book that have had the most impact on you so far?

2. How do you plan to take these ideas and put them into action?

3. This book mentioned several missiological authors/books. Make a list of those you plan to read and study in the coming year.

4. What is one idea, like Sophia's coffee shop theology night, that you could implement immediately in order to put into action a more missional lifestyle and youth ministry?

WORKS CITED

Anderson, Rufus, and R. Pierce Beaver. 1967. *To Advance the Gospel: Selections from the Writings of Rufus Anderson*. Grand Rapids: Eerdmans.

Barrett, Lois Y. 2004. *Treasure in Clay Jars: Patterns in Missional Faithfulness*. Grand Rapids: Eerdmans.

Bartholomew, Craig G, and Michael W Goheen. 2017. *The Drama of Scripture: Finding Our Place in the Biblical Story*. London: SPCK Publishing.

Benedict, Ruth. 1934. *Patterns of Culture*. New York: Penguin Books.

Bevans, Stephen B. 2002. *Models of Contextual Theology*. Maryknoll, NY: Orbis Books.

Blevins, Dean G., Maddix, Mark A. 2010. *Discovering Discipleship: Dynamics of Christian Education*. Kansas City, MO: Beacon Hill Press.

Boas, Franz. 1911. *The Mind of Primitive Man*. London: Forgotten Books.

_____. 1929. *Anthropology and Modern Life*. London: George Allen and Unwin.

Bosch, David Jacobus. 1991. *Transforming Mission: Paradigm Shifts in Theology of Mission (American Society of Missiology Series)*. Maryknoll, NY: Orbis Books.

Clark, Chap. 2011. *Hurt 2.0: Inside the World of Today's Teenagers*. Grand Rapids: Baker Academic.

Clark, Francis E. 1923. *Memories of Many Men in Many Lands: An Autobiography*. Boston/Chicago: United Society of Christian Endeavor.

Corduan, Winfried. 2012. *Neighboring Faiths: A Christian Introduction to World Religions*. Downers Grove, IL: IVP Academic.

Dean, Kenda Creasy. 2010. *Almost Christian: What the Faith of Our Teenagers Is Telling the American Church*. Oxford; New York: Oxford University Press.

Donovan, Vincent J. 2003. *Christianity Rediscovered*. Maryknoll, NY: Orbis Books.

Du Bois, W. E. B. 1897. "Strivings of the Negro People." *The Atlantic Monthly*, August. https://www.theatlantic.com/magazine/archive/1897/08/strivings-of-the-negro-people/305446.

Edgerton, Robert B. 1992. *Sick Societies: Challenging the Myth of Primitive Harmony*. New York: The Free Press.

Epstein, Robert. 2010. *Teen 2.0: Saving Our Children and Families from the Torment of Adolescence*. Fresno, CA: Quill Driver Books/Word Dancer Press.

Flemming, Dean E. 2005. *Contextualization in the New Testament: Patterns for Theology and Mission*. Downers Grove, IL: InterVarsity Press.

Glenn, H. Stephen, and Jane Nelsen. 2000. *Raising Self-Reliant Children in a Self-Indulgent World: Seven Building Blocks for Developing Capable Young People*. New York: Three Rivers Press.

Goheen, Michael W. 2014. *Introducing Christian Mission Today: Scripture, History, and Issues*. Downers Grove, IL: IVP Academic.

Guder, Darrell L. 2004. *The Incarnation and the Church's Witness.* Eugene, OR: Wipf & Stock.

Guder, Darrell L., and Lois Barrett. 1998. *Missional Church: A Vision for the Sending of the Church in North America.* Grand Rapids: Eerdmans.

Gutierrez, Gustavo. 2011. *A Theology of Liberation.* 15th anniv. ed. Maryknoll, NY: Orbis Books.

Herskovits, Melville J. 1958. *Acculturation: The Study of Culture Contact.* Gloucester, MA: P. Smith.

———. 1970. *Cultural Anthropology.* New York: Knopf.

Hiebert, Paul G. 1982. "The Flaw of the Excluded Middle." *Missiology Missiology: An International Review* 10 (1): 35–47.

———. 1985. "The Missiological Implications of An Epistemological Shift." *TSF Bulletin* 8 (5): 12–18.

———. 2001. *Anthropological Reflections on Missiological Issues.* Grand Rapids: Baker Books.

Hiebert, Paul G., R. Daniel Shaw, and Tite Tienou. 1999. "Responding to Split-Level Christianity and Folk Religion." *International Journal of Frontier Missions* 16 (4): 173–82.

———. 2000. *Understanding Folk Religion: A Christian Response to Popular Beliefs and Practices.* Grand Rapids: Baker Books.

Hughes, Philip. 1984. "The Use of Actual Beliefs in Contextualizing Theology." *East Asian Journal of Theology* 2 (2): 251–58.

Hunter, George G. 1996. *Church for the Unchurched.* Nashville: Abingdon Press.

Kraft, Charles H., and Tom N. Wisley. 1979. *Readings in Dynamic Indigeneity.* Pasadena, CA: William Carey Library.

Larson, Donald N. 1978. "The Viable Missionary: Learner, Trader, Story Teller." *Missiology: An International Review* 6 (2): 155–63.

Lee, Jung Young. 1995. *Marginality: The Key to Multicultural Theology*. Minneapolis: Fortress Press.

Maxey, James A. 2009. *From Orality to Orality: A New Paradigm for Contextual Translation of the Bible*. Eugene, OR: Cascade Books.

Middendorf, Jon. 2014. *Worship-Centered Youth Ministry: A Compass for Guiding Youth into God's Story*. Kansas City, MO: Nazarene Publishing House.

Moon, W. Jay. 2009. *African Proverbs Reveal Christianity in Culture*. Eugene, OR: Pickwick Publications.

Moreau, A. Scott, Gary Corwin, and Gary B. McGee. 2015. *Introducing World Missions: A Biblical, Historical, and Practical Survey*. Grand Rapids: Baker Academic.

Muck, Terry. 2011. "Interreligious Dialogue: Conversations That Enable Christian Witness." *International Bulletin of Missionary Research* 35 (4): 187–92.

Newbigin, Lesslie. 1989. *The Gospel in a Pluralist Society*. Grand Rapids: Eerdmans.

Nida, Eugene A., and Benjamin Elson. 1960. *A Synopsis of English Syntax*. Norman: Summer Institute of Linguistics of the University of Oklahoma.

Perkins, John M. 2001. *Restoring At-Risk Communities: Doing It Together and Doing It Right*. Grand Rapids: Baker Books.

Priest, Robert J., and Joseph Paul Priest. 2008. "They See Everything, and Understand Nothing." *Missiology: An International Review* 36 (1): 53–73.

Reeves, Michael. 2012. *Delighting in the Trinity: An Introduction to the Christian Faith*. Downers Grove, IL: InterVarsity Press.

Rynkiewich, Michael. 2012. *Soul, Self, and Society.* Eugene, OR: Cascade Books.

Sanneh, Lamin O. 2009. *Translating the Message: The Missionary Impact on Culture.* 2nd ed. Maryknoll, NY: Orbis Books.

———. 1995. "The Gospel, Language and Culture: The Theological Method in Cultural Analysis." *International Review of Mission* 84 (332/333): 47–64.

Schreiter, Robert J. 1985. *Constructing Local Theologies.* Maryknoll, NY: Orbis Books.

Senter, Mark H. III. 2010. *When God Shows Up: A History of Protestant Youth Ministry in America.* Grand Rapids: Baker Books.

Smith, Christian, and Melinda Lundquist Denton. 2005. *Soul Searching: The Religious and Spiritual Lives of American Teenagers.* Oxford/New York: Oxford University Press.

Snyder, Howard A. 1996. *Radical Renewal: The Problem of Wineskins Today.* Houston: Touch Publications.

Sumner, William Graham. 1906. *Folkways: A Study of the Sociological Importance of Usages, Manners, Customs, Mores, and Morals.* New York: Dover Publications.

Tennent, Timothy C. 2010. *Invitation to World Missions: A Trinitarian Missiology for the Twenty-First Century.* Grand Rapids: Kregel Academic.

Tucker, Ruth. 2004. *From Jerusalem to Irian Jaya: A Biographical History of Christian Missions.* 2nd ed. Grand Rapids: Zondervan.

Turner, Victor. 1977. *The Ritual Process: Structure and Anti-Structure.* Ithaca, NY: Cornell University Press.

Twibell, Simone Mulleri. 2020. "Contributions, Challenges, and Emerging Patterns of Short-Term Missions." *Missiology: An International Review* 48 (4): 344–59.

van Gennep, Arnold, Monika B. Vizedom, and Gabrielle L. Caffee. 1960. *The Rites of Passage*. Chicago: University of Chicago Press.

Venn, Henry. 1971. *To Apply the Gospel; Selections from the Writings of Henry Venn*. Grand Rapids: Eerdmans.

Volf, Miroslav. 1996. *Exclusion and Embrace*. Nashville: Abingdon Press.

Walls, Andrew F. 1996. *The Missionary Movement in Christian History: Studies in the Transmission of Faith*. Maryknoll, NY: Orbis Books.

Whiteman, Darrell L. 1984. "Effective Communication of the Gospel Amid Cultural Diversity." *Missiology: An International Review* 12 (3): 275–85.

_____. 2003. *Anthropology and Mission: The Incarnational Connection*. Chicago: CCGM Publications.

Wright, Christopher J. H. 2006. *The Mission of God: Unlocking the Bible's Grand Narrative*. Grand Rapids: IVP Academic.

Wright, N. T. 2013. *The New Testament and the People of God*. London: SPCK.

Zahniser, A. H. Mathias. 1994. "Close Encounters of the Vulnerable Kind: Christian Dialogical Proclamation among Muslims." *The Asbury Journal* 49 (1).

Zahniser, A. H. Mathias, ed. 1997. *Symbol and Ceremony: Making Disciples across Cultures*. Monrovia, CA: MARC Publications.